VENETIA AND NORTHERN ITALY

THE COVERED BRIDGE OVER THE PICINO AT PAVIA.

VENETIA ❧ ❧ *AND* NORTHERN ITALY

being the STORY OF VENICE
LOMBARDY & EMILIA *by*
CECIL HEADLAM
Illustrated by GORDON HOME

LONDON : J. M. DENT & CO.
NEW YORK : THE MACMILLAN COMPANY
MCMVIII

PREFACE.

THE object of this book is to recall familiar scenes to those who have visited them, to suggest them to others, and to be of use upon the spot. It deals in outline with the history, architecture, and art of the towns of Northern Italy which lie within the triangular plain bounded on the north by the Alps, on the west by the Apennines, and on the east by the Adriatic Sea— roughly, "with the pleasant land that from *Milano* slopes to *Rimini*." It embraces the Lombard Lakes and the Lombard Plain; the chief towns that lie in the valley of the Po and its tributaries, and along the great Æmilian Way, which the railway follows, from Como and Milan to Bologna, Rimini, and the sea. Following the railway northwards through Ravenna, Ferrara, and Padua to Venice, and omitting the north-eastern portion of the Veneto, it treats of the towns that lie at the foot of the Alps from Vicenza, Verona, and Brescia to Bergamo.

In each Italian town there is a distinct personality, an individual charm, the outcome of a history and development so curiously individual and distinct. For throughout the period when, apart from Roman times, the art and architecture of these towns were in making, and with which I have therefore concerned myself, whilst the South of Italy was a feudal kingdom, and Central Italy was composed of the States of the Church, we find in the North an interminable series of independent Communes and petty autocracies. Diversity of history and constitution led, with other influences, to individuality of art and architecture. I have endeavoured in this book to show how the history of each town, of which it treats, is illustrated by its art and architecture; and I have endeavoured to show how the various styles of art and various buildings enumerated are the direct and natural outcome of history and tradition, of despotism or independence, of invasion or commerce, of political, social, and geographical environment, or of the dominating, fascinating personalities who guided the destinies of these towns.

It is not possible fully to understand or appreciate a single building, monument, picture, or mosaic in Italy without some knowledge of the circumstances under which the artist was bred and his work was begotten. It is useless to be told that a particular building is in the Lombard, Italian-Gothic, or Renaissance style, that a thing is Byzantine, or even that a particular picture is by a particular artist, unless we know or are told something of the characteristics and the pedigree of that style, and something of the influences which formed the artists who wrought it.

The monuments which survive in these tiny Italian towns date from the times of Etruscan and Roman greatness, of early Christian Emperors, of the barbarian invaders, of the independent Communes, and of the Italian despots, who witnessed and inspired the glories

and the decadence of the Renaissance, and were responsible for the loss of Italian independence. It was not
necessary or possible to repeat the main outlines of events in
telling the story of each town ; and part of the difficulty of
writing this book has been that of playing a hand at bridge,
to discard with skill, to indicate history without much vain
repetition. It has been possible to regard several cities as
representative of a period : Ravenna, clearly, is a mummy
of Early Christian Art ; Bologna's Leaning Towers point
to the recurrent story of family feuds and factions ; Venice,
the city always putting out to sea, has her own peculiar
history and characteristics clearly reflected in her art. Milan
is the centre of the history of the Northern Republics, as it
is the central point of the Lombard plain. Its history is of
unsurpassable interest, and is representative. About the
story of Milan I have therefore allowed myself to linger, but
always keeping in view that the purpose of that story was in
part to illuminate the events connected with the buildings
and history of other smaller towns. And in the course of her
history I have dealt at length with subjects common to them
all—the peculiarities of Lombard Architecture, the Rise and
Fall of the Lombard Communes, the Age of the Condottieri, and the Age of the Despots in Italy. This note
will serve to explain both the scope and aim of this book,
however unsuccessfully achieved, and also the amount of
space allotted to Milan, which might otherwise have seemed
disproportionate. I have to deny myself the pleasure of
acknowledging the many sources from which I have drawn ;
the mere enumeration would run to many pages. The
good wine of Mr. Home's illustrations needs no bush.

Esthwaite Mount, Hawkshead.

CONTENTS.

xii   CONTENTS

LIST OF ILLUSTRATIONS.

IN COLOUR.

BLACK AND WHITE ILLUSTRATIONS.

CHAPTER I.

THE GATES OF ITALY.

LUGANO: COMO: LAGO MAGGIORE: MONZA: SARONNO.

THE Lombard Lakes are the Gates of Italy. But, for the purposes of this book, they must be regarded rather as fairy portals, through which we must pass quickly, without pausing too long upon the threshold of an enchanted land. There is, indeed, scarcely a yard of Italian soil, scarcely a year of Italian history, which does not call for comment from the historian or tempt the lover of art and nature to linger in admiration. We must early school ourselves to the task of omission and selection, in the hope that the result may be, if less comprehensive, yet more comprehensible.

Lugano is not yet Italy. But the scenery of its Lake, after the opening page of the St. Gothard Pass, will serve as the frontispiece to the wonderful volume that lies before us, beyond the mountain pass which divides the basin of the Lake from that of Como. The atmosphere of Lugano is German-Swiss, than which, perhaps, no harder thing can be said; but it has the supreme merit, apart from the possession of two frescoes by Luini, of being the best starting point for the ascent of Monte Generoso.

The view from the summit of Monte Generoso has been often described, but it baffles and surpasses description. Sheer beneath, smiling woods and pastures drop down to the flashing waters of the Lake. Richly wooded hills, and valleys veiled in gauze-like mist form a soft and sylvan foreground to the vast semi-circle of the mighty Alps, to the huge network of snow-clad peaks, which rise above the blue waters of the lakes they feed. From Monte Viso, in the far west, to the Ortler Spitz, in the east, the " mountain tops that freeze " glow and glitter in the sunshine, like warriors clad in mail of ice, grouped about the throne of the Queen of Snows. For there, enthroned indeed, smiles Monte Rosa, draped in an ermine mantle, radiant in her queenly diadem of five-fold peaks ; Monte Rosa, with her

> " thousand shadowy-pencilled valleys,
> And snowy dells in a golden air."

From this Pisgah-height of Monte Generoso the whole scheme of the tour we contemplate is laid out clearly as in a map. Across the Lago d' Iseo and the Lago di Garda, the Alps join hands with the mountains behind Verona. Beyond lies Padua, lies Venice, and the Sea whose Bride she was. And past Como and Varese, the fair, rich plains of Lombardy and Emilia stretch out to the southernmost point of our journey, to where, beyond the Po, the towering Apennines guard Bologna.

We see how this great basin of Lombardy, enclosed by the junction of the Alps and Apennines, may once, perhaps, have been a gulf of the Adriatic, now silted up with the detritus of the Alps, and drained, 400 miles from east to west, by the great river Po.

Little wonder if, at the vision of such a Promised Land of art and beauty, the heart even of the modern traveller throbs with something of the · same passionate desire as the starving hordes of Celtic invaders, as Hannibal's motley troops, as the armies of Frenchmen, of Germans and of Switzers must have felt, when, after enduring untold hardships on the Alpine heights, they gazed down at last upon the rich and smiling lands at their feet. The modern traveller, however, has no such preliminary hardship to endure ; he has no need for Hannibal's elephants and vinegar to cross the Alps withal ; he merely takes the train from Charing Cross—and some *vin ordinaire*. The South-Eastern railway and the P.L.M. may be trusted to do the rest.

The Gates of Italy have been forced by innumerable invaders. We can almost hear the tramp of the Roman legions as they march, under Scipio or Marius, to hurl back the tide of invasion, or, under Caesar, to conquer Gaul and distant Britain ; we can almost hear the echo of the warlike cries of the Celtic barbarians, or of the *Marseillaise* chaunted by Napoleon's troops. The fair plain at our feet has been the battle-ground of Europe.

Catholics and heretics, Guelfs and Ghibellines, Romans and Teutons, Frenchmen and Italians have deluged it in blood, fighting to the death in lust of hate, in religious frenzy, in frantic greed for the possession of the white villages and gleaming towers, and the silver winding streams that mark and intersect this fruitful Lombard land.

Far away the lake of Varese and the Maggiore are dwarfed to the measure of a tiny tarn ; and the fretted pile of Milan Cathedral beckons the traveller to the Capital of the North.

At Porlezza the steamer lands us upon Italian soil. Thence we pass through wooded glades and vineyards,— vineyards still cultivated in the old Roman way, so that they seem but vivid illustrations of Vergil's *Georgics*,—till we come upon the Larian waters, the Lake of Como, *Te Lari Maxime*! There lies Menaggio, veiled in a delicate blue haze, looking to where Varenna dreams voluptuously beneath her castle-crowned hill and white cascade, "beckoning up the Stelvio Pass." The grim heights and precipices of Monte Codeno and Monte Legnone, and the wooded slopes of Legnoncino lie beyond it. There in the sunlight twinkles Bellagio, nestling on the wooded peninsular, Serbelloni, and clearly earning its title *Bi-lacus*, as it divides the lower half of the lake into two broad streams. Above, the wide expanse of blue waters melts into the distant frame of blue mountains tipped with white.

A mountain-girt lake, seen by moonlight, is perhaps the most beautiful thing in Nature, and, when the colour fades from the azaleas and oleanders that flush the villa-gardens of the shore, after the rose tints of sunset have died from off the snow-clad peaks, and the green background of the wooded slopes has turned to black, singularly beautiful is Como, when the moon rises over its dark and placid waters. Fishing boats with blazing torches at the bows glide along the shores in search of fish to spear ; fireflies float through the immeasurable blue ; patches of brilliant white light mark such hotel-paradises of *forestieri* as Cadenabbia. Suddenly the searchlights of the custom-house boats streak the void and reveal for a second unsuspected heights and distances. The moonlight is dimmed, the darkness redoubled. But the silver music of the bells of Varenna mingles with the soft tinkling of the cow-bells by which, here as on far, peaceful Windermere, the fishermen mark their lines.

It was upon the wooded promontory of Bellagio, which rises so suddenly out of the Lake, that the younger Pliny, true *amateur* of country life, possessed a villa, to which, by a quaint conceit, he gave the name of *Tragedy*. For, so he fancied, the villa raised high above the surface of the water resembled a tragic actor, in his " tragic sock," raised high above the stage on which he trod. Another villa he had, touching the lake, resting nicely upon the comic buskin, which he called *Comedy*, and whence, so he tells his friend, Romanus ;—and the description at once calls up to the mind the picture of many a modern villa on Lake Como ;—" you may fish from your bedroom, nay, from your very bed."

So we leave Menaggio or Cadenabbia, overshadowed by the great spurs of Monte Crocione. On the deck of our steamer are bales of leaves stripped from the white mulberry trees, with which Lodovico il Moro clad the plain of Lombardy, and on which, as the food of silk-worms, the modern prosperity of the whole Comasco district is based.

We set forth upon our voyage, perhaps, beneath blue skies, on a blue lake ; green woods and flower-lit balconies are visible on the shore through a delicate haze, and the ballad-burthen music rings in our ears of the " rich Vergilian measure, of Lari Maxume, all the way." And we think of Vergil and Pliny, those Lake Poets of the Roman world, preaching, and sometimes practising, the simple country life as the antidote to the enfeebling, soul-destroying atmosphere of a corrupt and over-busy capital.

Well, the world has followed their example and their advice. Como is the villa-paradise of Milan and of the northern world, as once of Rome. But, as the day wears on, the aspect of the water changes. The outlines of the shore grow hard and sharp ; the warmth dies out of the rich colouring ; villas and villages stand out in harsh contrast of white on the green background of timbered hills and gloomy ravines.

For, as upon all lakes mountain-bound, the storms on the Lago Lariano are sudden and violent. The fitful gusts of the north wind, the Vento di Colico, forcing their way out of the gulleys, burst upon the lake with all the fury of pent-up passion, and quickly lash its waters into no mean waves. Each pass and valley is a bellows, and, whipped by the blasts that escape from them, under a changing sky the lake turns deep blue, lurid purple or metallic green beneath the white horses of the storm.

So Como yields us all the joy and unceasing change, all the vigour and repose, the passion and pathos, the colour and gloom, the light and shadow of a lake in mountain country. One day, one hour it is still and mirror-like ; its sole function seems to reflect the blue sky and the green forest, the gleaming villages, the skimming boats, the villas poised amid their gorgeous gardens above the shores, and the snow-clad peaks above, flushed with the glow of sunset. Next hour, next day, it is the kingdom of the clouds ; greys and purples and silver lights pass over the face of the waters, and the deep shadows of the ravines intensify the threatening aspect of the lake. The storm breaks with a flash and a roll of thunder ; and, whilst the heavens roar and flame, the rising wind rushes down the gorges and lashes the inky waters into a dangerous whirl of wave and foam.

It was in such a sudden storm, near the Punto di Bellagio, in 1493, that Bianca Sforza, Il Moro's niece (*see* Milan), but four days past newly wed to Maximilian, King of the Romans, had almost lost her life. A sudden, violent storm scattered the fleet, and only after tossing all day and part of the night did the Queen's barge succeed in putting back into Bellagio.

We pass the grand mediaeval Castle of Rezzonico (*Rhaetionicum*), home of the great Della Torre family, and the village of Cremia, which boasts a S. Michael of Paolo Veronese, magnificent in movement as in colour, of which the story is told that a tempting offer from a collector was refused, thanks to the speech of an old villager—" Our fathers left us two great inheritances,—that picture and our communal debt. Let the noble Count take both—or neither."

North of Cremia, upon the summit of a precipitous mass of rock, hang the remains of that Eagle's Nest, the Castle of Musso, which once the Milanese adventurer, Gian Giacomo de' Medici, "Il Medeghino," rendered the strongest fortress in Lombardy, the key of the whole Larian district.

Round this castle the troops and fleets of Medici and Sforza met in perpetual conflict, until at last Il Medeghino agreed to abandon it in exchange for 10,000 gold scudi a year and the title of Marquis of Marignano. We shall see his tomb, prepared by order of his brother, Pope Pius IV., by the Menaggio sculptor, Leone Leoni, in the Cathedral of Milan.

Como has but one island, the Isola Comacina, so seques-
tered beneath the olive-fringed shores of the lake that, when
Alboin and his Lombard followers overran Italy, it alone
remained unsubdued ; the one big rock of refuge rising
above the flood of barbarian invasion.   Here, it is supposed,
the *Magistri Comacini* sought asylum, a guild of masons,
who preserved the traditions of building during this period
of ruin, and to whom all the architecture of northern Italy
and the development of an early school of Lombard art
have been attributed by some imaginative writers.

The lower part of the lake is long and narrow, and
resembles some majestic river winding its way through
forests and through mountains broken by ravines.   The
richly timbered banks, sometimes precipitous, sometimes
sloping gently down to the water, are fringed with laurels
and chestnuts, with myrtle, bay and wild fig-trees and olives,
self-sown among the rocks, between flashing waterfalls and
shadowy glens.   The shores gleam with villas and glow
with flowers and flowering shrubs, with lemon trees, vineyards, oranges.   It is in this narrow and over-populated
reach that Como contrasts least favourably with the flowing
grace of the broad waters, the majesty of mountains, sky
and distant shores, that form the chief characteristics of its
rival, the Lago Maggiore.   There soft, silvan landscapes
blend with the grandeur of towering rocks ; there the
monotony of breadth and distance is broken by those lovely
islands, Isola Madre, with its wealth of beautiful exotic
trees and plants, Isola Bella, with its artificial grottoes and
marvellous views of the lawn-like meadows, the glancing
becks and spring flowers of the lower slopes upon the
western shore.   But the Lago Maggiore lacks the

atmosphere and rich colouring and the historic interest of
the Lago di Garda and the Larian Lake. It has, for
instance, nothing so full of interesting associations as the
Villa Pliniana. This famous house lies near the villadom
of Como, on the edge of the lake, but lonely, mysterious,
in the cool shade of dark woods, beneath the silent guardian-
ship of the mountain crags, of Gargantuan laurel trees and
giant cypresses. The present sixteenth century villa is
built upon a succession of terraces rising out of the water,
at the foot of a semi-circular precipice overshadowed by
deep forests of chestnut. Beneath the exquisite Loggia
flows the curious intermittent spring, which rises and falls
at regular intervals each day, and baffles the enquiries of
modern scientists as it baffled that humane, intelligent,
Roman gentleman, the younger Pliny, who, leisurely break-
fasting by its edge and drinking of its icy waters one still,
hot, dreamy summer's day, first described and discussed
it in a letter to a friend, nearly two thousand years
ago.

Como, Pliny's "darling Como," where he founded a
library and endowed schools and baths for the poor, lies
at the southern extremity of the lake, and is now the
flourishing centre of the Lombard silk trade. Historically
and architecturally it deserves a chapter, nay, a volume to
itself. Ruled by the ancient Etruscans, colonised by Julius
Caesar, conquered by Belisarius and Narses, absorbed at
length into the Duchy of the Viper of Milan, it presents, in
the vicissitudes of its history and the variety of its buildings,
a typical example of a Lombard town. Monte Baradello,
the hill, crowned by a lofty tower, which lies above it, once
the headquarters of Frederick Barbarossa, was the citadel

round which the armies of Milan and Como waged their ten years' war.

The Cathedral, one of the most perfect examples of the blending of Gothic and Renaissance styles in Italy, is built, like the adjoining Broletto (1215), with its graceful pointed arches and octagonal piers, of mellowed marbles, black, white and red. Designed by Lorenzo degli Spasi, who had worked on the Duomo at Milan, it was begun in 1396 and completed in 1730. A plain tower of rough stone rises up in noble contrast to the lovely façade and portal designed by Bramante (1491). The rose window is superb. The portals are marvels of rich carving, fit introductions to the characteristic masterpieces of Luini and Ferrari within. Noticeable amongst much beautiful statuary is the discordant hideousness of a sculptured frog (north doorway) ; the figure of Cecco Simonetta (*see* Milan), who lengthened the nave ; and, by the central door, the two Plinies, patrons, if not saints, of Como and its lake.

If there were no Milan, I should linger long at Como. But I press on to Milan because she is the representative city of the north, and, by dealing with her history and architecture at some length, I hope to make clear, not only the general character of the peculiar buildings with which we shall be confronted in all the Lombard towns, but also the circumstances, social and artistic, which attended their birth and formed their style. This plan will save much vain repetition.

On the way to Milan the wise traveller will stop at Saronno and Monza, unless he elect to return hither from Milan. For at Saronno in the Church of S. Maria dei

Miracoli are some of the finest pictures of two great Lombard artists, Bernardino Luini and Gaudenzio Ferrari (*see* pp. 13, 96 ff.).

MONZA.

In the castle, which I have mentioned as crowning the wooded hill above Varenna, Theodolinda, the Lombard Queen, passed the last years of her life.

Daughter of a Bavarian King, her hand had been asked in marriage for political reasons by Autharis, King of the Lombards. But, so the story runs, before the marriage, Autharis secretly accompanied his ambassadors to see his betrothed. Her charm and beauty filled him with passion ; and the princess loved the man before she knew the King. He revealed himself to the astonished Bavarians upon the confines of Italy, when, raising himself upon his horse he hurled his battle-axe against a tree with incomparable strength and dexterity. " Such," he cried, " are the strokes of the King of the Lombards." The Lombards, too, recognised Theodolinda's charm, for upon the death of Autharis they agreed to recognise as their King any prince whom she should choose for her second husband. Her choice fell upon Agilulf, Duke of Turin, whom she converted to Christianity, whereupon Pope Gregory the Great presented her with a fillet of iron brought by the Empress Helena to Rome, and made, according to the pious tradition, from one of the nails which fastened Jesus to the cross. It was used to crown the German Emperors Kings of Italy. It was used, in succession to them, at the coronation of Charles V., of Napoleon, and of Emperor Ferdinand I. And wearing this very fillet of beaten iron, set in a gold crown of Byzantine workmanship, the King of Italy took his coronation oath and addressed his courageous speech to the united people of Italy.

The construction of the Strada Regina, on the west side of the Lake of Como, is traditionally attributed to Theodolinda, still the fairy godmother of the lake, as S. Carlo Borromeo, Archbishop of Milan, in gratitude for his truly Christian ministrations, is the saint who lives in popular memory on the shores of Como, of the Lago Maggiore, and in the Cathedral of Milan.

Theodolinda it was who founded the famous Basilica of San Giovanni at Monza, where a series of frescoes long preserved the tradition of Longobard attire. The present fourteenth century Cathedral of elaborate brickwork has been modernised, but here her body lies, and here in the Treasury, amongst other personal possessions of the great Queen, the Iron Crown of Lombardy is preserved. Both the handsome thirteenth century Broletto, with its fine windows and balcony, raised upon open arches, and the façade of grey and yellow marble, with its large rose window, have been recently restored.

SARONNO.

The presence of so grand a church, with its Bramantesque cupola (1498) and with decorations so magnificent, may seem strange in a tiny town like Saronno. But the funds for the pilgrimage Church of Our Lady of Miracles were begged of passers-by by one Pedretto, who had long been bed-ridden, but was miraculously cured by prayer to a statue of the Virgin, which stood in an obscure wayside shrine on the Varese road. And the sympathy of S. Carlo Borromeo, who visited Saronno during the plague, helped to carry the building to completion (1581).

It is said that having sought asylum here after killing a man in self-defence, Luini returned the hospitality of the brethren, who gave him food and drink, by painting the noble frescoes in the cloister and the church. It is a spot appropriate to his genius. Child of the water and the hills of Italian lakeland, Luini always paints the softer harmonies of life, telling the simple, direct story of human love and divine compassion, prophet of pure loveliness and unquestioning belief, poet of the primitive purity and of the tender piety born of the mountains and the lakes.

CHAPTER II.

ROMAN MILAN.

It is not by accident that Mediolanum,—capital of the oldest Celtic settlement in modern Lombardy after the Insubres had destroyed Etruscan Melpum ; the key which, when the Romans had seized it, enabled them to extend their growing Empire up to the boundary of the Alps ; the Court, when that Empire was declining, of the Emperor of the West ; the See of Archbishops when the Church of S. Ambrose rivalled that of S. Peter ; the Milan, which, sacked, attacked, destroyed a hundred times by Huns and Goths and Romans, by Lombards and Franks, and utterly blotted out by Frederick Barbarossa, rose again like a Phoenix from its ashes to be the centre of the history of the Republics of the North, the first throne of the Renaissance ; the city where the Saxon Emperors, and, 800 years after them, Napoleon Buonaparte were crowned Kings of Italy ; the town which led the way in the revolt against Austrian tyranny and oppression,—is the Milan of to-day, the Capital of the modern industrial, social, artistic and intellectual development, and the headquarters of the railway system of Northern Italy.

It has no natural advantages for defence. It does not lie immediately on any navigable river. But to the north the Alps form a vast amphitheatre, to the circumference of which the roads leading to the passes, the Séptimer and Splügen passes which the Romans preferred, the Simplon and St. Gothard of modern commerce, radiate from Milan like the spokes of half a wheel. It is the strategical point from which an army can best strike at any invader from beyond the Alps. It is the commercial centre of the great, fertile arena, stretching to the Apennines,

> " The waveless plain of Lombardy
> Islanded by cities fair."

It is *Mediolanum,* the central point of the plain.

The position of Milan, as a breakwater against the tide of barbarian invasion, determined Maximian's choice, when the Emperor of the West established his Court here, after the division of the Empire (303). The barbarians of Germany were the pressing problem of the day. Their movements could be watched from Milan better than from Rome. Milan became, in fact, the capital of Northern Italy until Honorius abandoned it for the safe retreat of Ravenna.

It soon assumed the splendours of an imperial city. Ausonius describes the houses as numerous and handsome ; the manners of the people as polished and liberal. A circus, a theatre, a mint, a palace, baths, which bore the name of their founder Maximian, porticoes adorned with statues, and a double circumference of walls contributed to the beauty of the new capital. The second city of the Empire dared to rival Rome.

The Roman Empire was not built in a day, and it did not collapse like a house of cards. *Tantae molis erat*

Romanam condere gentem, and the stability of the foundations was proved by the centuries which it survived even
the repeated and terrible invasions of the barbarians, who
alone existed outside this, the only civilisation of the world.
The greater number of the cities now existing in Italy
flourished in at least equal splendour under Rome.   Milan,
Bologna, Verona, and other urban centres of the districts
into which the Roman Provinces were divided, rivalled the
capital in luxury, and enjoyed a considerable degree of local
independence.   They were governed by Municipal Senates,
elected by the people, and by two annual Chief Magistrates.
Here dwelt the proprietors of the neighbouring lands, who
lodged in palaces attended by slaves and freedmen, whilst
slaves worked their fields.   A middle class of artisans and
shopkeepers, and a mob of slothful paupers, whom the
millionaire land-owners, gradually developing into an
immense and organised bureaucracy, pacified with doles of
corn and public entertainments, completed the population
of these cities.   They were all miniature Romes, these
military or civilian colonies, with their own assemblies,
magistrates, schools, baths, temples, aqueducts, bridges,
barracks and amphitheatres.   They spread in every direction
from the central point, the Forum at Rome, to the extreme
limits of the Empire.   Along the magnificent roads, which
connected them with that centre, were, every few miles
apart, wonderfully organised posting stations, which enabled
governors and merchants throughout the known world to
keep in touch with the Capital in a manner unapproached
till the days of railways, and in some ways unequalled now.
There was one tongue and one head.   But trade was in
the hands of slaves, and the army was largely composed

of slaves and professional soldiers, of the same nationality as those Barbarians, who were pressing more and more irresistibly upon the frontiers of the Empire.

And meanwhile the doctrine of one Jesus of Nazareth was steadily sapping the foundations of this social fabric, denying the gods of Roman patriotism, denying the inequality of men, denying that the maintenance of an earthly empire, made by men's hands, was the be-all and end-all of life.

The unerring political instinct of the Roman administrators recognised at once that this doctrine was subversive of all existing social order. The best and most conscientious of the Emperors strove their utmost to stamp out these " enemies of the human race," as Tacitus, the philosophic historian, called the Christians.

But persecution was in this case not successful. The blood of the martyrs was the seed of the Church. By his famous Edict of Milan (313), Constantine put an end to the persecution of the Christians, and established religious freedom and equality throughout the Empire.

The subsequent vicissitudes of her career will explain why Milan can boast of but few traces of her ancient magnificence. A few fragments of Roman and pre-Roman antiquities are preserved in the *Museo Archeologico*, noticeably the torso of a Venus, and in the *Corso Vittorio Emmanuele* stands the " *uomo di pietra*," the statue of a Consul. Vestiges of the massive masonry of the wall we have referred to have been found (*Casa di Risparmio*), and of the high round towers which the chronicler says guarded the six principal gates (*Monastero Maggiore*). And a vague tradition of past splendour survives in the nomenclature of the Christian Churches. S. Vittore al Theatro, la Maddalena al Cerchio, and S. Giorgio in Palazzo (with its Luini pictures) indicate perhaps the sites of the Roman theatre, the Roman " circus " and the Palace of the Caesars. Traces of this Palace have indeed been found between the Via Torino and Via Nerino. The severe Doric Porta Romana is, of course, much later. It was designed by Martino Bassi for the reception of Margaret of Austria, who married Philip III. of Spain, Duke of Milan.

But, in the middle of the Corso di Porta Ticinese, sixteen majestic Corinthian columns of white marble rise up in solemn and lonely grandeur above the surging tide of busy humanity that ebbs and flows through the modern street, resembling the mighty ribs of some stately vessel stranded on the shores of time. Like that still perfect bridge which spans the Kiakhta River in a remote Commagenian gorge, these grim, iron-bound columns stand to bear witness to the wreck of that stupendous Imperial system, whose work still endures.

They are probably fragments of the Baths which Maximian built, the club-rooms and luxurious meeting-places of Roman life. The old order changed, yielding place to new. Where the Romans had erected their baths or temples, the Christians often built their churches there, converting to the use of the true faith the atmosphere of religion that hung about the pagan fanes. Even the Parthenon was turned into a Christian church. The chapel of S. Aquilinus within the adjacent Church of S. Lorenzo, which contains the massive Byzantine tomb of Ataulphus, King of the Goths, successor of Alaric, and some notable rich mosaics of the fifth century, was probably one of the

THE ROMAN COLUMNS BY THE PORTA TICINESE, MILAN.

inner. rooms of the Roman *thermae*. S. Lorenzo itself is an octagonal building with a dome, the sixteenth century version by Martino Bassi of a sixth century basilica after the manner of S. Vitale at Ravenna.

THE SAINTS OF MILAN.

The adhesion of Theodosius the Great to the orthodox creed brought Church and Empire into close alliance. It was an alliance that lent strength to both, though of that very strength and union discord and weakness were the inevitable offspring. From that union at this period the Church sucked out no small advantage. It was the era when the Latin system of theology was established, which had for its object the maintenance of one faith and one authority based upon the political powers of the Church. Typical as a product of that momentous union and as a promoter of that resultant ascendancy of the Church, stands forth St. Ambrose, the intrepid Bishop, whose vigour and virtue gave to the See of Milan a position inferior only to that of Rome and Ravenna. A saint by virtue of his character and the strength of his faith, this Bishop gave the cue to the ambitious Popes of succeeding ages by his unbending attitude towards the Emperor.

Chosen Bishop of Milan by the people in response to the cry of a child "Ambrose Bishop!" unwilling, unbaptised, scion of a noble Roman family and son of a praetorian prefect of Gaul, he did his utmost to escape the burden of his office, but the people would not hearken to his "*Nolo episcopari*."

He hastened to his judgment-hall and had some criminals put on the rack. But the people were not deterred by the

shrieks of the victims of a merciless judge. He ordered
prostitutes to be introduced into his house. " We," said
the people, " will bear your sin." Once consecrated, he set
himself to study theology, and became the chief support of
Gratian against Arianism. The Arians held that Christ
was but the first of finite beings, the mere creation of the
Deity.

Such was his eloquence, that the legend, told of Plato,
Pindar, and since of many others, was fathered upon
Ambrose. A swarm of bees had settled on his cradle, it
was said, as he lay asleep, and the lips of the infant were
honey-laden. Hence the bee-hive which distinguishes him
in Art. Despising wealth, he sold without hesitation the
consecrated plate for the redemption of captives. He won
and retained the devotion of the clergy and people of Milan.
The Archbishop was brave as he was wise. When the
gleam of the arms and the dust of advancing cavalry first
announced the approach of Maximus to the walls of Milan,
Ambrose refused to recognise the usurper, just as in later
years, when Argobastes had set the renegade rhetorician
Eugenius upon the throne and, the old Pagan religion being
restored, the soldiers boasted that they would stable their
horses in the churches of Milan, he alone resisted the claims
of successful usurpation. Refusing Eugenius' gifts, he
withdrew from Milan and waited till Theodosius routed
Argobastes and Eugenius, as he had destroyed Maximus, at
Aquileia.

And when, in 384, the beautiful and spirited Empress
Justina demanded in the name of her son, the boy-emperor,
Valentinian, first the Portian basilica (now baroque sixteenth
century San Vittore) outside Milan, and then, in its stead,

the new and larger basilica within the walls, to be used for
Arian worship, resolutely, in spite of every menace,
Ambrose refused to yield up to Caesar what he held was
God's. He spent the night with his priests chanting
psalms in the " little basilica," the day in preaching with
fiery eloquence. The Empire, he declared, could dispose
of earthly palaces, but not of the House of God. The

ONE OF THE ARMS OF THE CHAIR OF ST.
AMBROSE IN THE CHOIR OF SANT'
AMBROGIO.

mother of the Emperor he likened to Jezebel and Herodias.
His eloquence inflamed the temper of the people to fever
heat. A large body of the Palace troops marched to occupy
the basilica. The Goths were met, on the sacred threshold,
by the bishop, who, undaunted, thundered against them a
sentence of excommunication. The Imperial authority
quailed before the resolute prelate. The soldiers were withdrawn, and the Catholics left in possession of all the churches
of Milan.

By the influence of Justina, however, an edict of toleration was now published, granting a free exercise of their religion to all who professed the faith of Rimini, and an Arian Bishop, Auxentius, was encouraged to claim the throne of Milan. Ambrose was summoned to plead against him in the Imperial consistory. He refused. The sovereign, he said, was young and unbaptised. A bishop could not place his rights at the feet of laymen. Ambrose was forced to take refuge in the Church. The faithful—Monica and Augustine too amongst them, perhaps—crowded round him. In the face of the soldiers Ambrose set them to sing the hymns he had written and to chant the Psalms antiphonally. He knew how mighty a strain was that doxology which "made all who sang it teachers." The soldiers were withdrawn. The enthusiasm of the people overwhelmed the malice of Justina. Ambrose was left free to dedicate a church—the Ambrosian—and by his direction, the relics of SS. Gervasius and Protasius, martyrs of Milan, were discovered and placed in the new basilica. The feeble sovereign of Italy was unable to contend with so pronounced a favourite of Heaven.

Under Theodosius, the bigotry of Ambrose became yet more aggressive. He refused to obey the Emperor's command to rebuild a synagogue, which had been burnt by the people. No house, he declared before Theodosius, must be rebuilt, where Christianity was denied. But there was another act of his which earned for the Milanese prelate the admiration of the Roman world, when, for the first time since the establishment of the imperial despotism, the voice of a subject was raised in public condemnation of an act of tyrannical vengeance, and for the first time an

Emperor of Rome humbled himself in contrite confession before a new moral power, strong to bow the highest, as the meanest, under its dominion. Stung to madness at the news of a murderous insurrection at Thessalonica, the pious but choleric Theodosius, at the instigation of his minister, Rufinus, had ordered a promiscuous massacre of the citizens, innocent and guilty alike. Such was the news which filled the mind of Ambrose with anguish and horror. He immediately left Milan and wrote to Theodosius, calling upon him to repent. Otherwise, he said, he could not admit him to the Temple of the Lord or allow him to receive the holy Eucharist with hands polluted by the blood of innocent men and women. The Emperor was deeply affected, and, after bewailing his fault, proceeded in the accustomed manner to perform his devotions in the great Basilica. He was stopped in the porch by Ambrose, who, laying his hand upon the purple robe of Theodosius, declared in the tone of an ambassador of Heaven that private contrition was not sufficient to atone for a public fault. He had sinned like David, and like David he must repent. The Emperor retired abashed, and remained excommunicate for eight months, weeping because the temple of God was open to slaves and beggars and he alone was excluded. His minister, Rufinus, after attempting to win the Bishop by flattery, declared that the Emperor would enter the Church with or without his consent. " He must first pass over my body," replied Ambrose. And before Theodosius did indeed enter the Church, he had made submission to Ambrose. He did penance, December 25, 390, removing his imperial ornaments and prostrating himself on the pavement, weeping and repeating the words of

the Psalmist, " My soul cleaveth unto the dust," whilst the
people prayed and wept with him.

Theodosius seated Valentinian upon the throne of Milan,
and it was here that the unfortunate youth was buried,
and Ambrose pronounced his funeral oration when he had
been murdered by the barbarian Argobastes.

" From his time forward, Milan is no more the imperial,
but the Ambrosian city. Throughout her mediaeval existence the consecrating memory of Sant' Ambrogio, her patron
and protector, set like a spiritual jewel in a hundred exquisite
and devoutly fantastic legends, is present in her government,
her struggles for liberty, her art and peaceful industry, the
daily life and the peculiar ritual of her religious worship "
(Noyes).

Every trace of that " new basilica within the walls,"
scene of the conflict between Justina and Ambrose, has
disappeared. But its site was that of the great Gothic
Duomo which is the glory of Milan.

A portion of the doors which Ambrose closed in the face
of Imperial intruders and Imperial sinners is preserved in
the church (with later twelfth century restorations), which
took the place of that which he himself founded and dedicated to the martyrs he " invented."   It was then dedicated
to him, Sant' Ambrogio.

The aisles and nave, with their ogival vaults, which are
evidently important links in the transition from the Italo-
Byzantine style to Gothic, are probably the result of French
influence in the twelfth century.   But this is a moot point.
The campanile dates from 1129.

Near this Church, whose founder humbled the temporal
power of Rome to do penance before the spiritual throne,

stands, beneath the lime-trees in the piazza, a solitary column, relic of some Roman temple or Pagan rite. It was here that the Lombard Kings, as the successors of ancient Rome, took their coronation oath before being crowned in the Church with the Iron Crown of Kingship, now preserved at Monza.

A fine atrium, the courtyard beyond which the unbaptised might not pass, but where they were instructed by the priests and bishops of the early Church, and whence they could watch the gorgeous ceremonies of the initiated within, is a rich museum of early Christian tombstones and inscriptions.

The graceful decorations of the entrance portal is the work of the Master Adam. The sculptors who decorated the church and pulpit have run riot in ornamentation.

The Chair of St. Ambrose, wherein he and his successors sat in synod, surrounded by the ancient bishops of the northern Sees, is preserved in the upper choir, the marble screen and the roof of which, aglow with a splendid mosaic, contrast with the plain, round brick arches of the Lombard basilica. Beneath the High Altar, which stands isolated in front of the upper choir, lies the body of the Great Archbishop. And the front of this altar, the Palliotto, as it is called, is the most precious monument of the Saint. This marvellous masterpiece of mediaeval metal-work, signed by the Master Smith, Wolvinus, circ. 850, repeats, in panels of beaten silver and gold, set in a framework of uncut jewels and enamel of the most exquisite colours, the story told in the contemporary Mosaics of the Tribuna, the episodes in the life of S. Ambrose.

The columns of red porphyry which support the twelfth

century canopy over the altar are said to have been taken from a neighbouring temple of Jupiter and presented by the Emperor to Bishop Ambrose for the altar in his new church.

We have seen how the Christians converted Pagan buildings into Houses of God. The construction of early Christian churches was also based, naturally enough, upon the traditions of Pagan temples. Their orientation was adopted; the churches were built on an axis of East and West, save where, as at Venice, the nature of the land forbade. The atrium we have just described is a feature borrowed from the forecourt of a temple. And the apsidal presbytery, with its altar for the Communion Supper, is derived from the *triclinia*, the dining-rooms of Roman private houses.

The truth of the miracles which attended the discovery of the Ambrogian martyrs is attested by Ambrose and by his proselyte, Augustine, who was at that time a lecturer on Rhetoric at Milan, though dissatisfied with all systems of philosophy which he had studied. Wearied, yet tied by the pleasures of the flesh, Augustine first heard of the living power of the love of Christ as manifested in the life of Antony, and told to him by an officer in the Imperial Palace. Stirred by the narrative, in the agony of a soul in travail, he rushed forth into the garden of his house, and flung himself down on the turf beneath the shadow of a fig-tree. And there in the midst of his emotion he heard a voice singing, " Take up and read! Take up and read! " the refrain, perhaps, of some child's game. He took and read the scroll at his side : his eyes fell on Rom. xiii. 13 : " Not in rioting and drunkenness, not in chambering and wantonness, but put ye on the Lord Jesus Christ."

Confirmed by Ambrose in the Christian faith, as he has recorded in his so vivid *Confessions*, the repentant sinner, not yet saint, presented himself, with his illegitimate son, for baptism in this very Church of Ambrogio.

THE BRONZE SERPENT IN THE CHURCH OF SANT' AMBROGIO
AT MILAN.

It is, according to tradition, the serpent held up by Moses in
the wilderness.

And it may be, as tradition records, that this occasion inspired Ambrose and Augustine to write, there in Milan, the triumph song of Christianity, the Te Deum (*see* pp. 106, 107).

Of a different kind was another and most popular Saint of Milan, Peter Martyr. Son of a citizen of Verona, he joined the Dominican Order in the year of the death of its Founder (*see* pp. 152 ff.). *Domini canes*, the Order was called, and is so indicated in Art, and like a keen " hound of the Lord," Peter Martyr entered upon the mission of chasing the world into orthodoxy. He flung himself with impassioned energy into the task of preaching the true faith and of suppressing those who dissented from it. At Milan he roused Archbishop and Podestà to exercise the laws in defence of orthodoxy. Many heretics were burned, and the enthusiasm of Oldrado, the Podestà, was recorded upon the walls of the Palazzo della Ragione—" *Qui solium struxit, Catharos ut debuit uxit.*"

Politics added fuel to the flames of theological hatred. The Ghibellines lent their support to the heretics. The Pope set Peter at the head of the Inquisition, and at the mercy of the Inquisition all heretics were placed by the Bull *Ad extirpanda*. The " scourge of the heretics " was not content with eloquent denunciation. He surrounded himself with a band of fanatics, and, aided by the Guelph party, fought pitched battles at Florence, struck down multitudes of heretics in Cremona, and roused such tumultuous warfare at Milan that a large part of the city was destroyed.

At last, when on his way from Como to Milan, to deal with a heretic whom the Inquisition held at his mercy, the career of this terrible Apostle of Orthodoxy was cut short by the daggers of assassins.

A sword transfixing his skull is the emblem in Art of the sanctified Inquisitor. Such was the career of the frenzied *fratre*, whose martyrdom so stirred the people that they sacked the house of the Podestà who had allowed his murderer to escape. Peter had extinguished heresy at

Milan.   He had been the last to rely on the force of miracles alone, but now a long list of miracles was attributed to him.

Of these, the miracle of the cloud which he called up to shade his audience when he was preaching, his healing of a dumb man and of the sick by the touch of his garments, and the stilling of a storm at sea by the invocation of his spirit, are represented by the reliefs on the superb sepulchral shrine in which the body of the Saint is laid.

The Church of S. Eustorgio, founded in the fourth century, and endowed with the bones of the Three Kings by the Emperor Constantine, who presented them to the Archbishop Eustorgius,[1] near the Porta Ticinese, outside the walls built by the Emperor Maximian, had by this time been made over to the Dominicans.   The large, round columns that support the roof may date from days before the rebuilding and restoration of subsequent centuries destroyed whatever of beauty and interest the original basilica possessed.   It was from the stone pulpit which overlooks the Piazza, that Peter of Verona had thundered his denunciations against the heretics.   Upon this pulpit his martyred body was exposed to the reverent gaze of the multitude, before being enclosed in a marble sarcophagus, which he had declared in his lifetime to be a fitting resting place for a martyred saint.   Pilgrims flocked to this shrine in ever increasing crowds, until at last enough money had been collected from them and the pious great to found for him a new and nobler monument.

This masterpiece of Giovanni di Balduccio, a sculptor

[1] The huge, plain stone sarcophagus, the *Sepulcrum Trium Majorum*, in which this treasure was kept, is preserved in the Cappella de' Magi.

trained in the school of Niccolò Pisano, was completed in
1339. The sarcophagus, adorned with eight bas-reliefs, is
supported by eight caryatid figures, typifying the Virtues.
These figures and reliefs must be admitted to be in execution
inferior to those on the Tomb of S. Augustine at Pavia,
but the exquisite grace and perfect proportions of Balduccio's
design, so delicately carved in marble ivory-white, render
it, as a whole, the most beautiful of the sepulchral shrines
we shall visit.[1]

This beautiful gem of sculpture shines in a setting equally
beautiful. The lovely Cappella Portinari, fairest offspring
of the genius of Michelozzo, was built by Pigello dei
Portinari (1462), a rich Florentine banker, representative
of the Medici in their beautiful Milanese Bank,[2] and it
recalls the Cappella de' Pazzi at Florence. Beautiful in its
proportions, it is beautiful also in its decorations and furni-
ture. With splendid bronze candelabra and a wrought-iron
gate Michelozzo the craftsman supplemented the loving
labours of Michelozzo the architect; Vincenzo Foppa, or
some other Lombard artist of the Paduan School, painted
the ceiling with frescoes, full of animation and vigour,
depicting scenes from the life of the Saint; the pilasters are
richly carved; and, above all, a frieze of singing angels and
a border of cherubs' heads in low relief crown the chapel
walls;—blond angels, dancing in happiest chorus mid fruits

[1] The monument of Lanfranco Settala, founder of the modernised
Church of S. Marco, is very probably also by Giovanni di Balduccio, or else
by Bonino da Campione, one of his assistants.

[2] A magnificent marble doorway with portraits of Francesco and Bianca
Sforza survives in the Castello Museum to bear witness to the former
magnificence of this famous house.

and flowers, so exquisite in their vivacity and grace, so richly endowed with the spontaneous invention and humanity of their creator, that they seem to fill the martyr's resting place with all the joyous harmonies of the music of the spheres.

One other Saint must here be mentioned, who lives in the hearts of the Milanese by virtue of his Christian charity. When the city was groaning under the Spanish dominion, San Carlo Borromeo, the Cardinal-Archbishop of Milan, (1565) set himself to reform, to educate and to discipline an ignorant, lazy and licentious clergy. He enforced the rigours of the Inquisition ; he forbade the frolics of the Carnivals. The *Umiliati*, an Order which had been enormously powerful and was now utterly corrupt, were suppressed, and their principal home, the Brera, was handed over to the Jesuits. Himself a model of all the virtues, trained in the school of the Jesuits, Borromeo renounced his princely revenues, devoting them to the relief of the poor and the erection of stately and useful buildings, in which to house and educate the new Orders he introduced. The Archiepiscopal Seminary, with its baroque portal and fine court by Meda, and the Jesuit Church of S. Fedele (Pellegrini), as well as the modern rotunda church called after him, record his name and work. And when Milan was scourged, first by the terrible famine of 1570, and then six years later by the plague, the Archbishop, remaining when all the rulers had fled, organised order, combated the contagion, visited the sick and gave his all to the relief of his famine-and-plague-stricken flock. When he had emptied his granaries and his cellars, he cut up even the tapestry, the curtains, and the scarlet and purple cloth, used for decorations, which he found in his palace. So he clad the shivering multitudes, who cried to him for help, in the gorgeous colours of ecclesiastical raiment. And the streets of the stricken city blazed forth like a flower garden in spring.

It was he who consecrated the Duomo, and there, in a subterranean chapel, is the much-frequented tomb of the Saint. He contributed to the history of Milan that touch of Christian charity expressed in his motto *Humilitas*, which is lacking alike in the fanatical intolerance of the Hound of the Lord and in the proud, unscrupulous ambition of the Vipers of Milan.

CHAPTER III.

THE LOMBARDS.

DURING the centuries of barbarian invasion which Italy was doomed to endure, Milan, capital of the Roman Province of Liguria, extending from the Adda to Piacenza, suffered cruelly. The true policy of the Empire, as recognised by Caesar's practical foresight and recommended in Augustus' will, was to establish and fortify the Imperial frontiers on the Danube and the Rhine. But even if succeeding Emperors had been content to do this, it would perhaps have proved impossible to withstand the inroads of the hordes beyond the pale, the hardy, warlike, nomadic, pastoral people, who annually shifted their quarters in the German bogs and forests, and who, pressed by other tribes from the North and lured by the scent of prey in the rich provinces beyond, might have broken through the frontiers that hemmed them in, however strong.

The hosts of Alaric swept over the open country, leaving the fenced cities for the most part intact. But the onslaught of the Tartar hordes under Attila, King of the Huns, proved more terrible.

After a prolonged siege, with which at the last moment he had been induced to persevere by the sight of a stork abandoning her nest in the doomed city, the " Scourge of

God " had taken and destroyed Aquileia. The richest and strongest of the maritime cities, capital of Venetia and Istria, was, like Padua, reduced to a heap of stones, so that a succeeding generation could scarcely discover its ruins. Terrified by this example, Milan and Pavia submitted without a blow, and gratefully applauded the clemency which spared their lives and their buildings. When he took possession of the royal palace at Milan, it is said that Attila was offended by a picture which represented the princes of Scythia prostrate at the feet of the Caesars. He took a humorous revenge, by commanding the painter to reverse the figures and the attitudes, and the suppliant Emperors were represented with greater truth emptying their bags of tributary gold before the throne of the Scythian monarch.

The Western Empire fell. The Goths and Vandals established their empire in Europe. It was reserved for Justinian to win back part of the inheritance of the Caesars and to deliver their subjects of the west from the usurpation of heretics and barbarians. The campaigns of imperial armies under Narses and the heroic Belisarius destroyed the name and nation of the Ostrogoths. Whilst Witigis and his Goths were occupied in their vain and disastrous siege of Rome, Milan, under her Bishop Datius, led the revolt of Liguria to the Empire. But on his retiring to find shelter within the walls and morasses of Ravenna, Witigis detached 10,000 men to punish the rebellious city. Ten thousand Burgundians descended from the Alps to join in that chastisement. The capital of Liguria was reduced by famine ; Datius fled to the Byzantine Court, and the clergy of Milan were slaughtered at the foot of their altars. Three hundred thousand males were reported, by an over-generous estimate, to be slain; the women were given to the Burgundians, and the walls of Milan were levelled to the ground. The Goths, in their last moments, were revenged by the destruction of a city second only to Rome in size and opulence, in the splendour of its buildings and the number of its inhabitants.

The overthrow of the Ostrogoths left Italy exposed to yet another barbarian invasion. In 568 the Longobards, or Longbeards, so Paulus Diaconus derives their name, crossed the Julian Alps. Clad in loose linen robes of various colours, with breeches laced up in front, with streaming beards and hair cut short behind, but parted over the forehead in long, shaggy, side locks, this motley horde of Bavarians, Saxons, Gepidae and Swabians advanced into Venetia under Alboin, and established a Duchy at Cividale in Friuli, one of the gates of Italy (*Forum Julii*). A train of waggons, in which their women and children journeyed, served for their shelter at night.

Under an Emperor whose extravagant policy was retrenchment regardless of cost, the Byzantines in Italy had been left without money, and therefore without men, to resist the new invasion, which was destined to leave so lasting a mark upon the nomenclature, the architecture and the social development of the country. One after another the cities of the North opened their gates, almost without a blow, to the barbarian, when he promised to respect Church property. Milan, whose ruined walls had been only partially rebuilt by Narses, was surrendered by Honoratus, who occupied the Chair of St. Ambrose. But Archbishop, nobles and clergy alike were driven forth by the perfidy

of Alboin to seek refuge in the distant ramparts of Genoa
(569). With this event the Lombard kingdom in North
Italy would have been established, had not Piacenza,
Cremona and other cities on the Po whom aid could reach
from Ravenna by river, still resisted, had not Pavia, strongly
fortified and strongly garrisoned, held out stubbornly for
two years more.

The Lombards proved incapable of uniting into a compact
nation. They paid for their incapacity by failing to complete the conquest of Italy, and finally by their own downfall.
Their kingdom fell before Charlemagne and his Franks—
Germanic tribes from the right bank of the Rhine—whom
the Popes invited to attack them. Italy was split into fragments, never again to be entirely united, and the struggle
between Church and State had begun, which was to last
through the Middle Ages down to the present day.
Such were the results of the Longobard Conquest. The
special characteristic of their kingdom was its division into
Duchies,—cities with adjacent territory determined by the
ancient Roman circumscription,—under Dukes appointed for
life by the King. The name *Cordusio* still used in the
centre of the city, a corruption of *Corte Ducis*, the Duke's
Palace, recalls this period at Milan. There almost independent Viceroys, always striving after greater independence,
wasted their own strength and the organising power of the
kingdom in perpetual strife and revolution, till at length
the Lombards, having failed to make Italy German, became
themselves absorbed into Italy and the Roman system.
Opposed to the Lombard were the Byzantine Dukes, holding for the Emperor all that the Lombards had failed to
seize. The chief representative of the Emperor in Italy

was the Exarch, who resided at Ravenna and bore, nominally
at least, the same relation to the Byzantine Dukes as the
King to the Dukes of the Lombards. After the death of
Charlemagne came revolution and counter-revolution, broken
by the horrors of the raids of Saracens and Huns. But
the result of the Germanic invasions, on the whole, was to
leave the Peninsular, which had been enervated by luxury,
strengthened by an infusion of Teutonic blood, and filled
with new vigour and new ideals. The fabric of an outworn
civilisation had been swept away. In the country, a land-
owning, warlike class, chiefly Teutonic conquerors, had
arisen, ruling over the descendants of the Roman *coloni*,
repopulating and subdividing the huge estates of later
Roman times. In the cities, the Roman element still predominated. The old municipal organisation was not wholly
destroyed. The late Roman institution of *Scholae*, or Trade
Guilds, in which were enrolled all the citizens who practised
manual trades, continued to exist, and reappeared later as
one of the leading features of municipal life.

The work of the Lombard, then, was to give hardihood
and system to the enervated body and enfeebled mind of
Christendom.

Devoted to war, to the pleasures of the bowl and the
chase, the Lombard covered every church he built with
representations of the sword, the hawk, the hound or his
prey. At Milan, in the churches of S. Vincenzo in Prato
and S. Satiro, of S. Calimero, S. Eustorgio, S. Celso, S.
Nazaro and S. Babila, can be studied the gradual evolution
of the Lombard style. And by the Lombard style of
architecture I mean the Italo-Byzantine style as it was modified by the influence of the Northerners not so much during,

as after, the domination of the Lombards. Some of the most characteristic Lombard buildings—apart from the Lombard Renaissance work—are as late as the twelfth century. Lombard architecture must, in fact, be regarded as a geographical rather than a dynastic expression. From the fourth century onwards the artistic capital of the world was Constantinople: with the rise of the Mohammedan Empire the centre of art passed farther east. From the sixth to the eleventh century the barbarian invaders of Italy, Goth or Lombard, absorbed and assimilated the Italo-Byzantine style of architecture which came through Ravenna, the seat of an Exarch representing the Eastern Empire, from the East. This style the Lombards modified chiefly, at first, by the addition of certain barbaric details of ornamentation, the knotted dragons, the fighting men, the hounds and falcons of the chase, the great lions tearing their prey, with which they decorated their porches and facades. But the large cruciform churches with a cupola over the crossing, a circular apse and radiating chapels, with which we shall grow familiar, these are the direct outcome of eastern influence, passing through Ravenna and Milan, to develop into the Romanesque, and finally into the Gothic of the north. Then, at the end of the twelfth century, a wave of artistic influence washed back from France. There was an outburst of Gothic architecture in Italy. The activity of the Cistercians and the need of the Franciscan and Dominican Orders for large churches to hold their increasing congregations led to the adoption of the alien style. The Lombard art was transmuted to the art of Verona, Milan and Venice. The ogival vault and the pointed arch were accepted for a while, but were quickly modified by the national genius of Italy into a kind of pointed Romanesque, before the return to the traditional, congenial horizontal line and rounded arch, which was the gift of the classical revival of the Renaissance. Strange, indeed, to the eye trained to the beauties of Northern Gothic, to the glorious proportions of Salisbury, the grouping of steep roofs and soaring spires as at Canterbury, Lincoln and Chartres, and to the immense windows of the cathedrals of the sunless northern lands, will the Italian Gothic churches at first appear, those long, low buildings, sparingly lit, with their flat, central domes, detached campanili, and façades, filled with elaborate ornament and circular windows, and crowned by heavily corniced gables, which screen rather than complete the whole. But we soon learn to love the simple, square, unbuttressed brick towers, with or without arcaded stages, which form no part of the structural combination ; the typical Lombard campanile, of which the square tower of S. Satiro may be regarded as the prototype. The development of the terra-cotta campanile may well be studied in the bell towers of S. Eustorgio, S. Marco, S. Antonio and in the rich and elegant tower of S. Gottardo (1339) in the Palazzo Reale, which recalls that of the Certosa of Chiaravalle, with its series of octagonal stages and round-arched windows crowned by a steeple. We grow interested, too, in the Lombard use of brickwork, the development of which was determined by the scarcity of stone and marble and the presence of clay-fields in the valley of the Po. The Veronese builders had ready to hand the quarries whence they could draw the *mandorlato*, whose rose tints suffuse their columned aisles ; Venice could ransack the east for the marble of her palaces and for the artistic ideas of Alexandria. But the Paduan towns must rely upon their native material, and Paduan architects, as at Crema, Chiaravalle, Pavia, confronted the problem of decoration in this medium. In the Paduan plain we are in a paradise of terra-cotta. We shall notice, again and again, how the facility of repeating the patterns of moulded bricks led to the multiplication of trefoiled, arcaded brick ornament, ornament that has no constructional use or meaning, but hangs beneath window sills or clambers up gables.

I have said that Lombard architecture is a geographical rather than a dynastic expression. No well-defined school of Lombard architecture arose till the eleventh or twelfth century. When it arrives, we find that its characteristics express the result of northern imagination wedded to the tradition of the round arch, the horizontal line and the severe ornamentation of the monuments of Roman greatness.

The pyramidal façade ; the domes rising tier above tier from the intersection of nave and transept and ending in minarets and pinnacles ; the long, low colonnades of marble pilasters ; the round and pointed arches so boldly, so deftly combined ; the open porches resting upon pink, life-like Lombard lions of stone that blends in colour and effect so harmoniously with brickwork ; the plain, square, detached campanili that suspend aerial lanterns ; above all, the weird, wild invention of the northern giant luxuriating in the sunshine of the south, carving each string-course and capital with lions and mermaids, with sphinxes and griffins, with serpents and harpies, with winged horses and lizards, with knights in armour and hounds on the trail, and the touch of northern humour that pervades it all, like a fresh wind from the Alps blowing over the baking plain ; these are the features of a thousand churches in the plain of Lombardy, bizarre, not beautiful as wholes, suggesting the imperfect union of north and south, of Longbeard Teuton with Italian, of imagination and humour with the sensuous delight in pure beauty, of the sense of proportion with the joy in detail, of dome, round arch and horizontal line with pointed arch and soaring pinnacle.

Charlemagne had substituted Counts and Marquises for the Lombard Dukes. In the wreck of·his Empire they established themselves as hereditary rulers. In opposition to them stood the Bishops, largely chosen by the people. They had become the largest landowners in their dioceses, which coincided with the counties. And by the beginning of the eleventh century they had acquired the authority which had formerly been vested in the Counts. The Church, the one stable power in the midst of chaos, emerged triumphant, supreme in temporal as in spiritual dominion. The Archbishops of Milan appear as the wealthiest and most influential of the Lombard prelates, great feudal princes, who stood forth as arbiters of the affairs of Italy, and, acting the part of king-makers, laid that potent emblem, the Iron Crown, now upon the head of some Italian prince, now upon that of some heir of the Carlovingian tradition. Their object was always to increase their own power and to oppose the imperial nomination to the See.

In 1018 there was elected to the See of St. Ambrose a most capable and ambitious statesman, Aribert. Under this militant prelate, Milan, which had greatly increased in wealth and population, embarked upon a career of conquest. The rivalry between Milan and Pavia, which was to give rise to no less than six wars, apart from chronic enmity, in the next 150 years, had already begun. And when, on the death of Henry, the inhabitants of Pavia invited the French King to take possession of the crown of Italy, Aribert hastened to Germany and offered the kingdom to Conrad the Salic. He came, and since Pavia refused to open her gates to him, he received the Iron Crown at Milan. Aribert was left as his representative in Italy. The Milanese gladly followed their militant prelate, first to reduce Pavia, and then to subjugate the little neighbouring city of Lodi,[1] which had refused to accept a bishop of Aribert's choosing.

The pride and ambition of Aribert, however, soon involved him in a conflict not only with the lesser nobles of the city, but also with the Emperor himself. He had joined hands with the *Captains*, or higher nobles, in their opposition to the attempt of the *Valvassors*, or vassals, to make their fiefs hereditary. The latter were driven out of the city: they found support in the country, and the struggle spread through Lombardy. It was a step in the coming emancipation of the people from feudalism and the episcopal rule. A fierce battle was fought at Campo Malo. Aribert was worsted. Conrad now intervened. He came to Milan to restore order. But his presence led to a violent tumult there. He was obliged to quit the town, and marched to Pavia, which was quickly converted to the imperial interest when it was known that Milan had attacked the Emperor. Here Conrad assembled the Italian vassals, and sent Aribert to prison at Piacenza. This act caused the utmost indignation at Milan, and at once put an end

---

[1] Laus Pompeii, so called in honour of its founder, the father of Pompey the Great.

to the internal dissensions there. The Archbishop plied his gaolers with the heady vintage of Lombardy, and, escaping to Milan whilst the intoxicated Teutons were "snoring terribly," he there defied alike the Emperor's army and the excommunication of the Pope. He armed and disciplined all the citizens, united now in his defence, and invented, it is said, the device of the *Carroccio* to strengthen their patriotism in the field. This was a sacred car, hung with rich scarlet cloth and drawn by white oxen. Upon it was fixed a tall mast, with two white pennants fluttering from the top, and the image of the Crucified hanging half-way down. At the base was an altar, round which stood the priests invoking the blessing of Heaven upon the warriors. Like the Ark of Israel, the *Carroccio* was regarded by the citizen soldiers with the deepest veneration ; round the emblems of their faith and their existence they would rally, bearing it forward to victory with enthusiasm irresistible in the moments of advantage, defending it with desperate resolution in the hour of adversity. The loss of it implied the most crushing defeat. This singular device was afterwards adopted by all the Italian municipalities, and became the guide and inspiration of the Lombard peoples in their noble struggles for liberty, as, alas! in their petty enterprises of greed and of revenge.

It was, perhaps, the echo of an ancient Lombard custom. It was, doubtless, a symbol which would be likely to appeal in a peculiar degree to the instincts of a race, for whom, in their nomadic days, a waggon had been their only home. Certainly at this juncture the Milanese needed every encouragement. For Conrad, before departing for Germany, had caused all his adherents to swear to lay waste the lands of the rebellious city once a year. The burghers of Lodi and Pavia were ready enough to fulfil their obligation. Conrad's death put an end to hostilities. Aribert was left master of Lombardy. But the greatest of her ecclesiastical princes, who had "disposed of the whole kingdom at his nod," and who had thus triumphed over the head of feudalism, was also the last. In all the Lombard towns this rule of the Bishops had been preparing the way for municipal independence. In Milan we see clearly how the very victory of the Archbishop prepared the way for his fall. He had irretrievably weakened the feudal system, with which the episcopal and aristocratic power was bound up. He had stimulated the conscious existence and municipal organisation of the townsmen. He had disciplined the burghers and endowed them with the knowledge of arms.

Aware now of their strength, the people joined with the Valvassori, and broke into fierce revolt against the nobles. Under the skilful leadership of one Lanzone, a Captain who had espoused the popular cause, after months of rioting and bloodshed, they drove nobles and Archbishop together out of Milan. But the burgher forces could not meet the nobles in the open field, and they, to reduce the burghers, built a castle before each of the six gates of the city. Two years of siege, of famine and sickness were endured. Then the dread of imperial interference led to a reconciliation. The nobles returned, but the power of the Archbishop was in great part eliminated. The burghers had come into their own. The Commune of Milan was in being (1066).

The growth of the independence of the Milan, as of the other Lombard Communes, was furthered by the events of the succeeding years, the memorable struggle between Pope and Emperor on the subject of investitures, and the consequent movement for the reform of the clergy under Gregory VII. In Italy, the struggle centred round Milan, where Guido, an immoral Archbishop forced upon the people by the Emperor and supported by a lax and vicious clergy, was opposed by the people and the Pope. All tended to the emancipation of the Communes. For simoniacal Bishops, living in concubinage, vied with reforming, celibate rivals in bribing the citizens to support them, by granting away their privileges of government and their tolls ; by conceding to the burghers the care of their fortifications and the election of their own officers.

By the end of the eleventh century, then, Milan, with the other Lombard towns, had thrown off the yoke of the Bishops, and stood forth a free Republic, owning indeed the universal supremacy of the Emperor, but ready on occasion to ally herself either with him or with his resolute foe, Matilda, or defying Pope and Emperor alike, as suited best. The constitution of these new Republics was based on the organisation of the Trades Guilds with their representative heads, " Anziani," and corresponded roughly to the Governor, Council and General Assembly of our Colonial system. Two Consuls, reviving the old Latin tradition of the city, were chosen for the chief civil and military command ; there was a Council of chosen burghers to direct their policy, a Senate or Grand Council taken from the various classes, and a General Assembly of burghers, a Parlamento, which was summoned on grave occasions by the tolling of the City Bell to discuss and decide in the great Church or the City Square the questions of highest importance.

At first, in the natural evolution of things, the nobles tended to monopolise the higher offices, but by degrees the people made their power and their numbers more and more felt. Continual revolts counteracted the oligarchical tendencies of the magistrates, and vindicated the pretensions of the *popolo* to an increasing share in the direction of their own affairs.

It was characteristic of the Italian towns that the cities at once used their newly won liberty to fight each other. Commercial jealousy and quarrels over tolls, boundaries and waterways involved them from this time forward in unceasing fratricidal strife. Jealous of her flourishing trade, Milan turned first to crush her weaker neighbour, Lodi. An excuse for war was readily found in the disputed claim of the Archbishops of Milan to special authority there. Now and henceforth the quarrel between Empire and Church was embraced by the Communes, who called themselves Ghibelline or Guelf, according to their convenience, tradition and antipathies, and warred with each other under the banners of the Emperor or the Pope.

Aided by the Brescians, Milan ravaged the territory of Lodi, and utterly defeated first Pavia and then Cremona, her allies. The Cremonese prisoners were treated somewhat cavalierly. Their hands were tied behind their backs, and torches were fastened beneath. Then, when they had been assembled in the Piazza, the torches were lit, and the prisoners were driven forth through the open gates back to their own city, amidst the jeers of the Milanese.

Milan paid no heed to the Emperor's interference on

behalf of Lodi. The city fell at last into her hands. It was razed to the ground, and the inhabitants, forbidden to rebuild their homes, were scattered amongst six open villages. The prosperity of Como, strong on land and lake, next roused the envy of the Milanese. After ten years of war, which are likened by the chronicler to the Siege of Troy, Como was taken and sacked, and her fairest buildings destroyed.

The burghers turned their arms to wiser account in suppressing the feudal nobility who dwelt in castles in the surrounding country. These, after many years of struggle, the citizens compelled to come into the towns, build residences and dwell there, exchanging the semi-sovereign rights of freebooting, blackmailing robber nobles without the walls for full citizenship within them. But they brought their manners with them, and it was only after prolonged struggles that their power was extinguished and lawlessness checked by the increasing strength of the middle class of citizens.

A terrible day of retribution awaited the aggressive and tyrannical Commune. Frederick Barbarossa was elected Emperor, and the young King, "half barbarian, half Paladin," determined to convert his nominal Italian monarchy into a real one. But at the foot of the popular ramparts of the Lombard Republics, defended by the bands of intrepid citizens aflame with the love of liberty and eagerly responding to the summons of the bell from the Broletto and to the sight of their city standard erected upon the *Carroccio*, the pride of the Caesars was humbled. But not before the stately capital of Milan had been razed to the ground.

Milan's aggression had given the Emperor a pretext for reducing his chief vassal to obedience. One day, whilst he was dispensing justice at Constance, two citizens of Lodi, bearing heavy crosses upon their shoulders in token of their affliction, flung themselves at his feet and besought him with tears to deliver them from the yoke of Milan. The Emperor swore to punish their cruel and arrogant foe. But his letter, bidding the Milanese to restore the liberty of Lodi, when read out to the Assembly of the people, was received with the utmost indignation. The citizens prepared themselves for the inevitable struggle. The Naviglio Grande was constructed, canal and moat in one, encircling the suburbs with a new enceinte, and ramparts with gates of stone were built within it. At length Frederick arrived, having forced the passage of the Adda and established the citizens of Lodi in a new home, some four miles from the site of their former town. The second Lodi was strongly fortified, and has survived. The Emperor, supported by levies from all Lombardy, save Crema, Tortona and Como, laid siege to Milan. The defence was long and obstinate, but at length the proud city was humbled. " I love to reward rather than to punish," said Frederick, and granted lenient terms. But they were not observed. The Milanese rejected with contempt the Podestà, or foreign Governor, whom, in accordance with the regalian rights granted to him at Roncaglia, Frederick sent to administer justice in place of the Consuls ; they sprang at the throats of the German garrisons who held the passes of the Adda. The desperate defence of Crema delayed their punishment. But at length the might of the Emperor, aided by his Italian allies, wore down the rebellious city. With ashes on their heads

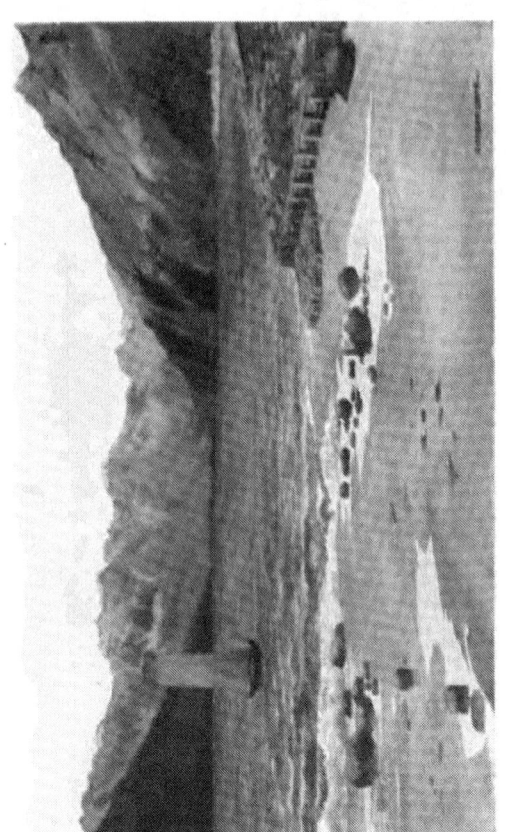

SUNSET AT LAKE COMO.

and ropes about their necks the famine-stricken burghers came out from the walls of Milan to prostrate themselves before Frederick. After a period of suspense he ordered the whole population to leave the city. Then he marched his army into the deserted town, and gave it over to utter destruction. To Lodi and Como, Pavia and Cremona, and all her bitterest enemies the work of annihilation was safely entrusted.

After the first surrender of Milan, Frederick had held a Diet at Roncaglia, where four famous jurists of Bologna decided that in the Emperor were vested all the regalian rights, or ordinary prerogatives of kingly government. Frederick's ideal was to establish an organised central government throughout Italy, administered by Imperial Governors (Podestà) in each city. It was an admirable ideal. If realised, it would have given peace and prosperity, in place of faction and rapine, to the land. But it had two drawbacks. It meant the crushing out of the beloved individual liberty of the towns, and it involved conflict with the Pope, who saw the privileges of the Holy See thereby infringed. Moreover the rule of the Imperial Governors proved oppressive. Opposition to Frederick's encroachments began with the machinations of the Greek Emperor, Manuel Comnenos, who was supported by the Venetian Republic and the confederacy of the four cities of the Veronese Mark—Verona, Padua, Treviso, Vicenza. It grew into the famous Lombard League (1167). Its object was to refuse to pay tribute or render services greater than had been rendered to Henry. As a declaration of war, it was decided to rebuild Milan. The burghers of the confederate cities, laying aside their quarrels for the nonce, assembled beneath their banners and marched to the desolate site, whither the outcast Milanese flocked from their scattered villages. The allies remained till the walls were in a state of defence. The limits of the town were marked by the present canal, along which the old walls ran. The central arch of the Porta Ticinese, and the arches of the Porta Nuova in the new enceinte [1] survive to illustrate this effort of individual independence and national resistance to a foreign oppressor. And, in the *Museo Archeologico*, in the *Castello*, are preserved representations of Frederick Barbarossa, astride a dragon, and of the Milanese returning to their native city, which were rudely carved by a contemporary sculptor upon the Porta Romana of that day.

The Imperial army, decimated by pestilence at Rome, could make no resistance to the Confederates. Frederick slunk back across the Alps. Lodi even, and even Pavia, were compelled to join the victorious League, which now numbered thirty-six towns. And in all the wide valley of the Po no feudal lord, be he Este or Montferrat, dared to remain on the side of the Emperor. Frederick, indeed, returned to enforce his claims, but at length the glorious day of Legnano (1176), waged about the Carroccio of Milan, defended by a devoted company of youths—the Company of Death—sworn to conquer or to die, proved to the Emperor that German feudalism could not crush the citizen militia of Lombardy. A truce, preliminary to the concession by the Peace of Constance of all that the cities had been fighting for—their customs, the regalian rights within their walls, and the right to make war upon each other—

---

[1] The city was enlarged by the Visconti in the sixteenth century. They built outside this enceinte and called the district beyond the walls the *Cittadella*.

GORDON HOME

SANT' ARCANGELO [See p. 178]

was arranged at Venice. And there, amid scenes of utmost splendour, the Emperor received, upon the threshold of St. Mark's—the spot is still shown—the Holy Father's kiss of peace.

Barbarossa's vain endeavour was repeated by his grandson, Frederick II. He failed again before the arms of the Communes and the thunder of the Vatican. The Lombard League was revived to resist him. The terrible disaster of Corte Nuova, near Crema (1237), seemed at first to have ruined the fortunes of the Guelfs. But, in spite of that overwhelming defeat, where, outmanœuvred by Frederick, the Milanese had lost their *Carroccio* and ten thousand men, the Lombard Communes would not yield up their independence. The Milanese, voicing the determination of the rest of the League, declared that, rather than submit to the Emperor's oppression, they would perish sword in hand beneath the ruins of their city. Brescia, with characteristic courage, withstood the Emperor's host for two months, and paved the way to his failure.

For the next sixty years no Emperor appeared in Italy. The Lombard Communes, that had been united for these brief moments in the presence of a common danger, having secured their autonomy and wrested themselves free of feudalism, were now left at liberty to fall upon their neighbours with renewed vivacity, attacking, defending, combining and disuniting with brilliant, kaleidoscopic changes, born of fratricidal greed, which it is quite outside the scope of this book to follow.[1]

[1] The curious reader—who should, however, have a head for halma, if not chess—is referred to the pages of Lanzani, of Sismondi, or of Professor Butler's *Lombard Communes*.

Henceforward the independent towns of Lombardy, now grouped in leagues, now separate, torn by faction within and without, losing their liberty by degrees in the blind intoxication of hatred of Guelf for Ghibelline, were to be ruled by oligarchs, more or less exclusive, on a basis of republican constitutions.

The occasion when the terms Guelf and Ghibelline—derived from rival German houses that claimed the Empire, and of which the former (Welf) supported the Papacy, the latter (Waiblingen) opposed it—came into use in Italy as the rallying cries of faction, is disputed. They represented, originally and in the abstract, the opposing ideals of the independence of the Church and Italy and of loyalty to the Empire. But these ideals were quickly subordinated to the petty motives of party advantage and municipal intrigue. Whenever introduced, the terms Guelf and Ghibelline were seized upon by the rival cities and the rival classes within, as convenient phrases under which to marshal their opposition. If their opponents were labelled Guelf, then they were Ghibelline ; if Parma changed, then Piacenza changed ; if nobles were Ghibelline, then the *popolo* were Guelf ; and, when the rivalry of people and nobles was forgotten, and the rivalry of one noble house with another had taken its place, if Montagu was Guelf, then, and for so long, Capulet was Ghibelline.

Party strife proved fatal to liberty. Lombardy, torn by factions, " a bark without a pilot 'neath a stormy sky," soon bowed beneath the yoke of tyrants. The age of the Communes was succeeded by the age of Despots. The heroic spirit of the twelfth century was exchanged for the ease and splendour of the fourteenth. But meantime, as a symbol of their Communal life, there had sprung up in every little town, at the beginning of the thirteenth century, a municipal Palace or Town-Hall, called in Lombardy *Broletto* or *Palazzo della Ragione*, the centre of council and of judgment, where the affairs of the little city-state were transacted, with its balcony (*Aringhiera—Arengo*) projecting over the piazza, whence the burghers, assembled below, summoned by the great Town-bell, which swung in the campanile alongside, were addressed by their chosen representatives. In the centre of the Piazza de' Mercanti stands the Palazzo della Ragione of Milan, begun in 1228 by the Podestà, Oldrado da Tresseno, that chastener of heretics to whom we have already referred, and to whose honour there was here erected (1233) an equestrian statue, by Benedetto Antelami, a thing notable in art, for it marks the first appearance of an equestrian statue since that of Theodoric at Ravenna. The Town Hall of Milan resembles that of Monza in design: a lofty arcade bears a huge hall above, which is approached not by a staircase but by a union gallery over an arch. The beautiful double Loggia of black and white marble was added by Matteo Visconti (1316) to the arcade of the Osii ; the balcony and the façade, decorated with the arms of the quarters of the City, and the statues in niches above lend grace and lightness to this charming building.

CHAPTER IV.

THE VIPER OF MILAN.

By this time Milan had built her walls and closed their circuit with the sixteen gates that showed she loved magnificence combined with strength. She had yoked the torrents of the S. Gothard and the Simplon, which had hitherto run wasteful through a wilderness of pebbles to the sea ; the Naviglio Grande was completed. The pasture-land of Milan, breeding-ground of much prized war-horses, was rendered the richest in the world.

Silk weaving and the woollen industry extended the commerce of Milan far and wide ; Milanese armour was famed throughout the world ; these and subsidiary trades and the agricultural wealth of the surrounding country fostered the great Milanese families, like the Borromei, who, as bankers and merchants, rose to power on the wings of commerce. The Princes of Milan succeeded to a heritage of wealth that placed them on a level with the sovereigns of Europe. We shall see how they applied this wealth, outcome of Republican works, in part to the aggrandisement of the Duchy, in part to the splendour of their courts, and in part to the adornment of the city.

Despotism in Italy, Mr. Symonds has observed, as in ancient Greece, was democratic. It recruited its ranks from all classes, and erected thrones upon the sovereignty of the peoples it oppressed.

The Carraresi at Padua, like the Gonzaghi at Mantua, the Rossi and Correggi at Parma, and the Scotti at Piacenza, erected their despotic dynasties on a basis of popular authority. Nobles charged by the Communes with military or judicial power, as Capitani or Podestas, they used their authority to enslave the cities they had been called upon to administer. These officers were either powerful citizens or nobles from a neighbouring Commune, called in to conduct a war or to promote peace between the parties. Often they were professional rulers, passing at first from town to town. Gradually they made their hold secure, and established their Lordship (*Signoria*) as hereditary. Then the Signore usually tried to legitimise his power by obtaining the title of Imperial or Papal Vicar, and finally, the regular feudal investiture, which admitted him into the circle of the legitimate princes of the Empire. Thus the officers of the free burghs developed into the tyrants of the Renaissance.

At Milan the Della Torre family had acquired great influence with the people ever since Pagano della Torre, Lord of the Valsassina, between Bergamo and Como, had succoured the Milanese fugitives who fled, wounded and starving, into the mountains from Corte Nuova. His nephew, Martino, led the people in their struggle with the nobles, and ruled the city as Signore, in spite of the continual attacks of the exiled aristocracy who lived in their Castles in the Contado. But the Torriani were destined to be supplanted by the Vipers of Milan. The Visconti had come early into the Viscountcy of the City. Their famous cognizance—a serpent of sevenfold coils devouring a child—

is said to have been won by a noble Crusader of the House, who, having slain a Saracen in single combat, adopted his terrible device.[1] It was transmitted to his descendants with who knows what mysterious and persistent curse of cruelty and of guile? Strong, crafty, determined, with that gift of biding his time singularly characteristic of his line, it was Otto Visconti, Archbishop of Milan, who, after years of forlorn struggle and intrigue at the head of the Ghibelline exiles in Lombardy, succeeded at length in ousting the Torriani. He seized Milan and shut up the captured Della Torre in iron cages in that lofty castle of Baradello, of which the ruins form so striking a feature on the way from Como to Milan. The Archbishop was chosen Lord of the city by the fickle crowd. He was succeeded by his nephew, Matteo Visconti—Matteo il Grande. Conducting his affairs with extraordinary skill, this cunning despot used the weapons of diplomacy and state-craft to establish and extend his sway and to accumulate treasure. With the aid of his warlike sons, he overwhelmed King Robert's general, and planted his banner upon the walls of Cremona, Milan's ancient rival. He seized Pavia, and built a fortress within the walls of the proud capital of the Lombard kings. There was indeed an interlude in his prosperity. The Torriani came back for a while. The story runs that Guido della Torre, in the height of his success, sent to enquire of his fallen rival, when he hoped to see Milan again? Matteo had retired to a remote country villa near the Lake of Garda, where he was wisely passing his time a-fishing. " I

---

[1] " O'l forte Otton, che conquisto lo scudo
In cui da l'angue esce il fanciullo ignudo."—*Tasso*.

shall return," he said, " when the sins of the Torriani have reached the measure of mine." Surely enough the new tyranny soon exhausted its popularity. The opportunity arrived when the Emperor, Henry of Luxemburg, came, as he thought, to bring peace to the faction-torn cities of Italy ; to restore exiles, to abolish parties and depose despots in favour of Imperial Vicars. Then the indignation of Guelfs and Ghibellines alike was boundless. Matteo Visconti, with peculiar cunning, used the situation to make his family secure in the mastery of Milan. The city was in a ferment, partly because of the sum levied for Henry's necessities, partly because he proposed to take a hundred young nobles as an escort—or hostages—for his coronation at Rome. It was rumoured that armed men were assembling at the houses of the Visconti and Della Torre. Henry sent his Germans to search them. Matteo was found conversing peaceably with his friends in the loggia of his palace ; the Della Torre were surprised in arms. Their barricades and palaces were burned ; the Torriani were expelled for ever, and Matteo, who had apparently concerted a rising with them, remained triumphant in his Macchiavellian treachery.

In his old age, the ban of excommunication, under which he had long been laid as leader of the Ghibelline party in Lombardy, began to prey upon his mind. At the first sign of weakness, his terrible sons rose up and forced him to abdicate. His grandson, Azzo, bought the city with the title of Imperial Vicar from the Emperor Louis of Bavaria, who, on the occasion of his visit to Milan, 1327, had thrown his father, Galeazzo, into prison.

He reduced many Lombard towns to subjection, and—for he was a martyr to gout—spent some portion of the Visconti wealth upon the tower of San Gottardo, that lovely, octagonal, terra-cotta campanile, with its delicate marble pilasters and arcades.[1] He was succeeded by his uncle, Lucchino, who, before his faithless wife had succeeded in poisoning him, added Parma and Pisa to the dominion of Milan. His government was continued by Giovanni, Archbishop of Milan, the friend of Petrarch. In this remarkable man were combined all the rarer qualities of the Visconti. Patience in politics, coolness, self-control and great tenacity, guided by most subtle brains and supple consciences, were the characteristics of this extraordinary race, resulting in a state-craft so passionless, so perfidious and so effectual, that the Snake upon their 'scutcheon became for all Italy a symbol of their methods as it was a sign of their horrible power. Profound intellectual cynicism strengthened their genius for political intrigue, and, whilst permitting free play to their abominable lusts, rarely allowed their passions to override their prudence. Physical cowardice, superstitious fear and inhuman cruelty were the weaknesses to which they were prone, but of which they were not ashamed, so long as they did not dim their bright intelligence. So skilful were they in their conduct of affairs, so unrivalled in their grip of politics, that, in spite of their record of crime, slow-footed retribution never overtook their dynasty. The race died out, and the last of the Visconti sank into the grave under the burden of a Duchy as great as many a Kingdom. Under the Archbishop Giovanni the House of Visconti rose to be recognised as a dynasty of self-made

---

[1] The brickwork, like that of nearly every other historic building we shall visit, has been recently restored. The new pointing has unavoidably destroyed for a while much of the charm of their colour-effect.

sovereigns, whose power extended over the greater part of Northern Italy. For Bologna and Genoa were now added to the tyranny of the Milanese despots, in whose scheming brains the ambition was henceforth ever burning to extend their principality beyond the Apennines, as a step towards the complete subjugation of all Italy. Giovanni's encroachments roused the Pope, who summoned him to Avignon. But the Archbishop felt himself strong enough to defy his master. Ascending his throne in the Duomo he unsheathed a flashing sword which he had girded to his thigh. In his left hand he brandished a crozier, and so gave his answer to the Papal Legate. "This is my spiritual sceptre, but with this sword will I defend my temporal empire." He would go to Avignon, he said, but it would be at the head of 12,000 cavalry and 6000 infantry. The Pope declined so embarrassing a visit.

Giovanni died, much beloved for his benevolence, and for the joyous open Court that he had kept. Three grandsons of Matteo divided his inheritance. Of these Bernabò and Galeazzo soon caused the third, a foolish glutton, to be murdered, and then ruled the Duchy between them. Galeazzo held his Court at Pavia. Tall and graceful, with long golden hair of which he was inordinately vain, he delighted in the magnificence of display. He married his daughter, Violante, to the Duke of Clarence, son of Edward III., and the welcome which he gave to the Prince's English retinue is recorded as a marvel of splendour and extravagance. Such was the profusion, we are told, of the banquet at which they were entertained, and at which Petrarch sat, that the remains were more than enough for 10,000 men. Equally dazzling was the entertainment given when his son, Gian Galeazzo, married Isabella, daughter of France.

Milan was now the richest, most populous and luxurious city of Italy. No kingdom in Europe could boast a capital with palaces so sumptuous, streets so splendid, and gardens with such fair fountains and noble pleasaunces.

No sooner was Galeazzo dead than Bernabò, who reigned at Milan, began to plot in order to obtain the estates of his son. The man against whom Gian Galeazzo was pitted was a monster of cruelty and oppression. He was strong in the wealth he had wrung from his subjects, he was strong in the cruelty with which he overawed them. In the intervals of conducting his wars of aggression and wars with the Pope, or of making the Papal Legates eat the bulls of excommunication with which they served him, he kept peace within his borders by publishing in elaborate detail the prolonged series of tortures, varied by every diabolical device of torment, which he had prepared for the edification of State criminals.

Without hesitation he would set his dogs to devour a poaching peasant—for he was devoted to the chase—and would burn a friar should he chance to protest. Like his brother, he was conspicuously devout, and founded many churches and convents. But in the youth whom he now chose to attack, this monster had to deal with one of the most remarkable and terrible of mankind. In him was concentrated all the intellectual force of the Visconti and none of their physical vices, save that of personal cowardice. In him was exemplified all the cold, intellectual cynicism and cunning of the Italian despot. Beyond the fascination of women or the chase, his sole recreation was in the conversation of men of letters, his only extravagance was to be in the erection of magnificent buildings.

Quickly aware that his uncle and cousins were intriguing against him, Gian Galeazzo dissembled whilst he determined in his turn to supplant them. He buried himself in the Library of Pavia ; he pretended to be absorbed in religious devotion ; he lived, rosary in hand, before the shrines of saints. This pose seemed natural enough to Bernabò in one who made no disguise of his abject physical cowardice, and who lived surrounded by a numerous bodyguard, in whose midst he would often give way, at the least unexpected movement, to paroxysms of agonising terror. Presently he announced his intention of making a pilgrimage to Our Lady of Varese. He passed near Milan ; Bernabò came forth to meet him. Gian Galeazzo embraced him tenderly, and then gave an order to his German guard. Bernabò was seized.[1] Gian Galeazzo marched into Milan, poisoned his uncle, and, discarding the mask of devotion, stood forth sole Lord of Lombardy.

Once established at Milan, Gian Galeazzo, cold, false, pitiless, immovable, set himself to fulfil the Visconti ambition of reducing all Italy beneath his sway. It was an ambition which he might have achieved had there been no Florence to check him. And even so, the Viper of Milan might yet have swallowed all the lesser snakes of Italy, had not the abhorred shears cut short his life.

Though he did not shrink from undertakings of the greatest daring and magnitude, as for instance a scheme for

[1] The equestrian statue of Bernabò Visconti standing upright in his stirrups, by Bonino (Museo Archeologico) is reminiscent of that of Can Grande at Verona.

reducing Mantua and Padua, by diverting the Mincio and Brenta, and, perhaps humbling Venice by thus drying up the lagoons, the minute and skilful way in which he administered his Duchy as an estate gave him the wealth needed for all his projects and the wherewithal to pay those armies which he durst not lead himself. But the brain of the schemer was fearless and his will of iron. Fraud, violence, and plots of diabolical cunning, he chose his weapons with unerring skill, and used them with remorseless precision. When plague struck down the tyrant in the plenitude of his powers, his acquisitions seemed well cemented, but when the guiding brain was gone, the dukedom crumbled to pieces. With him the force of the Visconti was exhausted. Of his sons, Gian Maria, after a brief career of inhuman lust and cruelty, was murdered by some nobles, relatives of men on whose flesh he had fed his hounds, and Filippo Maria, a prey to the nervous terror of tyrants in general and the Visconti in particular, vacillated so fatally in his excess of caution, that he paralysed his own clever policies, and foolishly turned against himself the able instruments whom he had wisely chosen to accomplish them.

It is to Gian Galeazzo that we owe the two great foundations of the Duomo and the Certosa of Pavia. There had always been much of the studious and of the devout in the composition of the scheming statesman, as there was always something intellectually artistic in his duplicity and plots. He encouraged literature ; he stimulated every form of Art which might glorify his State. To his magnificent patronage the University of Pavia owed a period of great prosperity. To Milan he summoned the greatest scholars of the day to read poetry with him and to discuss the literary movements of the day and the new discoveries of antiquity.   Emanuel Chrysoloras came to the University and brought the newly reviving knowledge of Greek to Milan.

Partly, perhaps, as an expiation of his crimes, partly as a votive offering for an heir, chiefly perhaps as a monument of his greatness and ambition, Gian Galeazzo began to build, upon the site of the old basilica, a cathedral which should be worthy of the capital of the new kingdom of Italy, whose crown, he felt, was now almost within his grasp. For this purpose he instituted a *Fabbrica del Duomo*, with its own revenues and organisation, a small, semi-independent community of artists and architects, devoted to the building of the great monument.

The work was begun in 1386.   Innumerable architects were destined to work at it ere it was completed, but it is not known who first designed it.   The Visconti's close connection with the Courts of France and Germany no doubt directed the choice of the Gothic style triumphant in the north.   But if the design was—as it must have been— the outcome of a northern mind, the alien style was soon modified by the native builders, most of whom belonged to the famous guild of stone workers from Campione.

The Duomo is the most magnificent specimen in Italy of Gothic, the Northern style unsuited to the genius and climate of the Italians, who were always looking back either to the horizontal lines and flat roofs of the basilica, or beyond, to the style of their ancestral Classic Age, which they were soon so triumphantly to revive.   And the Duomo in its very excellence exhibits most strikingly the faults of

MILAN CATHEDRAL.

their treatment of Gothic. The chief beauty of a Northern Gothic Cathedral—Salisbury, for instance—lies in perfect unity, symmetry and proportion, each part being subordinate to the whole, and the whole soaring up to Heaven in serene, mystic expression of spiritual aspiration. In the Duomo of Milan there is no unity, no proportion in the design, no serenity, as there is no single idea informing and dominating the whole. It is a conglomeration of architectural devices, of a pyramidal Lombardesque façade and gossamer pinnacles, of long thin lights and heavy piers, of uprights that would fain be horizontal, and pointed, soaring details, which look back wistfully to the earth. Its shape, viewed as a whole, is flat and most ugly. The very excess of the multitude of vertical lines in all this pointed work, instead of giving an effect of soaring height and upward spring, gives exactly the opposite impression of a depressed, horizontal mass. Buttresses, pinnacles, and panelled walls alike are weak, decadent and purposeless. But the effect of the wealth of detail in this paradise of sculpture is marvellous. For in the opportunities which this insubordinate treatment of Gothic afforded, the Italian genius for sculpture and decoration was justified. Here is a multitude of statues, a regiment of saints, cut in white marble, who take shelter in a myriad niches beneath canopies the most delicate, as though fearing to lose themselves in the fairy forest of white marble pinnacles. And the effect of this wealth of ornament and detail, however disproportionate to the whole, is, when seen in the first flush of dawn or the afterglow of sunset, or by the pale, silvery light of the moon, a thing of beauty, unique and undeniable.

There is a magic, unearthly beauty about the delicate

changing colours of this fair marble raised against the blue vault of heaven. It is an exotic beauty, exotic as the loveliness of a white mountain bird that has settled in a city of the plain. For the marble was brought to a land of terra-cotta from the quarries by Lago Maggiore. It was used by a race of sculptors turned architects, who, revelling in the strange abundance of this noble material, made lace-work and confectionery of marble. And the style, as I have said, was exotic. The Duomo was planned, probably, by a foreigner, as though by prescience to prepare a welcome for the French, the Spanish, and the Austrian conquerors by turn. It was founded by a despot ; it was finished— with a bombastic façade and a battalion of pinnacles,—by Napoleon Buonaparte.

The extravagance of the ornamentation, sacrificing all dignity and strength, the marble frills and frippery of the elaborately pierced balustrade, and the endless crocketed pinnacles, upon which flocks of baroque saints have settled like cathedral pigeons, may reflect to some extent the love of gorgeous display which was so marked a characteristic of Gian Galeazzo and his successors. But this tendency to the exaggerated use of sculpture was greatly enhanced by the fact that the prosecution of the work fell into the hands of men who were sculptors first and architects afterwards ; men like Cristoforo Solari, Giovanni Antonio Amadeo, and Gian Giacomo Dolcebuono, and their decadent successors, who seem to have thought it a merit to compel you to climb to the roof if you wished to appreciate the beauties of the details ; men like the egregious Marco Agrate who inscribed on his statue of S. Bartholomew in the south transept—" *Non me Praxiteles, sed Marcus finxit Agrates.*"

There can be no greater contrast than that between the fussy extravagance of the exterior and the solemn breadth and grandeur of the interior of the Duomo of Milan. Here, for once in Lombardy, North and South have kissed each other, and from their union has sprung a harmonious whole, that comprises the Latin love of a severe spaciousness with the Gothic ideal of height and spring. Through the traceried windows of the outer aisles streams the glare of an Italian sun, tempered to a dim, religious light by the rich hues of magnificent stained glass, and illuminating the simple, immense distances of the vast echoing aisles, the soaring columns and mighty nave within. For the prodigious width and height of the nave and adjoining aisles are accentuated by the rows of clustered columns of immense size and height which support them, a forest of giant piers crowned by gigantic capitals.

The octagonal dome by Amadeo—so inadequate without, —which joins the nave and transepts, marks the transition from the Gothic to the Renaissance style.

It is not my purpose here to deal in guide-book detail with the monuments of Italian Art, but rather to indicate the broad outlines where history and architecture coincide. But one may notice here the tombs of the Archbishops Aribert and Otto Visconti, and the magnificent bronze pulpits and candelabrum ; notice, too, how the *absence* of ornament and chapels adds in this cathedral to the impressiveness of its grandeur.

CHAPTER V.

THE AGE OF THE CONDOTTIERI; THE SFORZA, AND LEONARDO DA VINCI.

When Filippo Maria set about the task of reuniting the crumbled fragments of the mighty Duchy, which the ambition of the first Duke had bound together, the success he achieved was largely due to the strong arm of the great Condottiere whom he employed, and who, since it is the natural tendency of the professional soldier to supplant his employer and to aspire to be the hammer rather than the anvil, succeeded to the throne which he had been hired to defend.

During the thirteenth century the art of war had undergone a change. The prevailing use of heavy cavalry began to render the burgher infantry of but little use. They were no match for heavily-armed war-horses and their mail-clad riders. It required the practice of a life-time to wield the lance. Soldiering became a profession or the occupation of the leisured nobility. Bands of English and German mercenaries, like Sir John Hawkwood's company, supplanted the citizen-soldier. The development of town life had further increased the unfitness of the burghers for the military career of the times. They found it more convenient, and erroneously deemed it safer, to get their fighting done for them. Meanwhile, the order established by the despots, depriving the idle Italian nobles of the opportunity of private brigandage, led them to adopt the career of Sir John Hawkwood and his mercenaries, and to do the military business of the Communes.

War became a trade and a profession. Hired troops brought their skill into the market, and were purchased for the occasion by the highest bidder. The enemy of to-day was the ally of to-morrow. Inspired by no patriotism, but only by a fellow-feeling for gain and the bond of a common profession, the condottieri and their hired followers reduced warfare to an almost bloodless science. Endless blockades and pillaging expeditions relieved the monotony of innumerable marches and counter-marches, by which one hired general having outmanœuvred another, thereupon claimed and was granted the victory. Thousands of prisoners were taken ; hardly a life was lost, save perhaps by the explosion of a gun fired to proclaim success.[1] The brutal realities of war were almost forgotten till French, Swiss and German invaders brought them home to the polished Italians, by that time grown incapable of resisting them. And in the meantime courage and force and piety, the old *virtue* of the Romans, had given place, in the national estimation, to intellectual superiority. To outwit, not to outdo, was the ambition of the hero. Superior fraud, based on superior cunning, fertility of invention and diplomacy, not superior force, gained the national applause. Francesco Sforza, says Macaulay, was the model

[1] Guicciardini, the Florentine historian, observes, when speaking of the battle of Fornovo :

"*innanzi a questa morivano pochissimi uomini in un fatto d' arme.*"

of Italian heroes. He made his employers and his rivals alike his tools. He first overpowered his open enemies by the help of faithless allies ; he then armed himself against his allies with the spoils taken from his enemies. By his incomparable dexterity he raised himself from the precarious and dependent situation of a military adventurer to the first throne of Italy. To such a man much was forgiven, hollow friendship, ungenerous enmity, violated faith.

One day it had chanced that a troop of mercenaries were riding through the flat marshy land that lies between Ravenna and Bologna. They came upon a lad, the son of a small noble, who was cutting wood near his native town of Colignola, that Colignola which Sir John Hawkwood had fortified. Struck by his appearance, the soldiers invited him to join them. He flung his axe into the branches of an oak. " If it stays, I will go," cried he. It stayed, and Muzio Attendolo went forth into the world, to earn by his great strength and fiery nature the nickname of " Sforza " from his hero and compatriot Alberico da Barbiano, to be the companion in arms and then the rival of Braccio da Montone as the chief of the Italian condottieri, a peasant lad to found a line of dukes. Francesco Sforza learned the trade of war in his father's camp, and when Muzio lost his life in the passage of the Pescara in a gallant attempt to save a favourite page who had fallen into the river, he quickly took his father's place as leader. His victory over Braccio at Aquila placed him in the forefront of the condottieri. All Italy competed for his leadership. Filippo Maria Visconti persuaded him to enter his service. He served beneath his banners in three successive wars against

Venice, Venice, the Queen of the Sea, who had now become a mainland power and was pressing upon the frontier of the disunited Duchy of Milan.

That war was ended by the coming of the Emperor Sigismund to Italy. The occasion of his receiving the Iron Crown of Lombardy at Milan (1432) was marked by the betrothal of Francesco Sforza to Bianca Maria, the illegitimate daughter of Filippo Maria. The betrothal was part of the price of his services ; the consummation of it was henceforth the goal towards which Sforza pressed with an intense and unscrupulous persistency ; for that consummation meant for him the throne of Milan.

He wrested the March of Ancona from the Pope, and there commenced despot. But, as Lord of the March and as mercenary soldier, he directed all his efforts, now warring for one side, now for the other, towards the celebration of that marriage, which Filippo Maria, shut up in his Castello, watched by double sets of mutually suspicious body-guards, a prey to indecision and mad terror, the victim of self-indulgence and the dupe of astrology, ever strove to avoid. At length, Francesco won his end, when he was called in to act as arbiter between Milan and Venice, and, for his reward, was married to Bianca, " whose pure nature no less than her fair face accorded well with her name." The ceremony took place in the Church of S. Sigismondo, outside Cremona, a church which in gratitude Francesco rebuilt, when he became Duke of Milan.

The death of Filippo Maria plunged Milan into the chaos of a disputed succession.

French troops arrived in Italy and proclaimed Charles, Duke of Orleans, heir to Milan ; but Filippo, on his death-bed, had appointed Alfonso of Naples his successor. Almost before he had breathed his last, the banners of Aragon were floating above the Castello. The hopes of Sforza were dashed to the ground ; but the triumph of the Aragonese was short-lived.

Weary of the rule of the Visconti, and inspired by the example of Venice, the populace gathered behind the Palace of the Commune and enthusiastically proclaimed the Golden Ambrosian Republic. The Aragonese were driven from Milan : the Castello of Porta Giovia, seal and sign of Ducal power, was destroyed.

In spite of two centuries of despotism, the Republican ideal still burned brightly in the breasts of the Milanese ; but because of two centuries of despotism, the people had become incapable of self-government. They elected twenty-four " Defenders of Liberty " to rule them. Suspicious, irresolute, and foolish, they plunged the city into disorder, political and financial.

To carry on the war with Venice, they were obliged to hire Sforza. The inevitable happened. Sforza made himself master of Milan. The old despotism was restored. The big bell of the Broletto summoned the Assembly of citizens to hail Francesco as their Duke, and to give to a tyranny won by the sword the elaborate sanction of a popular election. By the Peace of Lodi Sforza's position was recognised by the five chief Italian States. His claim to the Duchy was, indeed, as good as that of the House of Orleans.

True, Bianca was illegitimate, and Louis of Orleans had married Valentina, Gian Galeazzo's legitimate daughter. But, in Italy, bastardy was no bar to succession. In either case the investiture granted by Wenceslaus to the first Duke excluded females.   Could Venice, Florence and Genoa have joined hands now to support the independence of Milan, the freedom of the peninsular might have been maintained. Then these Republics might have stood four-square to all the winds of foreign aggression that swept across the Alps. But, engrossed in their petty jealousies and minor policies of aggrandisement, they let the golden opportunity slip, and by admitting a new dynasty to the Duchy, instead of combining to support a fourth Republic, they tacitly admitted the rival claim, which was to furnish an excuse for the advent of the foreigner and for the interference of France in the affairs of Italy.

Francesco's first achievement was to re-build the Castello, to be, as he said, " an ornament to the city and a safeguard against foreign enemies."   Carried away by their enthusiasm for the Condottiere, the people turned a deaf ear to Giorgio Piatti, who urged that, when Francesco was gone, the Castle would remain, perhaps to be the stronghold of a cruel tyrant, whilst for a benevolent despot the love of his subjects should prove an all-sufficient stronghold.

The *Castello Sforzesco* is one of the grandest examples of an Italian fortress.   It is a massive pile, as grim without as the palace within was gradually rendered sumptuous.

Dominating the city rose a mighty curtain-wall, defended at each end by huge, round, machicolated towers, their sole ornament the Visconti Viper and the initials of the succeeding Dukes.   In the centre a fortified gateway and clock-tower led to the parade grounds and dwellings of the garrison, to the citadel and Ducal apartments within.   It was elaborately decorated by Filarete, as if to relieve the threatening aspect of the towers, that frowned so grimly upon the suspicious citizens.

This gateway was destroyed by an accidental explosion of gunpowder in the sixteenth century; it has of late years been skilfully restored by Luca Beltrami. The whole was once surrounded by an outer line of fortifications, ramparts and ditch. The original palace of the Visconti had been on the site of the *Palazzo Reale*, near their chapel, S. Gottardo. Upon the foundations of their Castle, Francesco now built his inner fortress, the *Rocchetta*, and, to the right of it, the new *Corte Ducale*, or palace, of the Sforzas. To its adornment his successors loved to devote their resources. Under Galeazzo Maria, Ferrini added the graceful Renaissance Loggietta; under Il Moro, the decorations were continued on a magnificent scale, and Leonardo and Bramante alike lent their genius to decorating the home of Beatrice d' Este. But beauty was a secondary consideration in such a building as this. Strength was the first; and such was the might of the *Castello* that it survived six sieges in the Sforza era, and, subsequently, innumerable attacks by Spaniards, Austrians, French and Italians. It is now preserved as a Museum of Antiquities, saved from destruction and restored by the efforts of enlightened citizens of to-day.

It is here that the fragments of the tomb of Gaston de Foix are preserved, and the exquisite recumbent statue of the young Condottiere, whose death at the battle of Ravenna, when fighting for Louis XII. against the onslaught of Venice, the Pope and the King of Aragon (1512), robbed a most brilliant victory of half its value for France. " His countenance," as Vasari says, " seems full of joy, even in death, at the victories gained by his hand." It is the touching work of Agostino Busti (Il Bambaja), recalling inevitably in its beautiful serenity that marvellous master-piece, the dead warrior at Ravenna, which is the highest poetic expression in marble of Death and his twin-brother, Sleep.

It was in such a gloomy fortress as the *Castello Sforzesco* that the Italian Despot lived his life of strenuous exertion and unremitting intrigue, expecting to die by poison or the poignard, and frequently abandoning himself to the wildest outbursts of lust and rage or to fits of ungovernable terror. Little wonder that, being, as a rule, a man of the highest intellectual ability, he endeavoured to lighten the gloom with the glories of Art, to supply the place of friends by the company of men of letters, men of science, and buffoons, whilst, to soothe the conscience, which made him tremble, like Filippo Maria Visconti, at the sound of thunder, or filled his fancy with the visions of starved and strangled victims, he endeavoured to bribe Nemesis by the foundation of beautiful churches and monasteries, where the pious might be at leisure to pray for his soul.

Filippo had extended his patronage to that querulous and disagreeable Humanist, Filelfo, and to Brunelleschi, the architect of the early Renaissance. It was the Sforza's cue to follow the example of the Visconti. He welcomed to his Court not only great writers, but artists also,—Michelozzo, Fioravante, Moretti, Bembo, and a dozen others,—who vied with one another in beautifying the houses and churches of Milan.

For a despot, Francesco was wise and beneficent. The soldier proved statesman in the task of consolidating the

Duchy he had won with such infinite pains. That vast
and beautiful foundation, the *Ospedale Maggiore,* one of
the best hospitals in Italy to-day, survives as a monument
of his practical care for the people. The lower storey was
built by Antonio Filarete, the Florentine, in the classical
style ; it was completed in transitional, late Gothic, style by
Guiniforte Solari, with additions by Bramante and Amadeo.
It affords a beautiful example of Lombard early Renaissance
terra-cotta work. The open *loggie,* the delicate terra-cotta
mouldings, the pointed windows, framed in a rich design
of *putti* playing amid the vines, are full of grace and light
and invention, born of the mingling of Gothic and Renaissance. Prompted, perhaps, by the devotion of Bianca,
Francesco founded several churches. S. Niccolo and S.
Maria Incoronata, like S. Maria delle Grazie and many
others, illustrate the Lombard transitional style, that blend
of Gothic and Renaissance, in which each style seems to
strive for supremacy. For the Renaissance era had dawned
at Milan—that era of universal genius and delight in the
fulness of life, of an immense capacity for the enjoyment of
all pleasures, physical and intellectual, newly discovered in
the springtime of the modern world. Dante's great poem
had heralded the dawn, when Italy shook off the slumbers
of the Middle Ages. Petrarch, with his passionate love of
ancient culture, had introduced the Revival of Learning.
And that revival in the knowledge, through the new-found
Greek, of the thoughts and ideals of the Greek and Roman
worlds, helped to guide the Renaissance spirit to its love
of classical art. The Italians revolted with delight from the
domination of the alien Northern Gothic, and took up the
story of their national style where it had broken off, in the

Roman monuments around them.   Renaissance is the style
of patriotic scholarship.

But this, too, was the age of great artists with horrible
minds ; when the profound intellectual cynicism characteristic of the Italians, inherited, I suppose, from the Romans,
and stimulated by the example of the careers of criminal
Popes, cruel, successful tyrants and prosperous *condottieri*,
burst into flower.

In Francesco's son, Galeazzo Maria Sforza, the vices of a
Renaissance tyrant appear in an exaggerated light.

Vain, luxurious, abominably cruel, and an exponent of
the vilest lusts, he abandoned himself without restraint to
the new delights of knowledge, power and beauty, which
the spirit of the age revealed to him, and in which his
position enabled him to indulge. This second Nero,
capable of ordering an artist to decorate a hall at Pavia with
portraits of the Ducal family in a single night on pain of
death, was charged with the murder of his mother and
of his betrothed. Music was his delight, and Europe was
ransacked for singing-men for his chapel. His courtiers
were clad in splendid liveries of mulberry, of crimson and
scarlet cloth. He took in hand the decoration of the Ducal
apartments in the Castello. The Ducal library was reputed
the richest in Italy, which Nicolò di Napoli, with a characteristic touch of Renaissance feeling, said he was gladder
to have seen than the Sepulchre at Jerusalem. Galeazzo's
wild extravagance and taste for gorgeous display knew no
bounds. His visit to Lorenzo de' Medici, with its vulgar
exhibition of splendour, was noted by Macchiavelli as the
evil communication which corrupted the austere manners of
the Florentines to luxury and license. Fifty palfreys for

his Duchess, fifty chargers for himself decked in trappings of cloth of gold, a body-guard of 600 soldiers, and 500 couples of hounds accompanied him and his suite of 2000 courtiers on horseback.

In spite of his unbridled passions, however, Galeazzo Maria had his virtues as an administrator. He held the gates of the Alps, with the keys of which Nature had entrusted Milan, firmly locked against the foreigner. His financial ability was great, and he fostered the industries of his dominion, as, for instance, the silk industry by minute regulations for the planting of five mulberry trees every hundred poles. He paved the streets of his capital, and under his patronage the first Greek books printed in Italy were issued from the presses of Milan.

Galeazzo Maria was assassinated by three noble youths of Milan, whom he had wounded, among many others, in their honour and in their property. Their imaginations had been fired by a new motive in history, the study of the Classics. For Montano, who had opened a School of Rhetoric in Milan, had taught to them the ardent love of liberty, which is the lesson of Greek and Latin history. The spirit of Harmodius and Virginius lived again in the breasts of the injured youths. In the garden of San Ambrogio, Carlo Visconti, Girolamo Olgiati and Gionnandrea Lampugnani met and prepared, amid prayers and offerings to the patron Saint of Milan, the death of the reigning monster.

Their daggers struck the tyrant as he was entering San Stefano (Dec. 26, 1476). The spot is marked by an inscription on the pavement of the existing church. When seized and subjected before death to the most inhuman tortures, Girolamo declared with a grandeur and constancy

that recalled the ancient heroes, the breath of whose
examples were now stirring the dead leaves of the dark
mediaeval forest, " The noble action for which I die gives
my conscience peace," and when the executioner was tearing
him, piece by piece, to death, he cried aloud *Mors acerba,
fama perpetua*—" my death is painful and untimely, but
my fame and glory will last for ever! "

On the death of Galeazzo Maria, his widow, Bona of
Savoy, and his minister, the Sicilian Cecco Simonetta, took
up the reins of government as Regents for the boy Duke,
Gian Galeazzo.   The task of Simonetta was a difficult one.

At the cost of the friendship of Naples, he abided by
the league which bound Venice and Milan to support the
Medici at Florence.   Ferrante of Naples and the Sforza
brothers revenged themselves by inciting Genoa to throw
off the yoke of Milan.   Then suddenly Lodovico Sforza,
Francesco's youngest son, appeared before the gates of Milan.
He was welcomed by a large party as the deliverer of his
nephew from the toils of the Calabrian upstart.   Bona
herself, in a moment of impulsive rashness, taking the advice
of Beatrice Sforza and her own lover, a handsome steward,
Antonio Tassino by name, admitted Lodovico into the
Castello by a garden door.   Cecco endeavoured to make
the best of it.   But he was under no illusion.   " Most
illustrious Duchess," he said, " I shall lose my head, and
you, ere long, will lose the State."   The prophecy was
accurate.   The aged Secretary was sent to the scaffold.   A
series of Palace intrigues followed, which ended in the flight
of Tassino and the departure of Bona, after Lodovico had
secured the person of the young Duke in the Rocchetta.

Lodovico Maria was now master of Milan.   In order

to procure for him the protection of the Virgin during his illness as a child, his mother had changed his second name, Maurus, to Maria. But the nick-name of Il Moro stuck to the dark-eyed boy, with his long hair and bushy eyebrows. And Il Moro he liked to be called, adopting, as he grew up, both the Moor's head and the mulberry tree as his device. Poets, painters, courtiers played with a theme so congenial to their flattering wit, providing themselves with black pages, and introducing Moorish costumes into every masquerade. Mulberry became the fashionable colour of the Court.

Lodovico is the typical tyrant of the Italian Renaissance. His alert and active brain had been trained in the tortuous paths of Italian diplomacy, the first principle of which was that the wise statesman should persuade his enemies that he means to do one thing, and then do another. Polished manners, a genuine love of art and letters, and an immense industriousness disguised and deepened his far-reaching political subtlety. His faults were a failure of nerve in great crises and the mistake of over-reaching himself in intrigue. "Born for the ruin of Italy," so those called him who remembered, amid the disasters which overwhelmed their country under a foreign rule, that Charles VIII., the first French King who invaded Italy, had crossed the Alps as his ally.

Gian Galeazzo was a weakling in mind and body ; he spent his days in drinking and hunting ; his only interest centred in horses and dogs. His brilliant guardian was the real sovereign. It was he who must some day be Duke of Milan.

Chief among Lodovico's trusted captains were " I gran

Sanseverini," as they were called by virtue both of their strength and their high position. Of these Messer Galeazzo was the most handsome and most accomplished. Lodovico, on his return from a successful campaign against the Forlì rebels, appointed him his Captain General, thereby mortally wounding the pride of that bluff soldier Gian Giacomo Trivulzio, whose big nose and rugged features live in Caradosso's medal. He was henceforth the Sforza's inveterate enemy. The great plain tombs of his warrior-race, with their armour-clad statues, are grouped in solemn dignity in the vestibule of San Nazaro. Upon the accomplished Galeazzo Lodovico heaped every honour, and bestowed upon this very perfect knight, ever foremost in the tourney and the fray, the hand of Bianca, his illegitimate daughter, that very beautiful and charming girl whose portrait by Ambrogio da Predis in the Ambrosian Library was long attributed to Leonardo.

Lodovico was not only ruler of Milan ; he was also the central figure of Italy. Milan was now one of the richest States, not only of Italy, but of the world. Lodovico carefully developed her resources. He rebuilt the Palace of Vigevano on a splendid scale, and established there a model farm. He did his utmost to improve the Ducal estates. The mighty *Naviglio Sforzesco* survives to indicate the vast system of irrigation by which he made a fertile garden out of a barren wilderness. At Milan, with Leonardo's plan of an ideal city in his mind, he laid out broad, paved streets and wide piazzas " to give the people light and air." In the heart of the city was the *Via degli Spadari*, the centre of the Milanese armourers, whose industry was so famous and flourishing that they were able, after the disaster of

Maclodio, to re-arm Filippo Maria's forces in a few days. Why this armour was so much sought after will best be understood by a glance at the *Poldi-Pezzoli* collection.

Amid prosperity so nurtured, when England and France could only present a frightful spectacle of poverty, ignorance and barbarism, Milan burst forth into the splendour of a New Athens. Wealth, drawn from teeming marts, busy factories and enlightened agriculture, poured into the treasury of the new Pericles. Fleets, which carried down the Po the rich harvests of Lombardy to the granaries of Venice, brought back the silks of Bengal and the furs of Siberia to adorn the palaces which Bramante was building. The Casa Borromeo is the most notable of the surviving fifteenth century palaces at Milan. Its noble courtyard is surrounded on three sides by a portico with broad, pointed arches, supported by octagonal pillars with shallow bases and capitals ; on the fourth side open the richly-decorated windows of the Palazzo.

For the pomp and luxury of the Court reflected the magnificence of Il Moro, as the splendid dresses of the nobles, represented in oil and fresco, sufficiently demonstrate. To this generous Court artists flocked, " as bees suck honey." Caradosso, sculptor, goldsmith, medallist, received Il Moro's generous patronage. Perugino painted for him the magnificent Madonna with the Archangels now in the National Gallery. The vaulted *Sala del Tesoro* in the Castello, decorated with frescoes by Bramante and Leonardo, was filled with priceless gems of art.

Lorenzo de' Medici had recommended to his friend Lodovico a young Florentine master, who played the lute divinely. Leonardo da Vinci came to Milan about 1483,

and, with all the confidence of genius, placed at the Duke's
service his gifts as a military and hydraulic engineer, as an
architect, sculptor and painter, being, he declared, "as
capable as any other man, be he who he may." He was
royally welcomed by one who could appreciate the breadth
and originality of his ideas and the universality of his
enquiries, one, too, who had this in common with the
greatest of the artists of the Italian Renaissance, that he,
also, was a far seeker, and a designer of things never to be
completed.

Vasari tells us that on his arrival at Milan, Leonardo
played to Lodovico upon a silver lute, which he had
fashioned like a horse's head, and tuned according to acoustic
laws discovered by himself, so that it surpassed in tone
every instrument at the Court. The Prince quickly became
enamoured of his admirable gifts and conversation, and
made him his adviser upon architecture and irrigation, upon
problems of military engineering, as upon pageantry and
painting. Leonardo brought to the Court not only
all the resources of his superb scientific intelligence,
but also all the charm of his social genius. The
perfect artist was perfect courtier too ; his manners
were most polished, his presence handsome ; he could
compose a song and sing it charmingly, and was ever ready
to apply his genius to the invention of some new elegance
or some new device for the theatre. The wit of the handsome Florentine was no less admirable than his learning ;
he could turn from discussing pure mathematics with Luca
Pacioli, or tactics with Galeazzo San Severino, to take part in
the conversation on literature or philosophy which Il Moro
perhaps had started, and to utter an epigram which flew

from lip to lip round the Court. But he was happiest, perhaps, in the pleasant home on the outskirts of the city, which Lodovico gave him, and where, in company of his favourite pupils, he could pass at will from painting to hydrostatics, from the Cenacolo to the construction of a flying-machine. But when the war with France was imminent, he abandoned his favourite studies and the decoration of the Castello, where that of the Sala delle Asse and the Saletta Negra is certainly at least from his designs, in order to superintend the waterways of the Duchy. His note-books were filled with mechanical projects and hydraulic dreams for the development of the agriculture of the Province.

He devised machinery for his hydraulic works on the Adda, invented and investigated in anatomy, optics, gunnery. And in every department of his many-sided activity he observed and worked unceasingly. He was, above all, a searcher. Intensely inquisitive as to the meaning and secret of things, his sketch books reveal him as an equally painstaking enquirer into the secrets of human personality as evidenced in human beauty or ugliness. His notes of ugliness and beauty as he saw them in the streets of Milan are the rough material of the Cenacolo. Lodovico first set this universal genius to model an equestrian statue of his great father, the Duke Francesco, and to paint a picture of the Last Supper in the Refectory of S. Maria delle Grazie. The model was completed, and hailed as a masterpiece : but for lack of funds the day never came when the bronze should flow into the clay. The model was used as a target by the French bowmen when Louis invaded Italy. And the fate of that stupendous masterpiece, the Cenacolo, upon which Leonardo would sometimes work without bite or sup from sunrise to sunset, sometimes paint but a stroke or two as the result of days of thought, or of the sudden inspiration of a moment when engaged at other work, has been almost as sad. The mischief arising from the damp of the wall began as soon as it was finished. It was characteristic of Leonardo that, probably in order to be able to work with deliberation, he discarded the customary methods and made an experiment with his masterpiece by painting in oil upon the plaster. The colour began to flake off almost immediately. The vandalism of the restorers and of the French soldiers again, who used the Confectory as a stable in 1796, has well-nigh completed the ruin of this first masterpiece of the Renaissance, the epitome of Leonardo's labours. Yet in no other Cenacolo do the figures express so perfectly the passions of the soul—to judge it by the artist's own test—as in this blurred remnant of the scene he imagined and shadowed forth, to represent the dramatic moment when, upon the ears of men so various in age and temperament, fell the dread announcement, " One of you shall betray me ! "

And even so, we can still feel the emotion of that painted moment ; still perceive that it is represented without sacrificing artistic composure or disturbing the atmosphere that surrounds Him from whose lips the word has fallen, the central figure whom the artist has spiritualised whilst humanising, and made more God-like because more real. The story is well known, how the Prior of this Dominican Convent outside the Porta Vercelliana, annoyed at Leonardo's delays, complained to the Duke that his highly-paid master had not yet begun the head of Judas. And

Leonardo replied that he had been searching Milan for a year to find the suitable type of criminal head, but now it occurred to him that the Prior's own likeness would suit excellently well!   The story implies the thought and pains which the artist took to individualise each type.   Achievement with him was retarded not by laziness, but by labour, born of desire for perfection.   And so it is that his creations, in their grouping and in their detail, bear the impress of work, of power, of thought so vividly, that their presence fills us with awe.   Standing before them, we speak in hushed tones of reverence and admiration, as in the presence of a God, a Creator among men, on the level of a Shakespere, a Rembrandt, a Beethoven.

When the Cenacolo was well-nigh completed Lodovico employed the artist to paint portraits of himself and his beloved duchess, Beatrice, with their children kneeling at their feet, on the opposite wall, where Montorfano had already painted his " Crucifixion." These portraits, too, painted in oil, were ruined almost as soon as painted.

" This," wrote the accomplished Isabella d' Este enthusiastically of Milan, " is the school of the master and of those who know, the home of art and understanding." For Lodovico was representative in his tastes and patronage of every side of the Lombard Renaissance. He encouraged men of letters, artists and men of science alike. The art of sonneteering was introduced from Tuscany: the Court became a nest of singing birds, musical with the songs and lutes of knightly lovers. Great efforts were made to revive the University of Milan, as of Pavia. The study of law, of Greek, of mathematics, of philosophy, as well as of medicine and art were enthusiastically encouraged by Il

Moro, who welcomed every modern development of thought. And in this atmosphere of new ideas won from ancient literature, born of the new vision of the pagan gods, Bramante, the great discoverer of new ideas in architecture, worked with Leonardo a revolution in Lombard art. Il Moro gave him the opportunity of impressing his genius upon the second period of the Renaissance style, when taste was chastened and wild indulgence in ornamentation checked, when the true principle was established and observed, that the beauty and luxuriance of details should be subordinated to the unity and simplicity, the symmetry and grandeur of the whole. In the Church of S. Satiro we can trace the germination of that idea which he was afterwards to develop at S. Peter's in Rome. Upon the baptistery Caradosso modelled a lovely terra-cotta frieze of putti and medallions which bear his own portrait and that of the architect. Bramante's pupil, Dolcebuono, designed the noble S. Maria presso San Celso. Lodovico again employed Bramante to adorn the Gothic buildings of the Ospedale Maggiore with arched windows and stately arcades, and enriched the cloisters with the marble shafts and terra-cotta mouldings that he loved. Bramante built the new cloister of the ancient basilica of S. Ambrogio, and added to S. Maria delle Grazie the apse and cloister and perfect cupola, which render it, though unfinished, the best example of Renaissance work in Milan, while historically every stone of it, as an inscription declares, proclaims Il Moro both Duke and Maecenas.

In 1489 Gian Galeazzo, the weakling Duke, married Isabella of Aragon. His wedding was celebrated with a splendour of pageantry typical of the Renaissance. At the

banquet, by which the meeting of the bridal pair at Tortona
was celebrated, each course was served by appropriate
mythological characters ; the fish by Naiads, the wines by
Hebe. Jason bore in the Golden Fleece, and Orpheus
offered birds, which, he declared in elegant verse, had
flocked round him to hear his musical praise of Isabella.
After the wedding had taken place in the Duomo, the
festivities were crowned by a masque, written for the
occasion by Bellinzione, and organised by Leonardo. Two
years later Il Moro himself was wedded in the Castello of
Pavia to his gay and charming girl-wife, Beatrice d' Este
of Ferrara. And then not only all Lombardy, but all
Europe rang with the splendour of the festivities with which
Milan welcomed the Regent's bride.

Beatrice was the personification of the new Renaissance
rapture in life. The bride of sixteen summers flung herself
with passionate delight into the task of living joyously,
as Matteo Bandello with his dying breath exhorted his
companions to do. Beautiful, accomplished, witty, singing
gay songs with her courtiers, dancing and hunting through
the livelong day, she was the life and soul of the New
Athens, as Milan so proudly styled herself.

Such was the influence which she acquired over her
husband, that she at once succeeded in persuading him to
give up Cecilia Gallerani, his beautiful mistress, the accomplished poetess, whose charms had caused him to delay his
marriage, whom Leonardo had painted and the Court poets
praised.

Isabella and Beatrice were first cousins. The wife of
Gian Galeazzo should be the first lady in Milan. But
socially Beatrice overshadowed her less brilliant cousin as in

real power Il Moro obscured his weakling nephew. That
playful boxing-match, in which, as a gossip records, the
Duchess of Bari knocked down her of Milan, is the symbol
of a natural rivalry between the two women which was to
have far-reaching consequences for Italy. The birth of
Francesco, Isabella's son, was celebrated by a small tournament ; that of Beatrice's Ercole was announced with all the
splendour due to the arrival of the heir to the Duchy.
Stung to the quick, Isabella wrote to her father, Alfonso of
Calabria, to come and rid her of the yoke of these
usurpers.

The answer was prompt. Ambassadors arrived from the
Court of Naples, who hinted that Lodovico should crown
his virtues as a Guardian by retiring in favour of his ward.
His reply was the formation of a league between Venice, the
Papacy, Milan, Mantua and Ferrara for the preservation of
the States of the Church and of the Government of Milan.
But neither the Pope nor Venice were to be trusted, and,
forgetting, as a contemporary historian writes, " that God
made the mountains as boundaries between ultramontanes
and Italians," and hearing that Charles VIII. and Maximilian had concluded a treaty which left the French King
free to come to Italy and prosecute his claim to Naples
without delay, Lodovico threw himself into the arms of
the French, and consented to become the " head and
director " of the Neapolitan expedition.

He opened the Gates of Italy to the foreigner, and from
that moment the end of the independence of the Italian
States was in sight, an end, too, of the petty wars and leagues
and intrigues by which they had been endeavouring to
maintain the balance of power between them. The Alps

became once more the highways of European armies, and
Italy a mere counter in the game of European politics.
For, once the great Powers of Europe had set foot on the
Italian stage, it was absurd to suppose that they would be
content to serve the petty despots. Italy, henceforth,
divided and rotten with the unscrupulous intriguing of small
states against each other, became but the arena where
Austria, France and Spain might fight their battles and glut
their appetite for spoliation. And Milan must pay, with the
rest, the terrible price of political disunion. The course of
events was to prove the most bitter commentary upon the
man who, in spite of his blind belief in astrology, prided
himself on his cunning, well-timed moves, and loved com-
placently to quote the flattering rhyme,

> "God only and the Moor fore-know
> What the future shall bestow."

For the moment, however, success seemed to crown his
intrigues. Charles VIII. passed through Lombardy with
his splendid host, and visited the wretched Gian Galeazzo,
who lay sick at Pavia. He resisted the importunities of
the Duchess Isabella, who, says the Venetian chronicler,
threw herself in tears at his feet and implored him to spare
the House of Aragon. Lodovico and the French King
left for Piacenza, and there news reached them that Gian
Galeazzo was dying. The timeliness of his death gave rise
to the rumour—it can never be proved or disproved—that
the past-master of intrigue had chosen, after years of
waiting, the correct moment for the aid of poison.

And now, when Naples had fallen, all Italy turned to
Lodovico to rid her of the French invader he had invited.
Commines, the French Ambassador at Venice, noting the

wry faces and terror-struck air of the Venetian Senators
when the news that Charles had taken Naples arrived there,
bethought him of the Romans after the defeat of Cannae.
But next morning, the bells of S. Mark's rang out to
announce the new League, of Pope and Maximilian, of
Venice, Spain and Milan, to drive the French out of Italy.

At Milan the Imperial envoys solemnly invested Lodovico
with the Ducal cap and mantle, and placed the sword of
State in his hands.   The end of his ambition was attained.
Yet within a week he had fled in nerveless terror to the
Rocca, on hearing that Louis of Orleans had sallied from
Asti and seized Novara.

But now Maximilian sent his long promised contingent
of Swiss and German troops, and the Venetian army under
Gian Francesco Gonzaga prepared to cut off the retreat
of the French King.   "Here I am," wrote the Marquis
of Mantua, "at the head of the finest army which Italy
has ever seen."   But that fine army only succeeded at
Fornovo in plundering the French camp, whilst Charles
continued his retreat across the Lombard plain.   Milan,
Mantua and Venice celebrated this disgraceful failure as
the most famous of victories.   Poets and artists vied with
each other to commemorate what was really the most deplor-
able proof that Italy could not combine to defeat the most
casual and ill-equipped foreign raider who chose to ravish
her rich cities and lovely lands.

For the moment Lodovico was arbiter of Italy.   He used
his position to invite the Emperor Maximilian to invade
Italy, regardless of the danger that the Germans might
prove to be even worse barbarians than the French.   He
had long cast covetous eyes upon Pisa, and when Venice

took that city under the protection of S. Mark (1496), Lodovico sought an ally to maintain the balance of power. A new league was formed to compel Florence to give up Pisa and Leghorn, and Lodovico could boast that the Pope Alexander was his chaplain, the Emperor his condottiere, Venice his chamberlain, and France his courier, who came and went at his pleasure. Poets proclaimed that there was one God in heaven and one Moro upon earth. Leonardo designed a series of allegories in his sketch-book, representing the Duke as Fortune, as Wisdom and the like. And frescoes were painted on the walls of the Castello, in which the Moro was shown brushing the dust off the skirts of the fair Queen Italy.

Suddenly, at the height of his prosperity, Fortune struck a blow at Il Moro. Beatrice died (1497). With the death of the " dearest thing he had in the world," a change came over his fortunes. The light and laughter of Milan was changed for silence and gloom. " Everything went into ruins," wrote a contemporary. " The Court was changed from a happy Paradise into a gloomy hell." The decoration of S. Maria delle Grazie and the adjoining convent absorbed the attention of the widowed Duke. Cristoforo Solari was commissioned to carve the tomb of the beloved Duchess, to the loss of whom Ariosto, the poet of the Renaissance, ascribed not only the downfall of the Sforza but also the captivity of Italy ;—

> " Beatrice bea, vivendo, il suo consorte
> E lo lascia infelice alla sua morte.
> Anzi tutta Italia, che con lei
> Fia trionfante, e senza lei captiva."

The death of Charles VIII. sounded the knell of the Sforza

dynasty. Louis XII. was determined to make good his claim to the Duchy of Milan. He would rather possess it for a single year, he declared, than spend a whole life-time without it. Against the arms of France, allied with Venice and the Papacy, not all the subtle diplomacy of Il Moro could avail. His preparations were made with feverish energy. He could boast that he was "strong in men, money and fortresses." But long wars and an extravagant Court had exhausted his finances, the fortresses did not resist, and the men scattered like chaff before the rapid advance of the French army under Trivulzio. Lodovico fled to Como. The Castello was yielded without a blow by the traitor Castellan, Bernardino da Corte. Louis XII. made his way in triumph, through streets decorated with fleur-de-lys, to the Duomo, where the representatives of the City-Gates welcomed him beneath their standards, Guelf and Ghibelline alike good Frenchmen now. Louis marvelled at the strength and magnificence of the Castello, and filled its Courts and Halls, which had so recently been crowded, as Castiglione put it, "with the fine flower of the human race," with the drinking booths and dung-hills of his debauched soldiery. All the treasures of art which Il Moro had so lovingly collected were scattered to the winds. But with the departure of the French King the tide of popularity turned. Exile had converted the tyrant into a martyr. Lodovico returned with an army of Swiss and Germans and rode into the Porta Nuova amid cries of "Moro! Moro!" For a moment it seemed as if Lodovico might drive the French across the Alps. But the mighty Castello raised for the defence of the Sforzas proved his undoing. It was gallantly held by the French.

The battle of Novara sealed the fate of the House of Sforza
Lodovico himself was taken captive, and ended his days
in the dark and dismal dungeon, cut out of the solid rock
at Loches.   True child of the Renaissance that he was, in
his passions and intrigues, his love of art and cynicism,
he beguiled the weary hours till death came to his release
by painting devices and mottoes in red and blue upon the
walls.   His only request—for a copy of the *Divina
Commedia* from the library at Pavia—was made in vain.
" The Duke," Leonardo noted in his book, " has lost State,
fortune, liberty, and not one of his works has been completed."   But in one hope, it is said, he, in his tragic end,
was not disappointed.

Solari had crowned the tomb of Beatrice with the recumbent figures of herself and her husband, for at her side he
hoped to lie.   And the brethren of S. Maria delle Grazie,
not unmindful of the benefits which the great, dead Duke
had showered upon their convent, brought his body home
by stealth to Milan and buried him by his wife's side.   The
tomb is now in the Certosa di Pavia.   In the altar-piece
of the Brera gallery, by Zenale (?), is a portrait of Lodovico
and Beatrice with their children, kneeling before the Virgin
and Child.

The raid of Charles VIII. had revealed the wealth and
civilisation of Italy to Europe.   Henceforth she was the
prey of successive invasions from the North.   The Swiss
unceasingly plundered the rich plains of Lombardy until
the Peace of Fribourg fixed the modern frontiers of the
Cantons ; the Germans raided the metropolis of Christendom ; France and Spain fought to the death for the
possession of so fair a mistress.   In the sixteenth century

Italy, and most of all Milan, had to endure the heavy hand of the political despotism and religious oppression of Spanish dominion, and to bear the yoke of Austrian Dukes. And, so far from uniting against the ravening foreigner, the Republics of Italy called him to their aid. They pitted Spaniard against Frenchman and paid the Germans to expel the Swiss, whilst, still intoxicated with the frenzy of internecine faction, Guelf and Ghibelline adopted the standard of France or Spain. For those parties survived the political interests which had given them birth, and lived on as factions ever ready to promote the dismemberment of each succeeding political organisation.

And so we leave the story of the fair city of Milan ere savage invaders had defaced its loveliness and the great developments of modern industrial prosperity had, to some extent, spoiled its charm ; whilst innumerable palaces with their tinted walls and rich porticoes still lined the Beautiful Way ; before time had dimmed the glowing tints of Leonardo's frescoes. In the struggles of the next forty years, before Milan reverted to the Imperial Crown and became a mere province of the vast empire of Charles V., the Duchy became a desert. The roads and villages were peopled only by wolves and robbers. Army after army had sacked the city. Her parks were destroyed ; her churches and palaces damaged by cannon-balls. French and German ruffians plundered and ravished. Men died of hunger in the streets ; grass grew in the piazzas. Silence and desolation reigned.

Not till 1848, when the citizens, almost unarmed, rose in heroic revolt and drove out the Austrian garrison, did Milan know freedom from the foreign yoke again. And her *Risorgimento*, accomplished not without dust and heat and blood, has rendered her to-day the most modern of Italian cities.

With the disappearance of Il Moro had disappeared also the Court of artists and humanists, who had made Milan the home of the new Lombard art. Bramante went to Rome, Leonardo to Venice. The influence of so titanic a genius as Leonardo was at first overwhelming. Amid the forest of statuary on the Duomo this is clearly traceable as in the work of Cristoforo Solari (*e.g.*, the Adam and Eve and Christ at the pillar), but the influence of Michelangelo predominates with Leone Leoni di Arezzo (façade of S. Celso; bronzes on the tomb of Gian Giacomo de' Medici in the Duomo). In painting, it is a delight to examine in those wonderful galleries of Milan—the Brera, above all, and the Biblioteca Ambrosiana, the Museo Poldi-Pezzoli, the Castello, the Palazzo Borromeo and the Palazzo Trivulzio—how, from a legion of slavish imitators of the Florentine Master, who reproduced the Leonardo face, the Leonardo grouping, the Leonardo tricks of style and technique, there emerge a group of artists, who had sufficient individuality to assert themselves and strike their own note, albeit in harmony with his. Vincenzo Foppa, indeed, deriving his inspiration from the Greek studies of Squarcione at Padua and the miniature work of Pisanello, seems to have remained entirely unaffected by Leonardo. But Bramantino, the suave Zenale, the devout and prolific Borgognone and Solario are instances of painters of the Lombard School, who admitted his influence and yet asserted their own personalities. But chiefly Bernardino Luini, the pure and brilliant colourist, the grace and sweetness of whose devotional sentiment rise at times to heights of true poetry, and his more full-blooded contemporary, Gaudenzio Ferrari[1] (Sta. Maria delle Grazie), who surpasses him in dramatic force as he is inferior in charm, are representative of Milanese art in the Lombard School. For great as is Sodoma, his greatness is, after all, Florentine and Siennese. Apart from the Brera in Milan, or at Legnano, Lugano, Saronno out of it, the simple, tender, idyllic charm of Luini can best be seen in those harmonious frescoes with which he covered the walls of S. Maurizio, the Monastero Maggiore, a Renaissance Church (1503), notable in itself for the beauty of its design and proportions. Here may be studied the rare union of Lombard architecture and Lombard painting, expressing the spirit of a single age. For as Giotto at Padua, Correggio at Parma, Giulio Romano at Mantua, Carpaccio and Tintoretto at Venice, so Luini and his pupils here had the rare felicity of decorating a whole building by his art.

It was in this Church that Giovanni Bentivoglio, of Bologna, after he had sought asylum in Milan, was buried, and here his grand-daughter took the veil, entering the convent of nuns long since founded. To adorn the Church, then rebuilt, Alessandro, his son, commissioned Luini, now at the zenith of his fame. He covered the walls, the choir and the chapels with the faces of fair, female saints and with gentle, mystical representations of their Suffering Lord, symbolising in the Marriage of Cana their divine union

---

[1] "The eagle of his art," as his pupil called him, so swift was he in execution, so strong in flight, had the faults as the merits of a most vivid and exuberant imagination ; his pictures throb with life and movement presented with tense dramatic vigour.

with Him. Catherine, Agnes, Lucy, Agatha, gem-like or star-like, gaze from their gallery upon the church below. "The Luinesque smile is on their lips and in their eyes, quiet, refined, as though the emblems of their martyrdom brought back no thought of pain to break the Paradise of rest in which they dwell" (Symonds). They are a sisterhood of stainless souls, the lilies of Love's garden painted round Christ's throne. Matteo Bandello records the curious fact that, as a model for his Catherine, Luini chose the features of the beautiful and abandoned Countess of Cellant, a sexual maniac of the day, one of those who share with the spider the strange instinct of destroying their lovers after they have enjoyed them.

In architecture the day of the "baroque" was at hand. Pellegrino Pellegrini (Tibaldi), who was appointed architect of the Duomo in 1567, represented here the ideals of the late Renaissance with its love of classical outline and detail, its mania for rich and overwhelming ornamentation. The small doors of the Cathedral, part of S. Fedele and perhaps S. Lorenzo, are his work. The sumptuous palace of the Genoese merchant Andrea Marino, now the *Municipio*, is the work of his contemporary, Galeazzo Alessi.

CHAPTER VI.

CERTOSA DI PAVIA.

WITHIN twenty miles of Milan, beyond the Cistercian Church of Chiaravalle, far from the madding crowd and noise of any city, alone amid the fields of rice and maize, in that happy solitude which is the sole happiness of the monastic ideal, stands the Certosa di Pavia. Alone it stands in the verdant plain, a suppressed monastery in an unbelieving age, a monument of the outworn creed of inhuman celibacy, a record of past ideals in art, and an eternal achievement of beauty. We pass within the tinted walls and frescoed vestibule which divides it from the monotonous, flat fields, the dusty, unkempt roads, the bare, muddy dykes, and behold the amazing façade of what has been called " the richest and most wonderful monument in the world." It owes its origin to the vow of Caterina Visconti, which her husband fulfilled after her death. Employing as his architects Bernardo da Venezia, Giacomo da Campione, Cristoforo di Beltramo, and other masters whom he had brought to work upon the Duomo at Milan, Gian Galeazzo laid the foundations of the Church in 1396. He bequeathed an annual sum to be devoted to the work, and, after its completion, to the poor at Pavia.

The monks concentrated their efforts at first upon building and decorating the domestic portions of their monastery. The political disturbances of the era of the Ambrosian Republic, which I have sketched above, led to further delay. But Francesco Sforza, eager to proclaim himself the true successor of the Visconti, as he set about rebuilding the Visconti Castello, so he encouraged the completion of this Church (1450), entrusting the task to Giovanni and Guiniforte da Solario, who had been at work upon the Duomo. And now, when the Northern influence, under which the original designers had laboured, was overpast, upon the Gothic foundations rose the gorgeous choir, the transepts and terra-cotta walls, which breathe the spirit of the Classic revival with which the Sforza dynasty is identified.

The Church, with its high nave and Gothic pillars, reminiscent of the Duomo of Milan, with its Renaissance transepts, choir and dome, and its culmination in the Renaissance façade, forms an epitome of Lombard architecture, and owes its existence not to one artist or to one patron, but, like the Duomo and Castello at Milan, to the continued patronage of the Visconti and Sforza dynasties and to the loving toil of generations of workers, who lived and died and handed on the tradition of their labours beneath the shadow of this mighty monument.

For upon the work of internal decoration a school of famous craftsmen was trained up.   Hither came artists from Venice, Verona, Florence and Brescia, Benedetto Ferrini, Antonio Rizzo, Vincenzo Foppa and others, to labour at altar-piece or terra-cotta detail, to advise on questions of construction, to stimulate and direct the growing art of the Mantegazza and Amadeo.   Within and without (this, I think, is the predominant impression the lavishness of the artistic treasures of the Certosa leaves upon our minds), there is at any rate nothing cheap or mean.   There is a harmonious luxury of material, of marble, paint and bronze, a cheerful extravagance of labour, as if no time or effort were too great to spend upon the polishing of this exquisite jewel of the Duchy of Milan, which go far to compensate for the lack of constructional meaning and true decorative power in much of the ornamentation.   Now this elaboration of ornament, and the extent of it, is, no doubt, largely owed to the material fact that no one at the Certosa was anxious to part with the revenues bequeathed by Gian Galeazzo " till it should be completed."

When we have passed through the long series of lovely chapels that line the nave, chapels built of finest marble, altars exquisitely inlaid with pietra-work, altar-pieces painted by Borgognone, the devout, Luini, the serene and tender, or Andrea Solari, Leonardo's pupil ; when we have stood in the Transept and looked upon the medallion portraits and stately statues of the Dukes of Milan slumbering, after lives so strenuous, feverish and passionate, upon their marble biers ; when, through doors enriched by magnificent reliefs, we have passed into the Sacristies, rich beyond price with the glories of illuminated missals, and into the gorgeous Choir, where bronze and wood and marble and glass have yielded all their sumptuous beauties to the hand of the decorative artist ; and thence to the superb Lavatory of the monks, where smiles a sweet, maternal Madonna by Luini ; we are dazzled and surfeited by this plethora of lovely detail.   We long for a quiet moment.   We escape through splendid doors to the sunlit cloisters without.   But least of

all may the eye rest here, in the presence of these lovely
arcades, the final triumph of Lombard brick-work, with
their slender marble shafts and the dark-red terra-cotta
friezes of cupids and angel-faces smiling through the foliage
of the vine, through woven lines of acanthus leaves, to a
chorus of Ave Marias beneath the deep blue of the sky.

But beyond, at last, *pax multa in cella!* In the tiny
gardens of the little cells that surround the Great Cloister
we can find a sanctuary of delicious peace, where once,
beneath the shadow of the central cupola, in the intervals
of regular offices, a monk might well excogitate a masterpiece of Theology, or execute such careful art-work as those
elaborate service-books and their wonderful notation.

Though the work, as it were, of a college of artists,
whose successive members found lifelong employment in
the decoration and construction of this marvellous monument, the Certosa of Pavia owes the peculiar character of
its rich and complex loveliness to two men in chief—
Giovanni Antonio Amadeo, sculptor and architect, and
Ambrogio Borgognone, the painter. Amadeo was the son-
in-law of Guiniforte. The decoration of the doorway
leading to the smaller cloister was one of his earliest pro-
ductions. There the charm of his angel faces marks the
arrival of a great sculptor.

The later artists of the Certosa echo and re-echo the
designs of Amadeo and of the Mantegazza, Cristoforo and
Antonio, his immediate predecessors, the first among the
Milanese artists to show, through a somewhat stiff and
ungainly realism, some signs of the Renaissance.

It was characteristic of Il Moro that he threw himself
with enthusiasm into the work at the Certosa. Precious

ONE OF THE SEPARATE HOUSES OF THE TWENTY-FOUR
MONKS OF THE CERTOSA DE PAVIA.

marbles were brought from every part of Italy. By his direction, Borgognone decorated the roof of the nave and the newly-added apse, designed the elaborate *intarsiatura* of the Choir-stalls, and painted the frescoes and altar-pieces of solemn, pale-faced Saints, and gentle, wan Madonnas, who still look down upon us from their golden harmonies in the side-chapels. By his direction Gian Cristoforo Romano began to work upon the Sarcophagus of Gian Galeazzo, near which, as we have seen, surrounded by portraits and mementoes of their race, lie Cristoforo Solari's beautiful recumbent effigies of Lodovico himself and Beatrice, the strong face of the Ruler pillowed by the side of the curling locks of his clever, joyous, girl-like wife. This monument, which he had ordered, was rescued from destruction in days of iconoclastic zeal by the monks of S. Maria delle Grazie, and brought by them to the great Lombard sanctuary, which the Duke had loved so well.

Amadeo developed his genius at the Duomo and upon that extraordinarily ornate façade of the Colleoni Chapel at Bergamo. Then, at the height of his powers, he was recalled by Lodovico to work upon the reliefs of the Monks' Lavatory, and Gian Galeazzo's monument, upon the medallions of the Sforzas, and, above all, upon the design and execution of that triumph of Lombard genius, the marvellous marble façade, with its great central portal and round-headed windows, its historical reliefs and its superb abundance of decorative sculpture (1494-1499). The sculptor Amadeo snatched the reins from Amadeo the architect. For six years he devoted all the energy of his exuberant imagination to this labour of joyous decoration, filling every available space with a boundless profusion of

Renaissance ornament, carving with infinite grace the burning censers, and the rich candelabra, which form the columns
of the windows, lavishing his invention and love of beauty
on the *putti* that bear the Sforza arms, telling stories and
allegories without number and framing them in flowers and
fruits and classical details, letting his fertile fancy run riot
in design, and, incidentally, illustrating in stone the glory
and the licence, the unchastened splendour and the uncurbed
delight in intellectual and artistic pleasures characteristic of
the Golden Age of the Court of Milan.

CHAPTER VII.

PAVIA; PIACENZA; RONCAGLIA; BOBBIO; BORGO SAN DONNINO.

FROM the Certosa we pass to where, upon the banks of Ticino, broad and swift, the red brick walls of Pavia, crowned by slender campanili and the tiled domes of her churches, rise out of the green plains. This is the old capital of the Lombard Kings, before the conquest of Charlemagne ; this, later, was the proud City of a Hundred Towers. The Romans set the ancient city a few miles above the junction of the Ticino and the Po, and called it Ticinum. The centre of a very fertile district, it is the point where the chief roads from France into Italy, passing over the little S. Bernard or Mont Genèvre, naturally converged and tapped the water-way. In its neighbourhood, therefore, many invaders, from Hannibal onwards, have had to fight for their right to advance into Italy. Theodoric the Goth seized Ticinum, and here, when he had made good his hold upon the peninsular, he built for himself a palace and baths, and, probably, the mighty fortifications which rendered it in after years " the last refuge of the Gothic name in Italy." For this stronghold of the Goths held out in isolation against the Lombard conquerors for nigh three years. It is said that Alboin, enraged by the obstinacy of the garrison, had bound himself by a tremendous oath that age and sex and dignity should be confounded in a general massacre. But, as he was entering the gate in triumph, his horse fell and could not be raised from the ground. The conqueror relented at this omen of the wrath of God. Sheathing his sword, he entered Theodoric's palace and proclaimed that the inhabitants should be spared and that Pavia should be the capital of his kingdom (572).

It was a later Lombard King, Luitprand, who, in 721, is said to have redeemed the sacred relics of S. Augustine for 60,000 gold crowns from the Saracens, and brought them from Sardinia to be deposited in the Church of S. Pietro in Ciel d'Oro. There, in the modern restored church stands, after many vicissitudes, the tomb which was begun in 1350 and which Gian Galeazzo Visconti directed his heirs to complete.

Superior in unity of conception, in the proportions of the design, and in delicacy of carving to the Arca of S. Dominic at Bologna, the beautiful Tomb of S. Augustine almost certainly must have been wrought by some Lombard pupils of Balduccio da Pisa, probably by Matteo and Bonino di Campione, sculptor and designer of the tomb of Can Signorio at Verona. It vividly recalls in the workmanship of some of the statuettes, with their highly polished surfaces and the elaborate borders of their robes, the statuettes by Balduccio on the Tomb of S. Peter Martyr at Milan.

The saint is represented lying on a couch covered with a sheet, which is held by six angels. About his head stand S. Jerome and S. Gregory, his saintly mother, Monica, who by prayer and precept wrestled with the powers of darkness for her beloved son, and S. Ambrose, the great Archbishop of Milan.

Above this central scene are reliefs representing the chief episodes in the life, death and translation of the saint ; others, again, in the crocketed gables above. Most of them are easily recognisable, but those which show him arguing with figures with the legs and feet of birds need a word of explanation. They represent the heresies against which the great Theologian fought, Manichaeism, Arianism, and Donatism. For the rest, the tomb is very richly adorned with architectural accessories and with statuettes of the Apostles and the Virtues, each and all of them worthy of minute study.

When the Popes invited the Franks into Italy and Charlemagne crossed the Alps as the ally of Adrian I., it was the fall of Pavia which marked the downfall of the Lombard kingdom. After eight months' siege the city yielded to the new invader. It is said that a daughter of King Desiderius, having become enamoured of Charles, conveyed a message to him by shooting it across the Ticino, tied to a projectile. Her passion was encouraged by the King's reply. In the dead of night she stole the keys of the city from her father's bedside, where they always hung, and opened the gates to the besiegers. But in hurrying forth to meet King Charles, she was thrown down and trampled to death, another Tarpeia, by the onrush of the Frankish cavalry.

Though the town was sacked and the inhabitants utterly destroyed by the Huns in 940, yet, such was the recuperative power of the site, that forty years later Pavia is mentioned as the richest and fairest in Italy. It was now that her rivalry with Milan began, which was to lead to continual and disastrous wars. The encroachments of that growing, democratic power, commercial jealousy and the ecclesiastical infringement of their privileges by Aribert, roused the opposition of Pavia, aristocratic and hotly Ghibelline. When Henry II., supported by Milan, was crowned at Pavia, a large party favoured Ardoin's claims. Only a spark was needed for an explosion, and during the coronation festivities a quarrel arose between the citizens and Henry's German suite. His army, encamped outside the walls, rushed to the rescue. They set fire to some houses ; in a short time the whole city was plundered and ablaze. In revenge, on Henry's death, Pavia rose, destroyed his palace, and invited the King of France to take the Crown. Nor would she bow to the German Conrad, to whom Aribert had disposed of the kingdom at his nod. Conrad must needs receive the Iron Crown at Milan, before bending proud Pavia to his will.

Ghibelline now by tradition, gratitude, and opposition to Guelf Milan, Pavia welcomed Frederick Barbarossa as the Chastener of her enemy. Here he wore the Iron Crown of Lombardy for three days ; here he held the Council by which he endeavoured to reassert the superiority of the Emperor to the Pope. And Pavia, in spite of her bitter feud with Milan, waxed in prosperity ; ring after ring of fortifications was made to embrace her expanding girth. But at length she fell, stung to death commercially, it would seem, in her death-struggle with the Vipers of Milan.

Her decline began early and suddenly. How quiet, now, and shrunken seems the town, which once could arm 3000 horse and 15,000 foot, when Messer Torffello d' Istria feasted the Saladin! Three square, gaunt towers alone survive of those famed 300, and but few of the 130 churches. But at least Pavia died fighting nobly and to the last gasp for her Communal independence.

The noble family of Beccheria, who led the Ghibelline *popolo*, were almost masters of the city. In 1356 they joined the confederacy of lesser despots to check the growing power of Milan. An army of 40,000 men at once blockaded Pavia. And now arose a young Augustinian monk, Jacopo dei Bussolari, whose fervid eloquence, amongst a people always easily stirred by rhetoric, encouraged the burghers to endure in defence of their freedom. He roused them to sally forth and rout the enemy ; to capture the besiegers' fleet on the Ticino, and seize their camp with all its stores. Fra Jacopo used the influence he thus acquired to preach a reform of manners and a crusade against all despots. The Beccheria in their alarm compassed his death ; were discovered and expelled. They returned with a Milanese army. Fra Jacopo roused the burghers by his inspired eloquence. Men and women alike made every sacrifice in defence of their restored Commune. The Marquis of Montferrat, elected Signore, came to their relief. But his mercenaries were bought by the wealthier Milanese. And ere long plague, famine and the Providence which is on the side of the big battalions won the day. Fra Jacopo surrendered, stipulating for a general amnesty and the internal liberties of the town. His conditions were granted, but not observed.

The enthusiastic monk, who had taken no thought for himself, died in the dungeons of a monastery at Vercelli, and Pavia passed under the rule of the Visconti.

The Rulers of Milan made of Pavia a royal residence. Under their patronage rose a new Cathedral on the site of the ruined basilica of Charlemagne's day ; marble palaces lined the Strada Nova, the stately Ateneo, with its halls and porticoes for the different Schools, sprang into being, and the mighty Castello was built and decorated. We still find in the Pavia of to-day echoes, faint but haunting, of this former splendour. The Castello stands close to the Milan Gate. Three sides, with characteristic forked Lombard battlements, and two square towers alone remain of the vast quadrangle with lofty towers projecting at the angles that once was here. This superb Palace of the Visconti, which had been built by Galeazzo II. (1360), which generations of artists under successive Dukes laboured to make the most splendid dwelling-place in Europe, which Petrarch pronounced " augustissimum," and of which Francesco Sforza declared that he had not seen the equal for its treasures in Italy, is now a barrack. On the interior of the quadrangle an open stone arcade is surmounted by fine Gothic windows of a later date, which light the corridor above, enriched with slender marble shafts and exquisite terra-cotta mouldings like those in the cloisters of the Certosa. Under Gian Galeazzo and his successors the vaulted halls were richly painted, and the vast Sala della Palla, where Dukes and Courtiers played " Pall Mall," the favourite game of the Renaissance, was decorated with frescoes by the best artists of Pavia and Cremona, representing those scenes of sport and hunting which the Lords of Pavia loved. The Library was filled with priceless treasures, collected and catalogued with loving care by Il Moro. And, without, a beautiful garden, with flowery lawns watered by crystal streams and groves of plane and cypress and myrtle that led to fair pavilions, was surrounded by a park that teemed with game, the sport of hound and falcon.

It was in this park that was fought the famous battle of Pavia, when France and Spain were struggling for supremacy in Italy. The French King was besieging the town. The Marquis of Pescara, in a desperate attempt to relieve it, forced on an engagement by attacking the French camp in the Park of Mirabello. The victory of the Imperialists was as overwhelming as it was unexpected. Francis I. was taken prisoner ; the shattered remnant of his forces was hounded out of the land, and Charles V. was master of Italy.

Under the fostering care of Lodovico Sforza, whose own Court, though unilluminated by any great genius in the world of letters, was so alive to the importance of literature that it is said that Jacopo Antiquario, going to his work as secretary one morning, found his clerks all neglecting the Duke's business to pore over a newly published book, and, when he would scold, found that the book was Poliziano's *Miscellanea*, and himself forgot business and scolding alike in the excitement of reading it, the University of Pavia naturally reached its height. Ninety professors and 3000 students studied there in the magnificent *Ateneo* built by Il Moro's orders. It became the University of the Milanese, and even when the town declined politically and commercially, the University, thanks to the consequent empty houses and cheap living, seems to have flourished the more.

Nor does Pavia owe her literary interest to an Academy

or even to the presence of Petrarch alone ; for here (*Vicolo San Zeno*) tradition says that Boethius, who, like Vergil at Mantua, was honoured at Pavia as a saint in the Mediaeval Cloister, confined by Theodoric, composed his great work on the " Consolation of Philosophy."

The Church of S. Michele (late eleventh century) is a typical building of the Lombard-Romanesque style, and is probably rather earlier than the twelfth century Cathedral of Piacenza, than S. Ambrogio at Milan and S. Zeno at Verona. The exterior presents the familiar features of the red-brick, domical Lombard basilica. As at San Teodoro and S. Pietro, a lofty, octagonal structure in diminishing stages rises above the internal cupola over the intersection of nave and choir and transepts. The roofs are flat-pitched, and under the eaves run open arcaded galleries. The single, broad-gabled façade is a mere frontispiece, screening the construction of the aisles. It is adorned with bands of sculptured reliefs. Within, there is a raised choir above a fine crypt. And, though the plan is basilican, yet, as at Sant' Ambrogio, the naves and aisles are vaulted, and the red brick walls, stone piers and broad round arches carry the ribs of the groined vaulting. Herein we perceive an important link in the transition to Gothic.

Typical of Lombard architecture are the rough but majestic round arches and the piers of clustered section ; typical, too, the added vaulting shafts, the distinctive feature, as Ruskin says, of Northern architecture, the " petrified " upright pilaster above the nave pier, representing in stone the necessary timber upright of a wooden church of the North. Typical, too, of Lombard work is the endless imagery of active life and fantastic superstition in which the sculptors have delighted, letting their Northern humour and love of the grotesque, and their fierce delight in the chase run mad in the sunshine of the South. There is one capital covered with a mass of grinning heads, heads that grow out of feet or out of two bodies. The creatures of the artist's imagination struggle and devour one another, fighting furiously, in fierce Lombard realism. They are alive and vigorous, as full of passion and spring, as savage, furious, hungry as the invading Lombard himself.

The vast, unfinished Duomo, which Il Moro founded, was begun by Bramante's pupil, Cristoforo Rocchi, to whom Francesco Martini and Leonardo were sent to give advice. The work was carried on (1498) by Amadeo, who presently resigned his post at the Certosa. The tragic close of Il Moro's career put a stop to the building, but not before Amadeo had enriched it with the graceful loggia and fine cupola, which recall the architect's training at the Certosa.

Such are the buildings, ruined or inchoate, of Pavia, and best we remember them as they group above the red brick walls, and the tiled houses of the town, beyond the green waters of Ticino, with the picturesque old bridge in the foreground. This bridge, with its grand oaken beams, carrying heavy tiles, its plain, worn stone pilasters and paved way, forms the most popular promenade of the town. It is part of the main artery of Pavesan life, and recalls to mind the prominent place which bridges took in Roman and mediaeval days, as the scene of games and religious rites. This picturesque bridge is the successor to a wooden one, which was seized by the people of Piacenza, ever eager to be at war with Pavia, and on this occasion fighting for the exiled Beccheria. They towed it twelve miles down the river, intending to hold it for a trophy at Piacenza, but there it stuck and they had to leave it to be burned by the mortified Pavesans (*see* frontispiece).

PIACENZA, RONCAGLIA, BOBBIO, BORGO SAN DONNINO.

Piacenza lies on a dusty, wind-swept alluvial plain, intersected by tributaries of the Po, often flooded in winter by

LAMP BRACKET IN THE PALAZZO DEL COMMUNE AT PIACENZA.

the swollen Trebbia, whose banks are famous as the scenes of victories by Carthaginian Hannibal and Russian Suvarof. But from this sandy plain, against the clear blue of the Italian sky, the red brick churches and palaces and the red-brown tiles of irregular houses, houses that line the winding streets, coloured every shade of green and pink and brown and yellow, and using to the utmost the artistic value of

shutters, rise up, extraordinarily effective in their colour
and picturesque grouping. At closer quarters the promised
charm is not denied. Piacenza is rich, even among Italian
cities better known, in lovely " bits " of street scenery,
and in the delicate terra-cotta tracery of the Paduan plain,
which contrasts with massive buildings, crowned by vast
projecting roofs that rest upon huge stone corbels.

The Romans founded Placentia as a stronghold to secure
the passage of the Po. River port and fort, the northern
point to which the Flaminian way was extended from
Rimini, under the name of the Via Æmilia (*see* pp. 138,
139), this frontier post was sacked, twenty years after its
foundation, by Hamilcar (B.C. 200), before he met his death
in the great battle of Cremona. It disappeared from its
leading position among the northern towns of Italy, when
Francesco Sforza, warring with the Venetians on behalf of
Milan, having breached with his artillery walls that had
been deemed impregnable, stormed and sacked the city, and
left Piacenza in ruins. Subsequently it fell into the hands
of the Farnese family ; from the vast, unfinished sixteenth
century Palazzo Farnese the body of Pier Luigi Farnese was
thrown into the ditch beneath, after it had been exhibited in
fierce triumph by his murderers to the people.

Its importance as a town in the days of the Lombard
League is indicated by the fact that the members of it
assembled here to approve the Peace of Constance. Their
meeting place was in Sant' Antonino, a church which was
founded on a spot where S. Barnabas is said to have
preached, and which boasts a richly decorated porch, called
Il Paradiso. The rival houses of the Scotti and the Landi
struggled for the rich prize of Piacenza ; it fell into the

power of the Visconti (1313). Gian Galeazzo refounded
the University, which dated its existence from a Bull of
Innocent IV., 1248, and he endeavoured to make it the
University town of the great Italian State which he was
building up. But in vain. Pavia was not to be ousted
by Piacenza from its position as the University of the
Milanese. Pavia, of course, and Parma, her neighbours
to east and west, were the chief enemies of the Commune.
It is in the days of her communal freedom that Piacenza
interests us most. It was in 1222 that the middle classes,
after prolonged and most violent faction fights, succeeded
in wringing from the nobles a share in the government.
And in 1281, as an inscription records, they began to raise,
in brick and marble, a monument worthy of their spirit of
municipal independence. The Palazzo Communale is the
most notable building in Piacenza ; it is one of the earliest
of such palaces of municipal life in Italy ; it is in itself a
most noble and harmonious building, boldly irregular, and
gloriously successful in its irregularity, in the colouring and
charm of the brickwork and marble, and in the richness of
the elaborate terra-cotta decorations. It is the typical
Broletto. There is an open ground storey ; five lofty
pointed arches on square piers of white marble carry an
upper storey of red brick, which is crowned by a marble
cornice and the familiar forked or swallow-tailed "Saracenic"
battlements. A delightfully harmonious transition of colour
is secured by lines of red and blue-grey marble above the
white, and below the string-course, which separates them
from the red brick of the upper storey. Six windows of
three lights, embossed under a round arch with a deep
archivolt very slightly recessed, are set flat in the wall.

PIAZZA DEI CAVALLI PIACENZA.

They vary in size and detail, and are very elaborately decorated with terra-cotta work. They illumine the Great Hall, where sat the Council of the State. From the richly-decorated balcony without, the rulers announced their decisions to the people in the Piazza below, appealed for their support, submitted to them, by a mediaeval rough-and-ready referendum, supreme questions of legislation, and the arbitrament of peace or war. Was it war, from under the great archway the Carroccio, bearing the banner of the town, was dragged forth by high-born women and children. And from the great tower adjoining, the bell rang out a summons to arms, a defiance to rival Parma or rival Pavia.

The piazza in which this building stands is still the centre and keynote of life at Piacenza. Peasants in brown cloaks, direct descendants of the Roman toga, commercial classes in plain black, officers in grey-blue cloaks, women in red shawls fill it with all the life and movement and colour of a typical Italian square. It is called the Piazza dei Cavalli, for at each corner of the Palazzo Municipale the rich bronze greens of two spirited—if strained—equestrian statues, by Francesco Mocchi (1620-5), pupil of Giovanni da Bologna, harmonise with the movement of the crowd and the brilliant colour scheme of the whole. They represent Alessandro Farnese, Prince of Parma, and his son, the cruel Ranuccio. At the western angle of the Piazza is the thirteenth century church of S. Francesco. To the south-east, down the Via Venti Settembre, towers the lofty campanile of the Cathedral, on which still hangs the iron cage, the *gabbia*, in which here, as in other Italian towns, criminals, heretics, or political opponents, were shut up naked, exposed to the fury of the elements and the mockery of mankind. The

Duomo itself is a notable monument of Lombard architecture (1122), exhibiting all the features which I have described as typical (*see* Milan and Pavia).

In the western façade are three magnificent projecting porches, and above them a circular window and open galleries. The newly-restored interior exhibits a grand simplicity, in marked contrast with the labyrinth of a hundred pillars in the crypt. Without the walls lies the Church of S. Maria della Campagna, by Bramante, which is filled with the paintings of Il Pordenone. The name of the Church of S. Sisto has some interest, since Raphael's picture now at Dresden, the " Sistine " Madonna, was taken from this building.

A few miles from Piacenza, in the direction of Cremona, lies Roncaglia, in the plain where the German Emperors held their diets.

Some thirty miles in the opposite direction is the Abbey-Church of Bobbio, which S. Columba founded, and where, a saint truly pious, a man truly great, he died (615), leaving his foundation one of the chief centres of intellectual activity in Italy.

From Piacenza we pass to Parma, but, short of Parma, the traveller interested in architecture will spare a moment, an he can, to view the unfinished façade and splendid porches[1] of the Cathedral of Borgo San Donnino, a little watering-place, which takes its name from S. Domninus, the Roman soldier who suffered martyrdom under Maximian. Here, as at Piacenza, we find a characteristic example of twelfth century Lombard art, when it had developed into a style easily recognisable as distinct from the Italo-Byzantine.

[1] " Taurus " decorated with bulls, " Aries " with lambs.

The barbaric element in the ornamentation imparts a marvellous, imaginative vigour to its spirit, and fills the spectator with a sense of a vast energy, struggling for expression, that has not yet found its soul. Here, as elsewhere, are dream fancies of knotted dragons and fighting men. Here, too, are pillars of porch or crypt that rest on mighty lions tearing their prey, or upon men, hunched and crushed beneath the weight they carry, riding upon lions. The little town was utterly destroyed by Parma in 1152.

CHAPTER VIII.

PARMA, REGGIO, CANOSSA, CREMA.

THE Roman Colony of Parma was founded on the right bank of the Po, amid the flat, marshy fenland which stretches up to the foot of the Apennines, as the immediate corollary of the newly constructed Emilian way. To-day, the Via Aemilia runs through the Piazza Garibaldi, dividing the city in twain. Under the military régime of Narses, the name of Parma was changed to Chrysopolis, the city of gold. It is not necessary for our purpose to follow its history seriously. There was a stirring year in the city's annals, when Frederick was trying to impose his rule upon Italy. Parma, seized by some exiled nobles, who surprised the German garrison, revolted from the Emperor.

Stung by the loss of this wealthy city, commanding as it did the road into Tuscany, Frederick hurried to recover it, gathering support on his way from all the Ghibelline towns. Meantime the Guelfs poured reinforcements into the town, and the citizens, animated by the Papal Legate, placed themselves under the protection of the Virgin and swore to conquer or to perish beneath the ruins of the city. Mantua and Ferrara ran supplies up the Po for the relief of the beleaguered town. Famine, assault and the atrocious

massacre day by day of two captive nobles and two burghers
before the walls failed to shake their constancy. Winter

crept on. Frederick, determined to continue the siege, built
a new town on the road to Piacenza, four bow-shots from
Parma. Walls and ditches were constructed, and a church,

palace and houses built from materials brought from the ruined villages. The proud name of Vittoria was given to these winter-quarters.

At length, when, after six months' siege, the situation seemed desperate, the keen eyes of a Milanese watcher from the walls observed that Frederick had quitted Vittoria and gone a hawking along the banks of the Taro. It was decided to stake everything on a sudden, desperate and concerted sortie against the beleaguering lines. The Legate himself, with the Standard of the Virgin, led the attack on Vittoria. A sea of citizens, old and young, women and children, surged up in one great wave of enthusiasm and broke upon the unready garrison. The Imperial army was routed ; Vittoria was burnt. In Dante's phrase, the Parmesans " *de Victoria victoriam adepti sunt.*" Frederick's hopes of crushing the Lombards were dashed for ever.

Parma passed from the sway of one despot to that of another, now Papal Legate, now Imperial Vicar ; falling under the foreign domination of the Visconti, whilst the feuds of the old families, the Rossi and the Pallavicini, the Correggi and Sanvitali, were still rife within the walls.

The city, which had hitherto been intensely Ghibelline, was reconciled with the Papacy 1115, when the Pope and Countess Matilda with a magnificent escort came to consecrate the new Cathedral. The old Duomo had been burnt down in the middle of the eleventh century, and Cadalo da Verona, Bishop of Parma, afterwards Honorius II., the Anti-Pope, had set about rebuilding it with vigorous enthusiasm. The broad screen of the rosy-coloured façade, with its arcaded galleries, is still incomplete ; the rest was not finished before the end of the thirteenth century, from

which period date the porch and its two mighty lions in
Verona marble by the Lombard sculptor, Bono da Bissone,
and the lofty campanile, to the low green spire of which
the golden *Angelo girante* was added a hundred years later.
At its side, in the corner of the Piazza, peaceful as an
English Close, nestles the octagonal Baptistery of reddish-
purple and grey Verona marble. This is one of the most
complete and one of the most beautiful of Lombard buildings. Begun in 1196 it was not finished till 1322 ; the
round arches of the first storey develop into the pure
French Gothic of the upper storey and crowning pinnacles.
Both the Baptistery and the Cathedral are indeed superb
museums which illustrate the development of Lombard
architecture, through Gothic to Renaissance, from apse to
cupola, from round arch to pinnacle, from terra-cotta gable
to marble balustrade. They illustrate, too, the rise and
fall of painting at Parma, from Benassi and Comune to
Correggio and his mannered successors, as well as the brief,
but glorious, episode of her sculpture. For the three
magnificent portals are adorned with sculptured stories. On
the North Portal is inscribed the name of Benedetto
Antelami, who began the work (1196). Here the history
of the Adoration of the Magi and of John the Baptist is
recorded, whilst on the door-posts are the genealogical trees
of Jacob and Jesse. On the West Portal is a curious Last
Judgment ; on the door-posts the six ages of man and acts
of mercy of Christ. On the South is the allegory of Life
and Death from the story of Balaam and Jehosaphat. A
frieze of symbolical animals and human-headed monsters
runs almost round the building. This sculpture is in itself
a sufficient answer to the extreme view of M. Reymond

that Tuscan sculpture was derived from France ; that Christian art owed little to classic models, and that Niccolò Pisano wrought in a virgin soil unstirred by any previous artistic effort.   In the face of this Baptistery, and of other early work at Modena and Ferrara, it cannot be maintained that the art of Niccolò blossomed forth suddenly and fortuitously like a flower in the desert.

On the other hand, such figures as those of Solomon and Sheba recall past a doubt the corresponding figures at Reims, and must be admitted to illustrate the very definite influence of French art upon the sculpture, as upon the Gothic architecture, of Italy.   The South door is later than the others—probably about 1260, the era of Niccolò Pisano.

The Baptistery within is a supremely interesting thirteenth century monument of Italian painting and sculpture in prosperous Parma.   Here took place the great annual immersions at Easter and Pentecost.   Something of the luxury of the Roman baths seems to have been intentionally reproduced in the artistic decoration, in the glowing frescoes or mosaics, in the glorious gates of bronze, in the porphyry pillars and coloured marbles of the pavement, in the lavish ornament of the richly sculptured doors of the Christian Baptisteries.   Here it will be noticed that the fresco in the cupola is strongly reminiscent of the style of the mosaic-workers.   There are two vast fonts ; the larger, which dates from 1299, rests upon a lion, full of tense energy, and is carved in a design of classic splendour and strength.

Modern Parma has cut adrift from its past.   It is a city of cheese and felt hats, of violets and aristocratic villadom.

THE CAMPANILE AND BAPTISTERY OF THE
CATHEDRAL, PARMA.

It has pulled down its old walls and bridges ; even the old Ponte Verde, thrown across one of the little encircling streams, which flow down from the Apennines and joining in the Parma river lose themselves in the Po, has been replaced by a modern serviceable bridge alongside. A fragment only, of the old Castello that guarded it, remains on the far side of the river. But Parma remains the city of Antonio Allegri, the work-place of the great painter, who, born in the little village of Correggio and trained at Ferrara, spent all his short life of fruition in covering the churches of Parma with the joyous creations of his sensuous imagination. He died at the early age of 38 (1534), and it is necessary, when we gaze at these wonderful frescoes, cruelly as they have suffered by time and restoration ; at the Christ in Glory in the dome of S. Giovanni Evangelista, which was hailed by contemporaries as the masterpiece of all painting ; at the labyrinth of limbs and medley of postures, which caused the contemptuous canon to denounce the Assumption of the Virgin in the Duomo as a mere " fricassee of frogs " ; at the life and light and vigour and mastery of technique which characterise all his work ; it is necessary to remember that this amazing artist, who could " so fleece with clouds the pure ethereal space," was but a youth. Uncurbed by patronage and the restraint of Courts, untroubled by such problems of thought as tormented Leonardo, untamed by the experience of life, he abandoned himself to a natural delight in portraying all its laughter and high-spirited joyousness. He is the most boyish and the most buoyant of painters. His world is a world of radiant, thoughtless wantoning ; his art, intoxicated by the light and life and colour of beautiful forms, revels in audacious attitudes and voluptuous movement. And these attitudes and these movements are portrayed with a delicate, sensuous colouring which raise him to the throne in his own kingdom of *Midsummer Night's Dream* ; they constitute the true " Correggiosity of Correggio."

Correggio was a poet, but also a realist ; not irreverent, but with a complete lack of reverence ; not consciously profane, but wholly untouched by ecclesiasticism.   Life and light, and the beauty of flesh tints and of the human form fascinated him ; these things he gloried in, reproducing and insisting upon them, sometimes even with a certain naïve naughtiness, and always triumphing in a proud display of his superb technique, his original draughtsmanship, his amazing mastery of chiaroscuro.   He painted, for the wise Abbess of that convent, the room in the convent of San Paolo.   Trellises of vine shadow the walls, as if with an actual arbour ; groups of *ragazzi*, peeping through the oval openings of the pergola, luscious in colour and faint in light, are ready to break through or hide behind the covert.   It is all as exuberant as it is young, as graceful as it is false. He painted the Assumption in the cupola of the Duomo, which precludes, as Ruskin says, all possibility of deception.

And here Correggio has made a dome of some thirty feet in diameter look like a cloud-wrapt opening in the seventh heaven, crowded with a rushing sea of angels.   There is nothing whatever of the spiritual in his picture of that spiritual event.   He paints clouds such as hardly even Shelley could have imagined ; he endows his youthful, cloud-encumbered cherubs with a superb fulness of sensuous vitality ; he so concentrates his force upon the surge of surrounding limbs that the meaning of the event is quite forgotten and degenerates into a tossing nightmare of tortured nudity. But at least Correggio is honest in his youthful exuberance and delight in his art. At least he never preaches. He honestly expresses his joy in the physical delight of human beauty and youthful loveliness ; he frankly proclaims the triumph of his own new-found mastery of technique. He is very young and very delightful. He had learnt in suffering no philosophy ; he had no moral lesson which he wished to teach. The moral of his painting, if we must seek one, is the advice of Matteo Bandello, " Live joyously."

It is in the magnificent Renaissance structure, S. Giovanni Evangelista, that Correggio's noblest achievement is to be found. The Benedictine monks, who preferred the baroque façade (1607) of this Church to that of Zaccagni, also destroyed the greater part of the painter's masterpiece, the Virgine Incoronata, in order to enlarge their Choir. But the building remains a fitting museum of Correggio's works. And he reached his supreme moment when he portrayed, in the guise of a youthful poet of singular beauty, the rapt Evangelist about to take his pen in order to describe the Apocalyptic Vision, the wonder of which is still perceptible in his far-off, ecstatic gaze. And this figure, and those Apostles, each of an ideal type, resting on clouds about the risen Saviour, lit by a divine light which never was on sea or land, in this, the first dome devoted to a general composition, were the work of a man under thirty years of age.

Alessandro Farnese had been Bishop of Parma in 1509. When he became Pope Paul III. he established the Farnese family as Dukes of Parma and Piacenza. Of these, Ranuccio I. built the Teatro Farnese and began the vast Pilotta Palace (1597), where, in the picture gallery and library, the art of Correggio (especially in Toschi's copies and engravings), of Francesco Mazzolo (Parmigianino), his contemporary imitator, and of his later mannered followers, may be further studied, as well as in the churches I have mentioned, and in S. Maria della Steccata.

From Parma to Modena the road runs through a luxuriant land, of maize and corn, veiled by the delicate drapery of the tendrils of the vines, which trail from tree to tree, rich in the glad promise of the Wine-god. And many streams, running down from the Apennines through the fenlands to the sea, blue or silvery white, intersect the brown, the green and purple plain. Reggio, birth-place of Ariosto, is more than half way to Modena. It has an interesting history, but is scarce worth visiting, save as the starting-point for Canossa. A day spent in driving, walking and climbing up to the ruined, ivy-clad walls of Matilda's Castle, on a

> "precipice encurl'd
> In a gash of wind-grieved Apennine,"

will never be regretted. The views and the experience amply repay for the fatigue and bother of making the *bundobast*, or *combinazione*, therefor.

Ruined forts and lonely towers, mediaeval strongholds once planted there in deadly earnest of defence, crown every eminence of the rising ground, which leads up to the spurs of the Apennines. These castles are, as it were, the out-posts that secured the gloomy and isolated rock of

Canossa. Chief among them are Bianello, and, upon a crest of red rock, Rossena, from whose battlements the unfortunate Everelina flung herself, that she might escape from the brutal embraces of her lord and lover. Beyond, aloft, at last Canossa is seen, lonely and repellent, gleaming white upon a distant and commanding rock. Here was the fortress of Albert Azzo, granted to him by Otho, as a reward for the shelter he had given to Adelaide, the Countess of Modena and Reggio. To these Azzo added the cities of Mantua and Ferrara; his son acquired Brescia, the next generation added the vast dominions of the Markgrafs of Tuscany. And the predominant position thus obtained by the Azzo family culminated in the person of its last representative, Matilda, the "Great Countess," who so devotedly defended the Papacy in the War of Investitures, and finally bequeathed her possessions to the Church.

This was that Matilda, *la gran' donna d' Italia*, the "Lady Beautiful," in whom, advancing towards him, "over the yellow and vermilion flowers," Dante, with, may be, more than a poet's wonted licence, chose to allegorise Devotion to the supremacy of Holy Church. But at least the stern and warlike chatelaine of grim Canossa was possessed by that one, consuming idea. And, when the monk Hildebrand was made Pope Gregory VII., a primitive Elizabeth, an earlier Joan d'Arc, she donned armour and led her troops to fight in the cause of the Papacy, to reduce the temporal power to subjection. She had her reward when Canossa became "a second Rome"; when, in the fortress of Matilda, the Emperor, in garb of penitent sought pardon of the Holy Father—sought pardon and received it not, till, clad in sackcloth and bare-footed, he had waited and fasted three whole days in the snow, the sport of the bitter blasts which sweep down from Monte Pellegrino to the coast.

The people of Reggio destroyed the Castle of Canossa in 1255.   But enough of the building remains for the imaginative to conjure up that scene, where the eternal conflict of spiritual and temporal power, the unceasing strife between secular and ecclesiastical authority, was fought out and focussed in one dramatic, thrilling act.

The view from the grass-covered ruins of Canossa has something of the poetic splendour and the historical associa-tion, though nothing of the surrounding architecture, which make Agra and Granada unforgettable.

The Lombard towns lie at our feet, Reggio, Parma, Modena, Mirandola, Verona, Mantua ; Padua and Ferrara, we know, are hidden from sight by the amethyst haze that bathes the Euganean hills ; the silver stream of the Po winds through the green Lombard plain ; and, to the north, sweep the eternal, snow-clad mountains, and the glittering needles of the Venetian Alps.

CREMA.

Crema was destroyed by Frederick Barbarossa after a siege conducted with the utmost ferocity.   The inhabitants retired to Milan : their territory was given to the Cremonese who had distinguished themselves in the siege by using the heads of their prisoners for cannon-balls.

The Duomo, which invites our footsteps thither, is one of the most beautiful and characteristic of Lombard thirteenth century Cathedrals. The rich terra-cotta decoration of the façade, combined with the delicate charm of the campanile, with its rare tints of yellow, form a picture unique and imperishable in the memory.

CHAPTER IX.

MODENA.

THE very strong and splendid Colony of Mutina, in Cicero's phrase, was founded by the Romans (B.C. 220) as an advance-post on the right bank of the Po, to hold the territory they had recently acquired from the Boii. It must be visited for the sake of its Cathedral and City square, and this the wise traveller, having found a really good hotel at Bologna (Hotel Brun), will do between two trains. Between the brick of Piacenza, Parma and Bologna is sandwiched the marble and stone of Modena. And the mellow tints of her marble Duomo and Campanile are of a rare and harmonious loveliness. The whole building is suffused with soft gradations of colour like the dawn in an Eastern sky or the tinted clouds at sunset in a land of lakes and mountains.

The Cathedral was founded in 1099, when Modena formed part of the estates of the Countess Matilda. The exterior, however, evidently belongs to the twelfth century.

The simple majestic construction of the outside walls, crowned by a superb, deep arcade, enclosed by round arches in each bay carried on half columns in front of the pilasters, recalls at once the surviving portions of the old Duomo at Ferrara. There are two doorways on the South side. The easternmost, with its shafts of white marble most delicately carved, is screened by a two-storied porch of red marble, carried on detached pillars cut out of one block and knotted together. It is evidently much later (1180?) than the other, ruder doorway west of it (c. 1100?). The pillars of the porch rest on the backs of lions hewn out of a marble so wondrous hard that the weather of centuries, and the rubbing of Italian children who play about them, or of the backs of girls, who, their heads draped in little black mantillas, choose this sunny spot to sit and plait straw, have only served to polish them *ad unguem*. The doorway and porch beneath the great rose window of the western front are still more remarkable. The jambs are sculptured with representations of the twelve months. And the façade is covered with figures and foliage by Nicolaus and Guglielmus, who worked on San Zenone at Verona.

Artus de Bretannia figures among the heroes in these quaint, rough carvings of the early eleventh century, which tell the story of " man's first disobedience and his fall " in a strangely humorous and vigorous style. The red marble Lombard Lions of this porch are full of life and vigour. They do not seem to feel their centuries of waiting or the oppression of the slender pillars they bear ; so fierce and full of spring and so alert they look that the children do not dare to play upon them as at the other porches. They bear their burden lightly, as becomes the King of Beasts, the Almighty whom they typify. Their feet claw a serpent, with the tense dominant grip of their race, of the Lombards who made them.

At the east end, the nave terminates in two massive

pinnacles topped by graceful open cupolas, which, with three semi-circular apses, group boldly with one of the noblest campaniles in Italy. Beautiful in strength, and height, and proportion, it rises through six stages of superb simplicity to two octagonal ones. It is called La Ghirlandina, " from the sculpture which encircles it like a garland," it is said. In this tower is preserved the famous bucket, which the Modenese, in a cavalry raid, carried off from Bologna, and which was the cause of a war and of a poem.

At the root of the prolonged quarrel and permanent rivalry of Modena with Bologna lay, in the characteristic fashion of the Communes, a difference over boundaries and a disputed claim to the tiny town of Nonantola. Many, and sometimes bloody, were the battles fought. Once (1228) Bologna made a huge effort, and collected contingents from Ferrara and Florence, from Milan, Piacenza and Brescia and others to crush her rival, who had embraced the Imperial cause. But, aided by Parma and Cremona, the Modenese first relieved Bazano, which the allies had besieged, and then, advancing into the Contado of Bologna, fought the Confederates at Sta. Maria in Strada, fought them " till the going down of the great evening star " and scattered them to the winds. And next year they again put the Bolognese to flight, and took their Carroccio. The Parmesans carried off in triumph to their Cathedral the captured battering train of mangonels.

It is noticeable that, in all this inter-communal strife, it was not usually a question of one city enslaving another, but of desultory warfare, of raids and prisoners, alarums and excursions, of schoolboy triumphs and trophies. The cities were too evenly matched, perhaps, and there was the

MODENA: THE DUOMO.

law of the Empire and the Peace of Constance behind them. As the Bolognese carried off the gates of Imola, and Piacenza the bridge of Pavia, so the Modenese horsemen snatched this bucket from the walls of insulted Bologna. The war which followed culminated in the disaster of Fossalta (*see* p. 149). It furnished Alessandro Tassoni with the subject of his mock-heroic poem, in which he celebrated with burlesque humour the amazing incident of the ravished bucket, but incidentally satirised with biting irony the petty dissensions which had ruined Italy. His description of Modena in this poem, *La Secchia Rapita*, is pleasing :

> " . . . Siede in una gran pianura
> Che da la parte d'austro e d'occidente
> Cerchia di balze e di scoscese mura
> Del selvoso apennin la schiena algente. . . .
>
> .   .   .   .   .   .
> Da' l'oriente ha le fiorite sponde
> Del bel Panaro e le sue limpid' acque. . . ."

The Torre Ghirlandina, like the Cathedral, is slightly out of the perpendicular—(very pretty, as the Yorkshireman said of the tower of Pisa, but it's crooked). Its beauty is partly spoiled by a spire, which it is wise to eliminate, as Mr. Home does, from the view ; it is wise also to put from one the thought that there is a project on foot, typical of the vulgarity of garish modern Italian taste, to illuminate the whole tower with little Earl's Court electric lights. There will have to be a society formed soon for the destruction of uglifications. The round-arched windows of the Tower harmonise with the arcading of the Duomo, as the orange and creamy tints of the main buildings blend with the rich pink and red tints of the marble porches. And beneath these simple, beautiful walls of the Cathedral all the bustle and colour of an Italian fruit-market lends life and vividness to the scene. The Piazza is completed by the appropriate porticoes and the Clock Tower of the *Palazzo Communale.* The interior of the Duomo is very good and characteristic brick-work. A splendid crypt with arches on slender shafts, supported on lions and men riding lions, and crowned by rich capitals, lies under the Choir. It is approached by stairs against the aisle walls, as in San Zenone at Verona. In the nave great piers alternate with smaller, circular columns of red marble. Above is a triforium with openings of three lights above the main arches, and a plain clerestory.

The note of beautiful simplicity, strength and harmonious colouring is echoed without by the mellow and soothing tones of the bells of the majestic Campanile—a word, by the bye, which does not rhyme with camomile, as some use.

The independence and rivalry of the Italian Republics led to the frequent imitation of the University evolved at Bologna. And amongst the younger rivals of Bologna, the University of Modena ranked with Reggio as the most formidable in the beginning of the thirteenth century.

From Modena a day is wisely spent in a flying visit to the picturesque old town of Mirandola, twenty miles away.

CHAPTER X.

BOLOGNA.

MOST, if not all, great towns owe their greatness in part, and many their decadence, to the facts of physical geography. Ravenna, marsh-girt, inaccessible Ravenna, lived by the sea, and died when the sea deserted her ; Bologna, by virtue of her position, has always been a town of importance since the date of her birth.   It was her position which made the Roman Colony of " Bononia " great ; this secured the success of her University—for to a fluctuating University population, accessibility was always a matter of great moment, and this in the days of railways keeps her busy and prosperous.   For Bologna lies necessarily on the main route of communication.   In the old days, when the road-making Romans began the business of linking up their empire by driving their great streets through the length and breadth of the known world, the Consul Marcus Aemilius Lepidus prolonged the Flaminian Road from its termination at Rimini, to the fortress of Placentia.

And through the centre of modern Bologna, with its miles of arches, its acres of colonnades, its sumptuous Renaissance Palaces and Christian Churches, the Via Aemilia runs, dividing that part of the town which slopes gently upwards to the Apennines from that which descends to the genial and fertile plain stretching to the sea.

On this broad, straight road, 258 kilometres in length, this Via Aemilia, which touches the Po at Piacenza and the Adriatic at Rimini, and gives its name, Emilia, to the whole district, Bologna was the halfway house. And not only so. For, forty years later, the great Postumian road from Genoa to Placentia, and thence by Cremona and Verona to Aquileia, connected it with the Tyrrhenian as well as the Adriatic Sea, and with the great trade route from the Venetian Alp-land. Thus Bologna became by the force of geography the central emporium of Cisalpine Gaul under Rome and of Romagna in the Middle Ages. For later, when the binding force of the Roman Empire was broken, Bologna lay at the intersection of four provinces, Lombardy, the march of Verona, the Romandiola and Tuscany. And to-day it is the point where all the great lines of communication between the centre of Italy and her northern gateways converge.

But before Bologna, through her University, had earned the title of " Learned " ; before Aemilius began his road ; before the Romans had founded Rome, other races, at the dawn of history, had pitched upon this favoured site and founded the most ancient of man's dwellings upon it.

In the eleventh century B.C. the Etruscans,—a nation, says Dionysius, like to no other in language and manners, —spread over the plains of the Po. Different in figure, character and language from the Italian, the Phoenician or Greek, it is not known whence they came, from East or West, from South or North, or to what stock they belonged, though most probably they came from the North over the Rhaetian Alps and belonged to the Indo-Germanic race. This warlike, town-dwelling people quickly subjugated the peaceful, pastoral, village communities of Umbrians whom they found in possession of the slopes of the Apennines.

They built brick houses in place of the mud huts they found: they laid out towns with streets at right angles to each other, as the excavations at Marzabotto show. They quickly developed a profitable trade, which led to commercial rivalry with the Phoenicians and the Greeks.

They spread over the South of Italy. They became a maritime power. The proceeds of privateering and commerce enabled them to command all the resources of luxury and art. They founded Ravenna, and on the green slopes of the Apennines, Felsina, surrounded by the waters of the River Reno and the streams Aposa and Savena, guarded by the snow-capped multitudinous peaks of the mountains in the rear, and looking through the blue mists over the brown and purple distances of the plain towards Ravenna and the sea. Bononia was called Felsina, says Pliny, when it was the first city of Etruria.

Of these people, of whom it is certain that they flourished, but of whom so little else is known, there are in the Museo Civico at Bologna many interesting relics. First, of the Umbrian cowherds and tillers of the soil, whom they subdued, excavations near the Church of S. Francesco (1877) revealed a huge urn of clay, containing some 14,000 bronze articles, needles, hatchets, saws, bridles and scythes, the implements of a peaceful agricultural population. And about a mile and a quarter outside the old Porta Sant' Isaia, on the site of the fourteenth century Certosa and modern

Campo Santo, tombs have been discovered in which were urns adorned with geometrical patterns and containing bangles, the ornaments of the departed mistress, or razors and broken bridles, symbols of the master, who had done with earthly things.

In the long, well lit and well arranged rooms of the Museo Civico (Room X) the tombs and artistic work of the Etruscans reveal to us how rich and powerful was this foreign nation that once dominated Italy.   But whilst the thousands of gold, silver and bronze ornaments here, the mirrors and necklaces, rings and brooches and vessels of all kinds bear testimony to the luxury in which the trade of the Etruscans with the Greeks and Phoenicians enabled them to indulge, and to the great dexterity to which their metal-workers attained, they show also how little originality they could boast as artists.   They found all their models in the art of ancient Greece and Egypt.   The painted clay vases of Etruscan artists, like the scarabaei of Etruscan lapidaries, are almost entirely imitative, and when they strive to depict scenes of daily life they are in no way inspired. The most beautiful thing here is the Attic Amphora on which Helen and Menelaus are painted.   But the Etruscan bronze candelabrum near it (Case H) is indeed a thing of beauty too.

These fragments, few and vague enough indeed, are filled with all the romance of forgotten grandeur, all the wonder and the pathos of the unknown : they linger here, in their cold, scientific cases, caught and preserved like flies in amber, like footprints of dead men in some ancient fossil-stone, like notes of a symphony still hovering in the frozen air. And, like the traces left in the fields, or like the lingering

love and memories of the old gods, which still survive
among the peasants, they illuminate the imagination as

> "departing sunbeams, loth to stop,
> Still smiling on the mountain top."

The Tuscan dominion, north of the territory which still
bears their name, came to an end when the Celtic tribes
poured over the Alps into the fair plain of Lombardy. Of
these tribes the Boii, who had come through the Great St.
Bernard Pass, pressed on beyond the Po and settled in
modern Romagna. And the old Etruscan town, under
the new name of Bononia, became their capital. After the
second Punic war, the Romans took in hand the subjugation
of the Valley of the Po. The Boii, who had sided with
Hannibal, disappeared before the armies of the conquering
Republic. Three thousand settlers were planted at Bononia
(B.C. 189) to make a Roman Colony. The boundaries of
the farms allotted to these colonists out of the territory of
the Boii are still traceable between Bologna and Cesena.
The town prospered in its trade and municipal self-government, rising even to the proud eminence of being chosen
for a time as the seat of the Imperial power and the residence
of the Imperial Court. Four hundred years after Christ,
Alaric the Goth was defeated by the Roman forces at its
gates. In modern Bologna there are few obvious relics of
those times. Roman municipalities were the Capital in
miniature. They were organised like Rome, with their
Senate and their populace. They were built like Rome,
with their theatre and temples, their forum and baths. The
Piazza Maggiore at Bologna is the Forum of Roman days.
Between San Stefano and the Porta Ravegnana stood the
Marcellus Theatre, which recalls to mind the Roman love

of the circus, and Martial's sneer at the cobbler, the Bologna
Boot-King, who gave a gladiatorial show here, and whom
he advises, now that he has taken to gambling in *hides*,
not to play the ass in the lion's skin, and not to spend on
the sword what he has won by the awl.   And there were
many temples dedicated to Roman and other foreign Gods,
which have been supplanted by the sanctuaries of Christian
Saints.   The temple of Jupiter stood near the Church of
S. Francesco, of Ceres on the site of S. Maria Maggiore,
of Janus on the rising ground where S. Giovanni in Monte
now stands.   Most noteworthy of all is San Sepolcro, one
of that curious cluster of little Churches which is called
after San Stefano.   The seven beautiful columns in this
circular, brick, tenth century church, originally supported
a Temple of Isis ; where once the naughty rites of the
Pagan goddess were celebrated, the tomb of S. Petronius,
copied from the Holy Sepulchre at Jerusalem, was erected
by the Christians, in the twelfth century.

San Petronio, who is honoured as the patron of the city,
was an ascetic who travelled barefoot through eastern wilder-
nesses, visiting and discoursing with Christian saints.   He
was appointed Bishop of Bologna in 430, and purged the
city, we are told, of Arianism.   He repaired the churches
that had been laid in ruins by Alaric.   It was in his honour
and to her own glory that Bologna, at the height of her
prosperous independence, now *docta e grassa*, both rich and
learned, began (1388) to build the great Gothic Cathedral,
which, raised on a noble flight of steps, forms the south side
of the Piazza.   It was begun, but never finished.   The
design, by Antonio di Vincenzo, aided by Fra Andrea
Manfredi, who built the Servite Church (Sta. Maria dei

Servi), with its graceful exterior colonnade and court,[1] contemplated a construction which should surpass in beauty as in size the Duomo of Florence and all the cathedrals of Italy. It would, doubtless, have yielded a truly magnificent effect of perspective. The interior does, as it is, exhibit extremely beautiful proportions. But neither the projected choir nor the intersecting transepts were ever completed. The task proved beyond the resources of the town. For centuries a-building, the Cathedral remains inchoate. Its growth ceased with the independence of the town at the beginning of the sixteenth century. The principal entrance is adorned with sculptures, full of the vigour and feeling for humanity characteristic of the early Renaissance. They are the work of the Siennese master, Jacopo della Quercia. Most notable among the statues here are, in the pediment, the life-like figures of the Madonna and Child and of S. Petronio, carrying the model of his cathedral. These statues, if not supreme master-pieces, have the proud distinction of having helped to train a supreme master. We shall see that Michelangelo must have studied them carefully.

The desire of the Bolognese to achieve in San Petronio a sacred building of such magnitude as they contemplated must not be construed and condemned as mere vulgar ambition to surpass all rivals and records. For there is something characteristically Italian in the desire for a vast enclosed area of space and light, wherein the whole city assembled might attend Mass or listen to the eloquent

[1] He designed it, he says, as a place where "the people might meet and sell their goods and at the same time learn from sermons the lessons of the life of the servite saint, San. Filippo Benozzi."

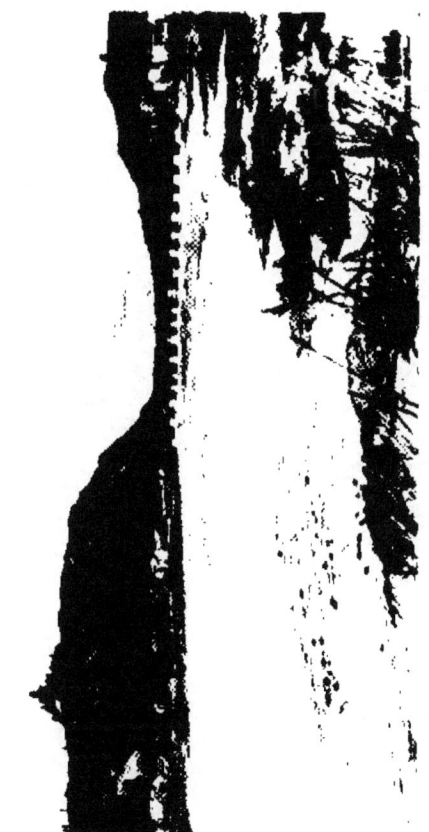

THE PONTE LUNGO, BOLOGNA.

exhortations of a preacher. It is a desire which is the direct inheritance of the descendants of republican Rome and the heirs of pagan art. And this characteristic, this humanism, which is always striving to express itself in Italian art and architecture, was fostered, one may think, by the democratic character of the societies which flourished in the Lombard Communes. To this point of view, to the desire to make their churches, like their piazzas, a centre of civic life, the Italian builders adapted the Northern Gothic style which the influence of France and the activity of the Cistercians had imposed upon them. They aimed, not like the builders of Durham, at erecting an edifice whose keynote is grandeur and might, "half church of God, half castle 'gainst the Scot ; " not like the builders of Chartres, at the expression of the mystic sacrifice of God ; not like the builders of Amiens, at the utterance of an exalted spirituality, soaring to Heaven ; but, sharing scarcely at all in the northern sentiments of reverence, mystery and awe, at the construction of a human dwelling, house of God indeed, but one which should take a very intimate part in the busy life of the city square.

Within, the almost total absence of ornament singularly enhances the sense of spaciousness ; there is here all the chaste simplicity of restraint, and the grandeur of the desert, the sweep of the down. It was in this church that Charles V. was crowned by the Pope with splendid ceremonies that disguised the loss of Italian independence.

Roman work may also be traced in the Romanesque basilica, SS. Pietro e Paolo, another of the S. Stefano group of churches, wherein are preserved in ninth century sarcophagi, the bones of the martyrs, SS. Vitalis and Agricola.

It is in the open court surrounded by a colonnade, called the Atrio di Pilato, that the chief reminder of the Lombard period is to be found in Bologna. This is the font which bears the name of Luitprand, the Lombard King. According to the pious legend, it is the basin in which Pilate washed his hands after surrendering Christ to the Jews.

The Piazza Maggiore, then, has its Roman associations: under its modern title, Vittorio Emanuele II., it recalls the era when that wise and moderate monarch worked out the union of Italy and harmonised the discordant elements which were represented by the grey-coated Piedmontese soldiery, and the red-shirted volunteers of Garibaldi. But the long Gothic façade, with its eight huge terra-cotta windows, and the clock-tower of the Palazzo Communale (1425-1444, Fioravante Fioravanti), which forms the western side of it ; the long, porticoed building of the former Portico de' Banchi (transformed by Vignola in the latter half of the sixteenth century) on the east, and, on the north, the tower and the arcades which support the great Hall of the Palazzo del Podestà (1201, 1492) ; —these all transport us to the days when Bologna was at the height of her prosperity and independence, when she claimed her motto of " Libertas " and earned the title of " Docta"—" Bononia docet." And though between the Roman Forum and the mediaeval Piazza the chasm of years is great, the continuity of spirit in the place is unbroken. It is fitly symbolised by the coincidence of site. For there is nothing fortuitous in the development of the independent Italian Republics from the independent Roman municipalities. Tradition counts for much in history, working through the minds and characters of the men who make it. The Italians were the *Socii*, the allies of ancient Rome ; their municipalities retained their self-government.

And when, in after times, the Lombardic kingship was absorbed in the Holy Roman Empire, and the Emperor's prerogatives could only be enforced by armed occupation of Italy, the towns, once they had emancipated themselves from the rule of their Counts, were free to develop on the lines of their traditional autonomy. This development was fostered by the struggle between the Emperors and the Popes. Both desired the co-operation of the towns : both therefore were ready to buy their aid by sanctioning their practical independence. Thus Bologna, which had been burnt by Berengar in his revolt against Otto I., was in 971 exempted by Otto from the power of the Counts, and put under the Bishops. But from the tenacious grasp of their spiritual lords, the townsmen, with their eyes ever set on liberty, availing themselves at each opportunity of the Bishops' difficulties, gradually wrested themselves free. At last, in 1116, Bologna received her great Charter as an independent Republic from Henry V. All the concessions she had won from the Bishops were ratified, and, glorying in her new freedom, she bore henceforth the device LIBERTAS in her coat of arms.

The town was governed by two consuls, chosen annually by the twelve chief men of the four wards of the town, who were known as Anziani, and who formed the Town Council. There was also a Council of 400 and an Assembly of Citizens for deciding important matters. But as the town developed into a State, the need of separating the Judicature and the Executive became increasingly felt. Bologna was the first to elect a Podestà for this purpose—a Magistrate who should be chosen impartially as a Judge, and who, therefore, according to the usual mediaeval plan, often also performed the function of General of the citizen soldiers. It was provided that only a foreign nobleman or a renowned citizen of another town should hold the office. For their first Podestà the Bolognese elected Guido Ranieri da Sasso from Faenza. It was with Faenza that Bologna allied herself in 1225, and subjected Imola: a feat which led to her being attacked by Parma, Modena and the Emperor, who defeated Bologna and her allies, Milan, Piacenza and Brescia, near Bazzano and again at San Cesario. This severe defeat led the citizens to rise against the nobles, who were steering the ship of state. An extension of the political rights of the Guilds of the Artisans resulted.

In the struggle between the Guelfs and Ghibellines Bologna made common cause with the Papacy, her constancy to the Guelf interest being perhaps determined by the Ghibelline policy of her near neighbour and rival, Imperial Ravenna. She was a prominent member of the Lombard League (1167), and under Gregory IX. and Innocent IV. became the centre of the Papal resistance to the Imperial power. When that monster of cruelty, Ezzelino da Romano, and Enzio, the Emperor's son, had established the Imperial control over North Italy ; even after the battle of Corte Nuova (1237), when Frederick II. seemed to have crushed the Guelfs once for all, Bologna remained steadfast. Within the sheltering walls of this, the chief stronghold of the Church, the Legate, Ugo degli Ubaldini, took refuge, but without his army. Resistance, however, gathered head, and when Enzio entered the territory of Reggio, his Modenese army of Ghibellines, supported by some

squadrons of German and Cremonese cavalry, allies from
Pavia and Reggio, and exiles from Ferrara and Piacenza, was
confronted by the citizen forces, the *quartieri* and *compagnie*,
of Bologna.

Hard by the bridge of S. Ambrogio over the Panaro,
the battle of Fossalta was fought from break of day to fall
of eve with equal valour and ardour on either side. All
day long the victory hung in the balance. At length the
Bolognese triumphed. Chief among their many captives
on that glorious day was Enzio, the Emperor's son, King
Enzio, the bravest and most ardent of warriors, Enzio the
most handsome of princes. His horse had been killed under
him, and he was forced to yield himself prisoner. On
August 24, 1249, the victors marched in triumphal procession into Bologna. From Unciola, where King Enzio had
been temporarily lodged, to the city, the road was thronged
with jubilant sightseers. Loud and triumphant sounded the
trumpets, gaily fluttered the flags and pennons, and brightly
glittered swords and lances and the trappings of the cavalry
as the victors, crowned with garlands of oak, wound their
way into the city through the old Porta Soteria (S. Felice).
But whilst they applauded their triumphant townsmen, maid
and mother alike turned their gaze upon their prisoner,
whose fair curls clustered about his shoulders, and every eye
grew moist in pity and admiration as they beheld his kingly
mien, so proud, so brave, so handsome, so wise, and so
undaunted in adversity. The captive King followed the
triumphal car, draped in purple, on which Filippo Ugoni
of Brescia, the conquering Podestà, clad in purple robes, led
the procession to what was then the new Palazzo del Podestà
(facing the Piazza del Nettuno, and now forming a part only

of the Communal Buildings). Enzio entered it, and the gates of that building closed on him for ever. For here all his life long was he kept prisoner. He who had entered it so young and strong and handsome never left it again, till his corpse was borne forth to its last resting-place in San Domenico. For years, and many weary years, he lived on immured in the rooms of the palace, fretfully pacing, we may imagine, that long upper room in which he spent his days, and which is now the Notaries' Library.

'Tis said that he found a friend and comforter in the daughter of a Bolognese noble, for lovely Lucia Viadagola elected to share his imprisonment and his solitude. 'Tis said, too, that he turned to literature to give expression to the chafing energy and the stifled romance of his nature, writing those Canzoni del Prigionero, which, if they are indeed his, have added to the prisoner's compensation of an immortality of pity, the immortality of a poet. For the Canzoni are among the earliest monuments of Italian national literature.

Perhaps, after all, if these traditions be true, his lot was not too hard. A beautiful mistress, the consolation of the Muse, and regular meals—these for him, as for the Persian poet, might well be " Paradise enow." His name is perpetuated in the (recently restored) Palazzo del Re Enzio, whilst the great Hall, to which I have referred, and in which the conclave for the election of Pope John XXIII. was held, 1410, is called after him the Sala del Re Enzio. Tradition adds that the great tower which crowns the Palazzo del Podestà was erected to guard against surprises and attempts to rescue the youth, for whom neither his father's entreaties, nor his own offer that for ransom he would gird the city

with a ring of gold, could obtain release. Nor were the
efforts of the devoted Lucia more successful: once he had
almost escaped concealed in a cask, but a lock of his bright
hair betrayed him.   His tomb and the monument above it,
whereon the implacable Bolognese boast so naïvely of their
prowess and determination in capturing and keeping their
royal prisoner, are in the Church of San Domenico, the
church where the bones of the great S. Dominic lie so nobly
entombed.

In the Piazza about this church are two noble tombs, the
canopied monuments of two chief Notaries of Bologna, one
that of Egidio Foscherari, and the other, richer and more
elaborate, with its elegant columns and arcades and
pyramidal roof, that of Rolandino Passeggieri.   He it was
who earned the gratitude of his fellow-citizens by virtue of
the letter which he was deputed to write to the Emperor
in answer to his imperious demand for the release of King
Enzio.   "We have taken King Enzio ; we hold him
prisoner, and we will hold him."   Such was the gist of this
letter ; and so firm was it in tone and so dignified, so cogent
in its reasoning in support of the policy which Passeggieri
had persuaded the Bolognese to adopt, that, in acknowledg-
ment of the lustre which it had added to the reputation of
the Republic, the citizens gave to his remains a magnificent
public funeral, and erected to his memory this splendid
monument.

These tombs wholly lack the skill and sculpture of the
Scaliger tombs at Verona.   But they are most interesting as
purely architectural monuments and as illustrating the
Italian adaptation of Gothic to the national manner, resulting
in a kind of pointed Romanesque.

But it is neither the tomb of King Enzio within, nor that of the clever Notary without, that draws the feet of the pilgrims to the church which was built in honour of St. Dominic. The church itself presents little attraction ; it was completely remodelled in the eighteenth century. But the tomb of the saint is a work of the rarest beauty and interest.

Dominic was born and bred in old Castille, but it was at Bologna that the first Chapter of his Order was held, and it was at Bologna that he elected to be buried.

He was born in an age when the Church was rich and the world was poor ; when the clergy were indolent and wealthy and their flocks industrious and starving ; when Bishops, luxurious and corrupt, jealously guarded their pre-rogative of preaching—and neglected to exercise it. The frightful persecution of the Manichees in the east had driven those worthy heretics into Lombardy and Languedoc. In Lombardy they were known as Patarines, in Languedoc as Albigenses. Their zeal and pure morals drew multitudes to them. To combat the increasing influence of the heretics and the justly failing influence of the Church, Francis of Assisi founded his Order of Mendicants, and Dominic of Caraloga, almost simultaneously, his Society of Preachers.

In 1212 Dominic visited Rome, and obtained from Innocent III. his approbation of the new Order, who should take up the work which the political, campaigning Bishops had so disastrously neglected—the work of preaching to the poor the glad tidings of Christ. At Rome Dominic met Francis, whom he had beheld the night before in a vision. He hailed him as a brother in his holy enterprise, embracing him and crying, " Let us hold together and none can overcome us." In 1220 the first Chapter of the Dominican Order was held at Bologna. On his way to attend it St. Dominic visited S. Francis at Cremona. S. Francis, too, founded a convent at Bologna. No sooner, says the chronicler, were the Dominicans settled near the gate of S. Procolo than the Franciscans made their homes outside the Porta Sterii. A Doctor of Laws was one of Francis' first converts at Bologna, and the Franciscan cemetery, like the " Frari " of Venice, was for centuries enriched with the tombs of the most distinguished men of the time. It was in Bologna, in the bosom of the brotherhood he had founded, that S. Dominic elected to die. He had fallen sick at Venice, and was removed to S. Maria degli Monti, near Bologna. He heard that the religious there had determined to retain his body for their church. " God forbid," he cried, " that I should rest anywhere but among my friars. Carry me into my own vineyard, that I may die therein." And he chose to be buried here in Bologna " under the feet of my friars."

He died in 1221, and was canonised thirteen years later. A series of six large bas-reliefs adorn the sarcophagus wherein the bones of the saint found a resting-place (1267), when they had been translated to this church. They illustrate the chief events of his life ;—that journey to Rome, which we have mentioned, when the Pope, hesitating whether he should extend the prerogative of the Bishops to this new religious fraternity, saw a vision of the tottering Lateran propped upon the shoulders of Dominic ;[1] the Apostolic vision, when S. Peter and S. Paul appeared to the saint and confirmed him in his mission of preaching ; his

[1] The story is also told of S. Francis. See Giotto's fresco at Assisi.

restoration to life of a noble youth—Napoleone, nephew of
the Cardinal of Torre Nuova—who had been thrown from
his horse and killed ; the ordeal by fire of the orthodox
and heretical books, when in the course of his campaign
against the Albigenses, his opponents' books were consumed
in the flames, and the doctrine of Dominic, flung thrice into
the fire, thrice leapt out unburnt ; the miracle that was
wrought when the fraternity was reduced to one loaf, which
S. Dominic began to divide, and, lo! two beautiful youths
entered the refectory bearing baskets filled with bread,
which they distributed, and then as suddenly disappeared ;
and lastly, the appearance of the Virgin to a youthful deacon,
Reginald. She, in answer to the prayers of Dominic,
restored him to health and revealed to him the pattern of
the Dominican robe as she willed it to be worn henceforth.
All these scenes, astonishing alike in their dignity and their
grace, in their vivacity and in the charm of their homeliness
and truth, are composed with great felicity and are presented
with great dramatic force. They are the work of Niccolò
Pisano (1270) and of his pupil, Fra Guglielmo, a Dominican
Friar, the Master of the Pulpit in San Giovanni Fuorcivitas
at Pistoia.

How much these reliefs owe to the labour of Niccolò
Pisano himself, how much to his pupil, cannot be said with
certainty. They certainly lack the vigour and virility of the
famous puplit reliefs at Pisa. The carving and modelling
is inferior : the spirit that inspires them is gentle and meek.
Probably Niccolò did little more than design or indicate the
designs of the reliefs. But what is important is that they
are beautiful in themselves, intimate, original and inspired
by the beautiful story they illustrate.

The tomb of S. Dominic necessarily lacks the unity and symmetry of the shrines of S. Augustine at Pavia and S. Peter Martyr at Milan. For it has been adorned by the hands of many artists of different ages. It rests on a base, with reliefs by Alfonso Lombardi (1532), the author of the colossal Hercules on the Palazzo Communale and the Death of Mary in the Church Sta. Maria della Vita. The rich canopy with bold volutes was executed by Niccolo dell' Arca (1469), who made the sarcophagus the centre of a design of his own. The kneeling Angel, by him, in front of the Arca on the left is a charming figure. It contrasts favourably with the more staid and formal Angel on the right, which is supposed to be an early work of Michelangelo, who certainly sought refuge in Bologna (1494), after the Medici had been driven out of Florence. By Michelangelo also is the statue of S. Petronius, church in hand. Superior as it is in detail and characterisation, this statue evidently owes the conception of its pose to the statue by Jacopo della Quercia in the pediment of the principal portal of San Petronio. Michelangelo owes little of his fame to Bologna, but to the seven remaining statues on pedestals about the tomb of S. Dominic — Francis, Dominic, Florian, Vitalis, Agricola, Proculus and John the Baptist—and to the exquisitely graceful festoons of fruit held by the most charming *putti*, Niccolo dell' Arca owes both his title and his fame. The beautiful terra-cotta Madonna in high relief on the Palazzo Communale, and the Mourning for Christ in S. Maria della Vita are also by this pupil of Jacopo della Quercia.

The fresco above the tomb of Dominic is one of the most effective works of Guido Reni, many of whose works are to be seen in Bologna. The master is buried in the

Cappella del Rosario here—the chapel which commemorates the fact that Dominic introduced into the Catholic Church that instrument of devotion. Two other works of art tempt us to linger in this church : the Marriage of Catherine by Filippino Lippi, and in the choir the magnificent inlaid stalls by Fra Damiano da Bergamo and Fra Antonio Asinelli (sixteenth century). The latter was a member of the family who built the taller of the two Leaning Towers, which form the most familiar feature in Bologna. Both were built in the twelfth century ; the smaller one, probably in emulation, by the Garisenda family. When Dante in his vision beheld the giant Antaeus stooping, the sight suggested to the poet's mind the image of

> "The tower of Garisenda, from beneath
> Where it doth lean, if chance a passing cloud
> So sail across, that opposite it hangs."—*Inf.* xxxi.

For faulty foundations or the unkindness of an earthquake threw both these family fortresses out of the perpendicular, and prevented their being finished in spite of many mechanical devices.

They stand, these Leaning Towers of Bologna, in their proximity and their strength, in their obliquity and their incompleteness, as monuments of misdirected energy, memorials of that most profitless form of stupidity, family pride. And they, with a dozen other survivors, serve to conjure up for us the aspect of old Bologna—Bologna of the thirteenth and fourteenth centuries—when within her strong girdle of walls and ditch, pierced by twelve gateways, there had been reared no less than 200 high watch-towers, or fortresses such as these, but strong and straight. For Bologna was a town of towers before she became a city of

THE TOWERS OF BOLOGNA.

colonnades, as Francesco Francia's fresco in the Town-Hall shows us. When every town in Italy was divided into opposing camps of Guelfs and Ghibellines, party spirit ran high in Bologna. And just as Florence was torn by the factions of the Amidei and Donati, of Whites and Blacks, of Guelfs and Ghibellines, so in Bologna the feuds of the great families, the Lambertazzi and Geremei, were fierce, and in them was centred all the political and religious division of the time. For all who favoured the Papal cause ranged themselves under the banner of the Geremei, whilst the supporters of Imperial law and order espoused the pretensions of the Ghibelline family, the Lambertazzi. The history of the town becomes a record—often a very romantic one—of the conflicts of these two families and their adherents. Each party was continually attacking the other, burning the houses and towers of their enemies, inciting the townsfolk to riotous assaults upon them and their property, and using every trick and treacherous artifice in order to score one point against hated Guelf or hated Ghibelline. In such troublous times every house must needs be a castle. Every great family strove to provide itself and its adherents with a strong tower of defence, adjacent to its palace, as a sure haven of retreat and a convenient starting point for projected attacks, as a sign, too, of their family greatness. The Leaning Towers are a vivid illustration of this period, and, as an example of the old palaces of these noble families, with their overhanging storeys, supported on huge wooden uprights, and vast inner courts, the (restored) Palazzo Isolani (Via Mazzini, No. 19), the Palazzo Ghislieri, now the *Hotel Brun*, and the Casa dei Caracci, live in the memory.

These internecine feuds, outcome of family pride, political

ambition, religious sentiment and the natural pugnaciousness of mankind, had great influence upon the history of the town as upon the lives of individual citizens.

Alberto de' Carbonesi loved Virginia, the beautiful daughter of the Guelf Cavaliere, Giampetro Galuzzi, who swore that she should never bed with Ghibelline. From the top of a tower which dominated all the houses of the Galuzzi, Alberto, undeterred, continued to watch and woo, until at last he won his beloved. Mad with rage, the old Galuzzi, when he heard of it, armed a band of cutthroats, and stealthily made his way with them into the bridegroom's house. Virginia awoke to find her husband bleeding to death in her arms, and to see the assassin, her father, disappearing from her room. She screamed and screamed in vain for aid, she rushed from room to room, and found that not one soul had been left alive in the house. Next morning her body was found hanging from the balcony. Galuzzi was merely banished from the city for a couple of years. And still the feuds continued ; Galuzzi fought with Carbonesi, Lambertini with Scannabecchi, Torelli with Delfini, Beccari with Preti, and Orsi with Orsi.

> " e l' un l'.altro si rode
> Di quei che un muro ed una fossa sera."

As Romeo and Juliet were working out their tragedy at Verona, thanks to the feud of Montecchi and Capuleti, Ugo and Parisina at Ferrara, and Francesca and Paolo at Rimini, so at Bologna Imelda and Bonifazio carried on the fatal tradition of Virginia and Alberto. Imelda, fair daughter of the Ghibelline house of Lambertazzi, loved Bonifazio, a gentle youth of the rival house of Geremei. Yielding to the passionate entreaties of her lover, she consented to receive him in her chamber. Her secret was betrayed to her brothers, who surprised the happy lover, and plunged a poisoned dagger to his heart. Imelda strove to save Bonifazio's life by sucking the poison from his wound. She was found dead across her lover's body.

The feud now blazed more furiously than ever. The course of events shows how these quarrels involved the fortunes of the town and gradually enlisted the services of outside powers. For, in a desperate endeavour to drive out the Lambertazzi, the Geremei allied themselves with the Duke d'Este and the Guelf nobility of Parma, Modena and Reggio. The Podestà and the Bolognese " Brotherhoods in Arms," which had been founded for the defence of the town, defeated their designs for the nonce, but their treachery was soon more successful. Alberto dei Caccianemici invited the Castellano degli Andali, with nine other Ghibellines, to a conference in the Palazzo del Podestà with a view to settling their differences, and there seized them and flung them into the dungeons. Then the common people, incited by the Geremei, drove out the Podestà, seized the armoury and began to storm the Lambertazzi Towers. The Lambertazzi retorted by setting fire to the towers of the Geremei. Full fourteen days the fight lasted, till the Geremei, reinforced by the Duke d'Este, overwhelmed the Lambertazzi and obliged them to fly with all their families and followers. They found an asylum at Faenza, where they were allotted the empty dwellings of the expelled Manfredi. Such was the savage bitterness of the feud that boys cut the bodies of the slain to pieces in the streets and carried them home in triumph. The expulsion of the Lambertazzi led to war with Faenza, Forlì and Guido Montefelto, Duke of Urbino.

The Captain of Bologna, Malatesta of Rimini, was not equal to the brave and experienced Montefelto, who defeated him severely on the bridge of S. Procolo.

Then Bologna turned for help to Florence, to Charles of Anjou in Naples, and to Pope Nicholas III. The Florentine army was driven back by Duke Guido over the Apennines: Charles of Anjou put off the Bolognese ambassadors with empty promises; but the Pope sent a Legate to Bologna, through whom a reconciliation between the rival parties was effected. Amid much pomp and rejoicing of the populace (1279), to the sound of sermons and blowing of trumpets, in front of the Palazzo, fifty Lambertazzi and fifty Geremei greeted each other with the kiss of peace. The ending of this family feud, however, had cost Bologna her complete independence. The Papal Legate remained to represent the supremacy of the Holy See.

It was not long before the city was divided into new factions, the Scacchesi[1] and Maltravessi, followers of the families of Pepoli and Gozzadini. The Crusades, from which other countries gained but wounds and relics, brought to the rising commonwealth of the Adriatic a large increase of wealth and of knowledge. Italian ships covered every sea. Italian factories rose on every shore. The tables of Italian money-changers were set in every city. Chief among those bankers who thus rose to fortune in Bologna, and strove for supremacy, was Romeo Pepoli. The rival factions were united at last in face of the unpopularity of the Papal Legate, Cardinal Bertrand de Poïet, Bishop of Ostia, who, after treacherously seizing the Duke d'Este, had led the Guelf forces to disaster before the walls of

---

[1] So called from the chessboard pattern of the Pepoli coat of arms.

THE TOWER BOLOGNA AT NIGHT.

Ferrara. Weary of his intrigues and of his French following, Bologna followed the example of Ravenna, Faenza,
Forlì and Rimini, and revolted from the Papal Cause.
Brandeligi dei Gozzadini and Taddeo, son of Romeo Pepoli,
the wealthy banker, headed the rising. The Legate, at the
head of his troops, was driven out. The citadel which he
had built outside the Porta di Galliera, and which he had
garrisoned with French mercenaries in order to terrorise
the town, was razed to the ground. The Republican
Government was restored. "Sacred Ordinances" were
passed to check the excesses of the nobles. Political power
was concentrated in the hands of the Trades Guilds and the
Companies of Arms. In place of a Podestà it was decided
to appoint a leader elected for life. The choice lay between
Brandeligi and Taddeo. Taddeo was elected, by an overwhelming majority, Signore and Captain General of the
City, and earned the proud title of Keeper of the Peace.
The Gozzadini, to avoid further faction, were ostracised.
Taddeo Pepoli was a man of remarkable character and
accomplishments. Rich and generous, courteous and wise,
himself a Doctor of Law, he won the affection of all classes
and steered the ship of state with a politic hand. He
reconciled himself with the Pope, who had laid the City
and University under an interdict, by consenting to a formal
submission. He agreed to a yearly tax upon the town,
but paid it out of his own pocket, and took the title of
Papal Vicar (1333). He restored the walls and gates and
improved the streets of Bologna. In the terrible year of
famine, 1347, he spent his own fortune in buying corn
from Sicily to feed his starving people. In the same year
Taddeo, the Magnificent, the Father of his Country, fell

v.n.   L

a victim to the plague which was devastating the city. He was buried in the tomb he had prepared for himself in the Church of San Domenico, executed by Jacopo Lanfrani the Venetian. Of the splendid Palace which he built to celebrate the grandeur of the Pepoli, the beautiful terra-cotta work of the gateways remains to indicate its former magnificence (*Via Castiglione*).

Taddeo Pepoli was succeeded in the government by his two sons Giovanni and Giacomo. But it happened that the Papal Captain General, Count Astorre, came to Bologna with a French troop of horse, collecting men to reduce Faenza and other towns beneath the sway of the Pope. After a conference in his tent, to which he had invited the brothers, he treacherously seized Giovanni and held him for ransom. Unable to raise the money demanded, the Pepoli sold Bologna and its inhabitants like chattels to Giovanni dei Visconti, Archbishop of Milan. Under the Archbishop's natural son, Giovanni da Oleggio, a cruel, avaricious and abandoned tyrant, Bologna suffered ten years of misery and oppression. First Giovanni set himself to get rid of the Pepoli. The Porta di Castiglione was found left open one night. The guards were tortured and forced to say that they had been bribed by the Pepoli. Giovanni accused them of intriguing with the Florentines. Giacomo was thrown into prison ; the property of the Pepoli was confiscated, and, aided by the Maltravessi, the tyrant waded deep in the blood of the Scacchesi. To secure himself against the hatred of the populace, he built a fort near the Porta di S. Felice, whence he ruled the city with a rod of iron and wreaked his vengeance on his enemies with the utmost cruelty. At last, on the most glorious day in the annals of her martial achievements, Bologna rid herself of the heavy yoke of the proud Visconti, when, in conjunction with her allies, she utterly defeated their forces in the valley of San Rofillo (1361). And it was at this period that, as though to mark her release from foreign rulers, she began to build the great church to her patron Saint, the Bishop Petronio.

To the end of the fourteenth century belongs also the Gothic brick Guild Hall of the Merchants, the Loggia de' Mercanti at the corner of the Via S. Stefano, the symmetrical proportions of which are composed of an open portico with two broad, pointed arches and an upper storey lightened by a decorated pulpit with a canopy of white marble, and two narrow windows framed in terra-cotta, with white marble mouldings.

The Visconti had held Bologna in spite of the Pope. Their expulsion opened the way for the rise of the Bentivogli, who for several generations now directed the fortunes of Bologna, nominally as Vicars of the Holy See, but in aspiration, and sometimes in practice, independent of all control. The star of the first of this line, however, Giovanni I., rose and set with equal rapidity. A counter-revolution, aided by the forces of the Visconti, ended in his murder in the Palazzo del Podestà (1402). Bologna was now in the hands of the great Gian Galeazzo Visconti, Duke of Milan. But not for long. A few years later Pope Alexander V. made it his headquarters and died there. And now Anton Galeazzo Bentivoglio, son of Giovanni, fired with ambition to rule Bologna as his father had done, seized the Palazzo del Commune by force of arms (1420), and, adopting the cry of *Viva il populo*, which his rival

Matteo de' Canetoli raised against him, established himself, banished the Canetoli and defied the Papal claims to the City. But the argument of force and the potent weapon of excommunication soon compelled him to come to terms. He gave Bologna up to the Church and received Castelbolognese in compensation. After fifteen years of a wandering life of adventure, the Pope allowed him to revisit Bologna. But so overwhelming was the popular demonstration with which he was received, that the Papal Governor, quite in the fifteenth century Italian way, invited him to review the army, and immediately afterwards had him assassinated in the courtyard of the Palazzo Communale. The Papal Governor also banished Battista Canetoli.

But the line of Bentivoglio was not extinct. Anton had left a son, Annibale, to succeed him. Offspring of a period of violence and change ; of banishment and repatriation ; of intrigue, treachery and ruthless crime—a period when the warlike school of Alberico da Barbiano was in high esteem, and professional soldiers of fortune like Pandolfo Malatesta, Facino Cane, or Sforza il Grande were in the hey-day of their sanguinary success, when the terrible Duke Gian Galeazzo Visconti was followed by the ferocious Filippo Maria, Annibale had learned eloquence at Castelbolognese and the prowess of arms under Michelozzo Attendolo, cousin of Sforza il Grande, in the Neapolitan wars. After the assassination of his father, the reputation of his rare gifts and noble character determined the Bolognese, who were weary of the cruel and avaricious Papal Governors, to invite him to return. He was received with the utmost enthusiasm. But hard on his heels returned

the malign Battista Canetoli, who had persuaded Filippo
Maria to release him from Milan in order to win back for
the Visconti the much coveted city of Bologna. It was
the time when the bigger States were extending their grasp
over the smaller. The territory of the Republic of Venice
was approaching that of the Dukedom of Milan. The Senate
weakly allowed Battista and his adherents to take up their
abode once more in Bologna, and once more, as the inevitable
consequence, Bologna was torn by the factions of rival
families ; once more the Piazza resounded with the clash
of arms, and the narrow streets were loud with the cries
and encounters of the partisans of Bentivogli and Canetoli.
The terrified Senate begged the Visconti for aid to preserve
order, and Francesco Piccinino, son of the famous Captain,
Niccolo, came.

Battista Canetoli failed in his attempts upon the life and
fortune of Annibale, and was recalled to Milan by the
Visconti, who now determined to secure his hold over
Bologna by allying himself with Bentivoglio, the real Lord
of Bologna. Donnina Visconti was brought from Milan
with the pomp of a Princess to be the bride of Annibale,
and great were the rejoicings in the city, and mighty the
bonfires that blazed before the palace of the bridegroom
in the Strada di S. Donato (1441).

But the rejoicings were soon turned to mourning. Francesco Piccinino, jealous of the success of Annibale, feigned
illness and persuaded him to bear him company to Persiceto,
for the pure air of which the invalid pretended to pine.
Annibale, in the goodness of his heart, consented, and the
treacherous Piccinino, on his arrival, seized him and his
friends and held them prisoners.

Annibale was released at length, thanks to the devotion of the loyal and single-hearted Galeazzo Marescotti de' Calvi, and four others, who scaled the Castle of Varano by night, surprised the Castellan and his guards, freed Annibale from his chains and carried him off to Bologna.

This daring deed was followed by an organised attack upon the soldiers of Francesco Piccinino and the ministers who held Bologna for the Visconti. The attack was successful. The foreigners were expelled. The Rocca di Galiera, the citadel of the Milanese garrison, was destroyed. From that time Galeazzo and Annibale were supreme, the former as the first Soldier of the Republic, the latter as its political head.

Two years later Bentivoglio began to build his famous Family Chapel in San Giacomo Maggiore.

His supremacy had not failed to rouse the envy of the Canetoli and Ghislieri. Peace, indeed, was apparently made between the rival factions, when Francesco Ghislieri asked Annibale to stand as godfather to his little son, and he, ever eager for unity and concord within the City, gave his consent, pledging good fellowship with Canetoli and Ghislieri. The ceremony, which was one of extraordinary magnificence, took place in the Duomo. When it was over the company set forth, with Annibale at its head, to the banquet to which Francesco had invited them. But on the way, at a signal given by Battista Canetoli, Annibale was surrounded by armed ruffians—Francesco seized his arms, bidding him with a satanic smile to have patience, whilst the daggers of the assassins pierced him to the heart.

The murderers then rushed to the Piazza to attack the

Palazzo, crying *Viva il popolo e la lega!* slaying on the way the four brothers of Galeazzo, who himself barely escaped after fighting like a lion. He succeeded in rousing the supporters of Bentivoglio in time to defend the Commonwealth and to take swift and terrible vengeance on the treacherous assassins. Many of the Canetoli and Ghislieri were slain there and then ; their palaces were sacked and burned.

The son of Annibale, this hero and martyr, as he came to be regarded, a presentment of whose features is preserved in the relief in S. Giacomo Maggiore, perhaps by Niccolo dell' Arca, was Giovanni II. To his upbringing and guidance the strong, single-minded soldier, Galeazzo Marescotti, devoted himself. He refused the Signoria for himself and determined to " nurse " it for the heir of the Bentivogli.

Nicholas V. had been a student and a bishop of Bologna. He was the first Pope who felt the inspiration of the new movement of Humanism, and it was under his direction that the Constitution of Bologna was slightly altered, the power of the State being kept in the hands of Sixteen annually chosen, as hitherto. But the Legate was given a Seat in the Collegium, and the Anziani elected, with him, the Chief Justice (Gonfaloniere), the Standard-bearers of the people, the Representatives of the Guilds, and the new Councillors. This constitution reflected the tendency of the time, which was towards an aristocracy of intellect and culture, who regarded themselves as the heirs of ancient Rome, and began to separate themselves from the ignorant masses in the leading-strings of the Church. The President of the Sixteen remained President for life, and his position was tacitly acknowledged as hereditary. If he kept in accord with the Papal Legate his position was secure.

To bridge the space of time before Annibale's son should be of age to take up the reins of government, the Sixteen now invited Ercole Bentivoglio's bastard son by a peasant girl, Santi, who was living in Florence and earning his livelihood as a clothweaver. Cosimo de' Medici gave the obscure tradesman God-speed and good advice ere he set out for Bologna to assume the office of Gonfaloniere.

In spite of many attempts and conspiracies to oust him, he ruled the city with a strong hand. In 1454 he espoused Ginevra, daughter of Alessandro Sforza, Signore of Pesaro. To celebrate his nuptials with this beautiful girl, who, though only twelve years of age, was renowned as much for her bright intelligence as for her looks, he invited to Bologna the Representatives of the Venetian Republic, the Dukes of Milan and Ferrara, the Signoria of Florence and Siena, and a host of nobles from all Italy. Later, the bastard weaver called in Pagno di Lapo Portigiano from Florence to build him a palace worthy of his magnificence. But the beautiful bride whom he had espoused under circumstances of so much splendour proved his undoing. Ginevra gave her heart to Giovanni II., when he was now twenty years of age. Was it fortune, so seldom propitious to lovers, or the surer use of poison which brought about Santi's death and left Giovanni free to marry the fair Ginevra six months later? From this time forward Giovanni, practically Lord of Bologna, ruled the city as President of the Council and Papal Vicar. He allied himself, by the marriage of his children, with the Lords of Mantua, Faenza, Modena, Rimini and Ferrara, and raised himself to a high pitch of power and importance. But the ruler for whom Bologna had waited so long and hopefully proved in the end but little better than the worst sort of tyrant. Pride, and fear resulting from the insolence and violence of his sons, and the terrible experiences of his daughters, rendered him moody and tyrannical. A conspiracy against him was betrayed in the nick of time. His sons hunted out the leaders and slaughtered them ruthlessly. Giovanni now shut himself up in his palace, having added a strong watch-tower to it and surrounded himself with a body-guard. Once he left Bologna to go to the aid of Caterina Sforza, the Virago of Forlì,[1] and again, when his daughter Francesca had in jealous resentment procured the murder of her husband, Galeotto Manfredi, Giovanni went to succour her. She had been obliged to take refuge in the fortress of Faenza. The people were enraged at Giovanni's attempt to restore her and her little son to power, and kept him prisoner in the Palazzo Municipale, until Lorenzo de' Medici persuaded them to release him. And now Bologna was threatened by the encroaching power of the Borgias, Pope Alexander VI. and his son Cesare, whose ambition was to found and consolidate a kingdom of Middle Italy. First Imola fell, then Forlì, which Caterina Sforza had held so bravely, then Rimini, Pesaro, Faenza, and Castelbolognese. But the

[1] She had married Girolamo Riario, who obtained Forlì, but not popularity. He was murdered in his private apartments by some malcontent courtiers, Lodovico and Cecco Orsi. The Castellan held the fortress for Caterina, and here she raised the Sforza standard and held out, unshaken by threats of Orsi to murder her children before her eyes. Galeazzo San Severino from Milan and Giovanni Bentivoglio established her authority.

French King, Louis XII., took Giovanni Bentivoglio under his protection. The hopes of the Borgia leader without, and of the Borgia party within Bologna were baffled. The Bentivogli organised a fearful massacre of the opposing party, which included the Marescotti. Galeazzo, indeed, was spared for the moment, but died soon after, at the age of ninety-six, poisoned, it was said, by Ginevra. By 1502 Bologna alone of the Church States had not succumbed to the grasping hand of Cesare Borgia. But when Pope Alexander had died of poison, mixed by his son but intended for Cardinal Castellesi, Julius II. outplayed Cesare, and then determined to reduce Bologna to complete submission, as the foundation stone of his Kingdom of Romagna. He was actuated also by personal hatred of Giovanni, whose tyranny he had experienced when Bishop. He issued a Bull of Excommunication against the Bentivogli from Forlì. Giovanni, forsaken by his French allies and hated by the people for his tyranny, fled to Ferrara. In 1506 the Pope entered Bologna in triumph. The palaces of the Bentivogli were sacked and destroyed. A Papal Legate was installed as a ruler, with a Council of forty citizens as a nominal Government. In place of a lay tyrant the fat sheep of Bologna now fell a prey to the more bloodthirsty and rapacious horde of clerical wolves. There was a moment of successful reaction, when Annibale II., who had married Lucrezia d'Este, was brought back by a French army (1510) and the old form of government was re-established. The mob wrought its vengeance on everything that reminded it of Papal rule. They destroyed the bronze statue of Julius II. by Michelangelo (1508), which had been erected on the façade of S. Petronio, and the metal was used by the Duke of Ferrara to cast

BOLOGNA FROM THE SOUTH.

" Giuliano," his pet piece of ordnance.[1]   But the statecraft of the Pope triumphed.   The French were forced to retreat from Italy.   Francesca Maria della Rovere, Duke of Urbino, entered Bologna, and the independence of the town was forever at an end (1512).

The chief memorial of the Bentivogli in Bologna—apart from the superb early Renaissance Palazzo Bevilacqua, with its court and beautiful portal by Francesco di Simone, which was bought by them in 1484, and in which sat for a short time the famous Council of Trent—is to be found in the family chapel and monuments of San Giacomo Maggiore. Here in the ambulatory is the tomb of Anton Galeazzo by Jacopo della Quercia, which seems to have served as a model for all the later monuments of the Professors of the University ; here, in the Bentivoglio Chapel, is the equestrian statue of Annibale ; here a small, lifelike relief of Giovanni preserves the features of that mighty tyrant ; here, above all, the votive picture of the Madonna enthroned with the family of Giovanni II. (1488), by Lorenzo Costa, recalls to us the success and the failure of his career.   In this chapel, too, hangs one of the finest paintings of Francesco Francia, Costa's chief follower in Bologna.   His Madonna Enthroned is distinguished by its brilliant colouring and characterisation, and the peculiar charm of the angels that surround the central group.   This fascinating and typical master of the quattrocento, through whose naiveté and unaffected charm sincere devotion and

[1] The Pope was seated with his right hand raised. The keys of S. Peter were in the other. The story runs that Julius asked the artist whether his hand was raised to bless or curse the Bolognese. " Your holiness," Buonarroti cleverly replied, " is threatening this people, if it be not wise."

sincere love of beauty shine, can be studied at Bologna, and can be studied thoroughly at Bologna alone.

Languishing and effeminate Francia may be, lacking he is undoubtedly in vigour and dramatic force, but the charm of his blue, mountainous landscapes, of his red-haired Madonnas and urchins playing musical instruments, and the truth of his representations as of his minute delineation of jewellery and vestments, make one picture of this master worth all Guido Reni's Chamber of Horrors, or the wretched daub, which was once Raphael's S. Cecilia, in the Accademia di Belle Arti. The presence of masterpieces by Costa and Francia in the chapel of the Bentivogli is not accidental. It was under the patronage of Giovanni II. that Lorenzo Costa, coming from Ferrara, worked at Bologna with Francia, the goldsmith. The art of Bologna is exotic ; just as, marble being an imported article and brick the normal material for ornament, all sculpture was wrought by foreign artists, so the school of painting which was founded at Bologna under the patronage of Giovanni, was imported from Ferrara by Cossa and Costa and developed under the unmistakable influence of Perugino and the Umbrian School.

A new school was started by Ludovico Caracci, and his cousins Agostino and Annibale, who had studied the great colourists, Tintoretto and Paolo Veronese, in Parma and Venice. Their Madonnas and ecstatic Saints abound in the Picture Gallery, but their most characteristic work is to be found in their fresco-illustrations of classical myths, of the Aeneid and Argonauts in the Palazzo Fava, of Romulus and Remus in the Palazzo Magnani, and, above all, of the Hercules story in the Palazzo Sampieri. They

seem to echo here the heroic notes of Tasso, as at Parma
Correggio illustrates his fancy and his grace.

The chief pupils of the school of the Caracci, the
" Accademia degli Incamminati," were Guido Reni, Dome-
nichino, Lanfranco, Albani, whose works, like their masters,
are best studied at Bologna.

I have said that the growth of S. Petronio ceased with
the independence of the town. As though to mark the
term of the ambitions of the citizens, Pope Pius IV., in
1562, commissioned Antonio Morandi (Terribilia) to build
a new University Building on the site which had so long
been designed for the East transept of S. Petronio. That
fine example of Renaissance work, the Archiginnasio,
remained the seat of the University till 1803, when it was
transferred to the Palazzo Poggi (*Pelegrino Tibaldi*), which
now contains the Library, the University being housed in
new buildings (*Via Zamboni*).

Side by side with the development of Bologna there had
waxed within her walls a little community within a community, that most elusive and characteristic growth of the
Middle Ages, a University.

In Italy the Cathedral and Monastic Schools had never
obtained a complete monopoly of education. A certain
number of lay teachers survived through the darkest ages,
and it was in the schools of independent, lay Masters that the
earliest buds of the Italian Renaissance opened into flower.

Thanks to the continuity of municipal life in the Lombard
Cities, the use and tradition of Roman Law had not been
obliterated by the successive waves of barbarian conquest.
The study of Grammar, Rhetoric and Logic, peculiarly
congenial to Italian minds, had not been wholly abandoned.

This side of the mediaeval curriculum was developed as useful for legal documents, legal pleading and legal precision. And with the revival of intellectual interest, mental activity turned into the channel prepared by the political and commercial development of the Italian cities, plunging, not as in the North into theological controversy, but into the study of legal study and Roman Jurisprudence. At the beginning of the twelfth century, thanks to the brilliant lectures of Irnerius, the School of Law at Bologna not only eclipsed that of Ravenna, but raised Bologna itself into the front rank as a cosmopolitan seat of learning. For with that great teacher, who, tradition says, used to lecture from the open-air pulpit in the corner of the great square in front of the venerable Basilica of S. Stefano, began, perhaps, the system of organised legal education, which soon drew men of good birth and mature years from all parts of Europe. The number and quality of the Students who soon thronged the lecture-rooms of Bologna, and the practical advantage they derived from the study of the profitable art of law, raised Doctors of Civil Law at Bologna to a position of great political importance. On their verdict Emperors acted, as, for instance, Frederick Barbarossa, when at the Diet of Roncaglia he attempted to impose upon the Lombard towns the "regalian rights" (1158). Princes and Cities, too, sought their advice upon points of constitutional law vitally affecting the lives and prosperity of their people. Gratian's *Decretum*, on the Church side, and momentous works on constitutional law by learned Jurists of Bologna on the other, decided crucial questions in the prolonged struggle between Church and State, and exalted the reputation of Bologna.

Numerous and most interesting are the tombs and monuments of these Doctors of Bologna, adorned in many instances with characteristic reliefs representing the learned teachers, as they sat in their hired lecture-rooms, or perhaps in the Church of S. Domenic, as in St. Mary's at Oxford, surrounded by their audience of students.

Out of the lectures of such Doctors of Law as Irnerius, delivered to men of means and position, grew up the Student University of Bologna, lay, scientific, democratic, the relation of which to the City is best understood by regarding it as on a par with the political Guilds of Guelfs or Ghibellines, or the Merchant Guilds, legal corporations recognised by the city.

To a Guild of Learning foreigners were allowed to belong, but of course without enjoying the valuable rights of citizenship.   Hence, students of the various Nations formed separate Guilds of Learning, from which the Bolognese and Doctors were excluded as being too much identified with the City.   They set up a University and elected a Rector.   The installation of the Rector, in later days, was an affair of great pomp, rivalling that of the Podestà himself.   Clad in scarlet and gold, preceded by Bedels with their ponderous maces, followed by a crowd of Doctors in purple and miniver and of Students in their black academical dress, accompanied by the inspiriting strains of the three University pipers and four University trumpeters, he was installed, probably in the Cathedral. Afterwards he was escorted in triumph through the city by the whole body of students, who set upon him and tore his clothes from off his back, and compelled him to redeem the pieces at an extravagant rate.   Exhausted and poorer, he arrived at last at his own house, where he entertained his electors at a banquet.

The position of the Students as aliens without the privileges and outside the jurisdiction of the City led to many conflicts and repeated collisions with the municipality. As in other University towns, the most potent weapon of the Masters and Scholars consisted in migration. It was always in their power to leave—and partly ruin—a town that proved too inhospitable. The last important conflict between Town and Gown at Bologna took place in 1321, when, in protest against the execution of a student, the University seceded to Siena. The citizens were compelled to humble themselves, and when they had persuaded the Masters and Students to return, they built as a peace-offering the University Chapel, the Scholars' Church of S. Mary in the Borgo of S. Mamolo.

Later on some of the " Nations " were provided with Colleges. The " College of Spain " (1367), (*Via Saragossa*), and the College for Flemish Students (1650) still survive as specimens of the mediaeval College.

It was under the Cardinal Legate Carlo Borromeo that the Archiginnasio was built, and he it is whose care for the well-being of the people and the provision of a good water supply is commemorated in one of the chief monuments of Bologna. The statue of Neptune, which surmounts the famous fountain in the Piazza Nettuno, a noble monument nobly placed, is not by a Bolognese, nor even an Italian artist. The art of Bologna, like her Generals and her Podestàs, was exotic. Giovanni da Bologna was plain Flemish Jean Boulogne, born at Douai, but a Florentine by training. But however that may be, this vigorous work, in which the splendid virility of the Sea-God harmonises with the force and decision of the whole design, and in which the freedom of exuberant fantasy does not degenerate into the licence of a tortured imagination, is wholly Italian in feeling, noble in its power and proportion, admirable for its joyous delight in life.

It is time to leave Bologna and to pass on to towns whose history is no less interesting and whose atmosphere is yet more individual.   But before we leave this fair jewel of Learning set in a coronet of hills, it is well to wander up past the vineyards, the villas and the cypresses, to the wooded lower slopes of the Apennines, flushed with autumnal tints, or the pure, subtle after-glow of a spring sunset across the snow.   To the East, on a high hill, stands San Michele in Boscc ; on the summit of a western peak, the pilgrimage Church of S. Luca, to which a sheltering colonnade three miles long conducts the devout ; in the distance, to the North, rise up the snow-capped Alps. Below, beyond the serpentine streams that encircle her, and across the leaning towers and campanili of Bologna, the level plain stretches down, a purple distance, to the sea.

Between Bologna and Rimini we pass Imola, and then pleasant Faenza, home of " fayence," " Lamone's city," with its palace of the Manfredi, scene of the famous murder of Galeotto, and its little gallery of the painters of the School of Faenza.   Next on the Aemilian Way lies Forlì, where Girolamo Riario was done to death, and his murderer, Count Orsi, torn to pieces in the Piazza (1488).   Forlì boasts the Cathedral of Santa Croce, which Carlo Cignani decorated, and a picture gallery, which students of Melozzo and his school must visit.   Then comes the sweetly placed

village of Forlimpopoli, and then Cesena, with her picturesque round Castle,

> "Whose flank is washed of Savio's wave,
>   As 'twixt the level and the steep she lies."—*Inferno*.

Next appears, ten kilomètres north of Rimini, with the huge
blue mountain rock of S. Marino behind it, Sant' Arcangelo,
a perfect little hill-town, unknown to guide-books, which
nobody, who is fond of colour and is free from heart-disease,
should omit to visit.   Wholly devoted to the commerce of
agriculture, the centre of all the industry of the surrounding,
wine-growing district, it is to-day very prosperous in its
small way.   Wholly Italian and ignorant of *forestieri*, its
inhabitants have none of the unpleasant manners which
tourists produce.

Perched upon a rocky excrescence rising sheer out of
the vine-clad plain, which stretches in purple distance to
the azure waters of the Adriatic, the houses of the village
group round mighty walls and frowning towers, about
gates whose grooves now lack the portcullis.   Up through
the steep winding streets you clamber, till suddenly there
bursts upon the sight, through a screen of cypresses and
olives and stone-fences, a wonderful view of the rock of
San Marino and of the Rimini river winding up into the
more distant recesses of the Apennines.   In the foreground
churches and villages crown each small excrescence in the
plain.   And this lovely picture is framed by the time-
coloured bastions on the right, and the walls of the Rocca
Malatestiana towering above us on the left.

CHAPTER XI.

RIMINI.

RIMINI, the ancient Ariminum, is said to have been an Umbrian Colony, seized first by the Etruscans and then by the Senones, and lastly held by the Romans as an outpost against the Gauls. This was the northern naval station, to which a Quaestor of the fleet was appointed when Rome was making her effort to master the maritime power of Carthage. This was the northern point at which the Via Flaminia terminated, and it was the starting point of the later Via Aemilia. The stately Arch of Augustus, which, as the mediaeval machicolations show, was afterwards used as a gateway in the fortifications of the town (Porta Romana), stands to record a truly Roman triumph, the paving of these great roads under his beneficent rule. Still grander in its massive simplicity is the bridge of Augustus, which spans the Marecchia with five gigantic arches of white Istrian stone and unites those two great Roman thoroughfares. An inscription plainly commemorates the names and offices of the Roman Emperor and his stepsons. Another interesting monument of Roman days is in the Piazza Giulio Cesare, the old Forum, where a stone marks the spot on which Julius Cæsar is said to have addressed his soldiers after crossing the Rubicon. This was one of the narrow streams between Ravenna and Rimini, probably the Uso, if not the Pisatello, two miles from Cesena, and it formed the northern boundary of Italy. To cross it with an army meant declaration of war against the Republican form of Government. It was at Rimini, according to Lucan, that Curio's speech " o'erwhelmed the doubt in Caesar's mind," and confirmed him in his wavering intention of marching upon Rome.

Rimini made a gallant defence against the Goths in 538, when Belisarius, Justinian's general, was winning back Italy for the Empire. She was relieved at the last moment by the hurried flight of the besiegers to Ravenna, when they beheld Imperial ships approaching the harbour, whilst the device of numerous camp-fires, lit along the Flaminian Way, scared them by the supposed approach of a relieving force. A few years later, however, they obtained possession of the town through treachery, but only to yield it again to Narses (549), in spite of their endeavour to arrest his advance by breaking down the furthest of the five arches of the Augustan bridge. Rimini now became part of the Pentapolis, which included Pesaro, Fano, Sinigaglia and Ancona. The record of a *cruciform* church of this date, S. Andrew's, is of interest.

The great family of the Wrongheads appear at Rimini in the twelfth century. For the ferocious, forceful Lords of the Castle of Verruchio early earned the name of Malatesta from the evil and violent humours of one of their race in the course of accumulating wealth and power during the struggles and disorders of the time. In 1239 a Malatesta was Podestà of Rimini ; by the end of the thirteenth century " the old Mastiff of Verruchio, and the young "

PONTE ROMAGNO, RIMINI.

(*Inferno*) were masters of Rimini, Cesena, Sogliano and Ghiacciuolo, ruling as tyrants, serving as condottieri, brave, cruel, diabolically perfidious, strong. So, clever and warlike, fighting chiefly for the Pope, and submitting generally to the Papal Legates in Romagna, the Malatesta dynasty maintained itself at Rimini for centuries. The grandson of the Podestà I have mentioned was Giovanni il Sciancato, the hunchback. To him was given in marriage Francesca, daughter of Guido da Polenta, Lord of Ravenna. Giovanni was deformed, but his brother, Paolo il Bello, was handsome and accomplished. Francesca loved him.

> "Love, that in gentle heart is quickly learnt . . .
> Love, that denial takes from none beloved,
> Caught her with pleasing him so passing well."

She yielded her beauty to her beautiful lover, and "Love brought us to one death." Discovered in their guilt, they were both slain by the enraged hunchback in a house which was afterwards removed to make room for Sigismondo's Castle.

These are the twain whom Dante beheld in the Inferno of carnal sinners, where, amid eternal wailing, unceasingly the tyrannous blast

> "With restless fury drives the spirits on . . .
> On this side and on that, above, below,
> It drives them; hope of rest to solace them
> Is none, not e'en of milder pang."

And these two wearied spirits, united still in punishment, but at least united, Dante has immortalised in one of the most famous passages in literature. The story has been told and re-told, amplified and dramatised, but the grand

LA ROCCA MALATESTIANA AT SANT' ARCANGELO, NEAR RIMINI.

pathos and reticence with which Francesca intimated her guilt to Dante has not been surpassed.

> "One day
> For our delight we read of Lancelot,
> How him love thralled. Alone we were, and no
> Suspicion near us. Oft-times by that reading
> Our eyes were drawn together, and the hues
> Fled from our altered cheek. But at one point
> Alone we fell. When of that smile we read,
> The wished smile so rapturously kissed
> By one so deep in love, then he, who ne'er
> From me shall separate, at once my lips
> All trembling kissed . . . That day
> We read no more." [1]

We can do no more than share Dante's compassion for two souls entangled in a mutual, forbidden love.   The Palazzo Ruffo is said to have been the home of Francesca. The House of Malatesta culminated at Rimini in Sigismondo Pandolfo, one of the strangest figures of the early Renaissance.   He it was who built (1438), on the site of the old fortress of the despots, the Castle, once held to be the strongest in Italy, of which so picturesque a fragment remains.   We can gather what it was once, from a medallion in the *Tempio Malatestiana*, Sigismondo's Church of S. Francesco.   There, too, carved in red Verona marble, medallions record the features of that corrupt and furious being, the man of murderous, unbridled lusts, the cruel and treacherous Condottiere, the husband who murdered three wives in succession and carved horns upon his own tomb with the cynical epitaph,

> "Porto le corna ch' ognuno le vede,
> E tal le porta che non se lo crede."

[1] Carey's translation.

Such was Sigismondo. But this frantic and licentious man, who was impeached at Rome, when quarrelling with the Pope, for heresy, parricide, incest, adultery, rape and sacrilege, was inspired by a genuine love of scholarship, and was ever ready, in the intervals of political intrigue and military duties, to converse with men of learning and, though intolerant of contradiction from a prince, to accept correction from the lips of those who spoke by right of scholarship alone.

It was characteristic of the man that, when he commanded the Venetian troops against the Turks in Morea, he brought back as his chief treasure the bones of the great Platonist, Gemisthus Pletho. This Renaissance despot worshipped the relics of a Scholar almost as the mediaeval princes worshipped those of a Saint. With loving care he placed the bones of the Byzantine philosopher in a sarcophagus and inscribed upon it words of admiration that may still be read, outside his Cathedral. Pletho was a prophet of revived Paganism. Of the Neo-Pagan faith of the fifteenth century the Church of S. Francesco at Rimini is the typical temple, devoted wholly to the worship of art and the deification of the tyrant and his clever and learned mistress, Isotta. Here the genius of Leo Battista Alberti has enshrined the memory of Sigismondo in exquisite reliefs in marble, has inscribed his name and emblems, the elephant and rose and the intertwined initials I and S, upon every scroll and frieze and point of vantage, and dedicated a shrine *Divae Isottae Sacrum*. " It is more like a Pagan temple than a Christian Church " observed Aeneas Sylvius ; and indeed, what with the triumphal arch of the unfinished façade, the chapels wherein Sigismond and Isotta are sancti-

fied, and the medallions and bas-reliefs and inscriptions in
Latin and Greek, the whole building bears so heathen an
aspect, that, as has been well said, we look involuntarily
towards the altar for a train of chaplet-crowned priests and
augurs, about to offer a milk-white heifer in sacrifice to the
god and goddess of Rimini.   To build and adorn his fane
Sigismondo devoted all his restless and unscrupulous energy.
He used the ancient Port, a basilica and a campanile as a
quarry ; he stripped Classe of porphyry and panelling ;
he plundered the people of Fano of the materials they had
collected for a bridge.   He employed the chisels of Matteo
da Pasti, of Simone Ferrucci, the pupil of Donatello, and
of Agostino di Duccio, the Florentine, to carve the charming
putti and angels, or the draped female figures in low relief
often upon a blue ground, that suggest Della Robbia.   But
above all, for the task of remodelling the Gothic shell of
the existing church into a building of the classic style, he
availed himself of the genius of Alberti, who, by his studies
in Rome, had mastered classic details more thoroughly than
Brunelleschi.   For the façade, with its Roman arches and
engaged orders and inscription, Alberti took the triumphal
Arch of Augustus for his model.   This architectural device,
full of possibilities in itself, but singularly inappropriate for
an entrance to a Christian house of prayer, he carried out,
we shall see, in S. Andrea at Mantua.   Within, the conversion of the Gothic building was accomplished by means
of sculpture and medallions, of Roman pilasters and mouldings applied to screen the pointed arches.   Panels were added
round the piers with bases of Renaissance design ; the
chapels were enclosed by screens of Veronese marbles with
beautiful columns resting on elephants, and bearing figures

of children. And everywhere, amidst all this wealth of lovely ornament, appear the arms, the emblems, the initials, the features of this Saint Sigismund of the Renaissance. In the third chapel on the right a beautiful fresco by Piero della Francesca represents him kneeling before his patron Saint, his favourite hounds and his castle in the background.

Pandolfo Malatesta sold Rimini to the Borgia, recovered it after Cesare's death, and ceded it to Venice for a cash consideration. Venice, after the League of Cambrai, was obliged to yield it up, and Rimini then became part of the legation of Ravenna, with Faenza, Forlì and Cesena, under the immediate rule of the Pope. The ruined and unfinished walls of the town, which include fragments of the old amphi-theatre, form a delightful walk, with views of the Apennines and the sea.

Two chapels commemorate the visit of S. Anthony of Padua ; one, the pretty octagonal chapel in the Piazza Giulio Cesare, is on the spot where, when he preached, the heretics stopped their ears ; the other is on the shore, whither he repaired in disgust, and, stretching forth his hand to the sea, " Hearken unto me, ye fishes," he cried, " for these unbelievers will hear me not! " " And of a truth it was a marvellous thing to see how an infinite number of fishes, great and small, lifted their heads above water," listened to the Saint, then bowed their heads in appreciation of his holy words. The port which Sigismondo destroyed has been rebuilt and the river canalised. In these days a little sea-side settlement has sprung up by the shore ; the sands are dotted with *chalets*, with the painted walls and green shutters that the Italian villa-maker loves.

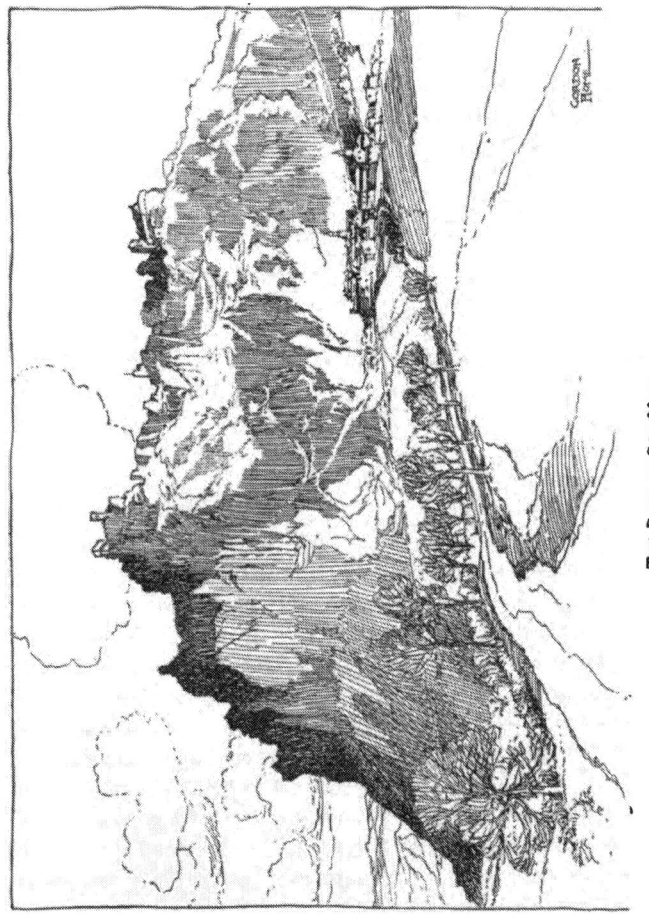

THE ROCK OF SAN MARINO.

CHAPTER XII.

SAN MARINO.

SAN MARINO and S. Leo are hill-set villages and castles, perched on sudden, sheer pinnacles of rock, so characteristic of the Umbrian landscape, beloved by the early painters. It may be thought that they are not worth visiting. There is nothing to see at San Marino ; there is only a view and an idea. But it is such a view and it is such an idea as may make the pleasant bicycle ride thither memorable. True, the existence of San Marino as an independent state in the heart of Italy is a mediaeval curiosity, and the fact that this pygmy Republic remains at war with Austria, because it is not worth while to make peace, is amusing. But the idea which its existence represents is the triumph of those principles of liberty and equality, which are the noblest ideals of man as a political being. The Republic of his fellow-Christians, which was founded by S. Marinus, a stone-mason, when he fled from Rimini, to escape persecution under Diocletian, to this lofty rock at the foot of the Apennines, survives to-day. When Napoleon proposed to increase its territory, the Republic wisely declined. It had always been small and wished to remain small. It has always been free, and remains free after a life-time as a Republic nearly three times as long as that of Rome.

SAN MARINO.

Centuries of actual independence have bred in the people
a notable independence of character and manners.   The
affairs of the Republic are announced and discussed in
General Assembly, as in the ancient city-states of Greece.
Each man is equal.   Two Regents are elected every six
months, and wear traditional costumes.   They have reason
to be proud both of the Republic and of the Idea which
they represent.

The upper town, perched on perpendicular cliffs, often
deep in snow, frowns above the suburb of Borgo.   Rough
mountain gorges, sheer rock and scree form a pleasing contrast to the soft scenery of the plain.   In the distance the
sunlight strikes upon the creamy villas of the plain and
illumines them, like sails of fishing-boats upon a purple sea.

CHAPTER XIII.

RAVENNA.

NORTHWARDS from Rimini the railway hugs the sea, skirting the sandy shore of the Riviera Adriatica. It is dotted with seaside villas, devoid of gardens, looking out on to the gray-green or azure-blue of the treacherous Adriatic Sea. We cross the Rubicon, and presently run through the juniper bushes and pine-trees that form the famous *Pineta* fringing the coast. Then we come to where Ravenna sleeps, a fossil-city embedded in the sands of time, a mummy of the fifth century, her face set towards the immemorial East. *Ravenna sta come è stata molti anni (Inf. xxvii.)* The receding sea has destroyed her prosperity, but the surrounding marshes saved her from the ravages of the barbarians. And the city sleeps on through a placid, regular existence, a living tomb of the mighty dead, bathed often, so characteristically, in fog and mist, as in the half-light of the underworld, pervaded by a mysterious, whispering silence, the silence, and the sound and the smell of dead leaves in autumn ; sleeps on, a mausoleum of past splendours and of regal memories. A ruined, unkempt city-wall fences ruined palaces. All the grandeur of " the Rome of the Lower Empire " is decayed. The pavements of the jewelled

churches are awash with marsh water ; the marble columns
are stained with the strange, lovely colours of decay.   But
the tombs of Theodoric and Galla Placidia are still almost
untouched by time, and, upon the glistening walls of S.
Vitale, Justinian and Theodora still hold their Court.
Ravenna is the Pompeii of the Byzantine era.   Scarcely anything of ancient Rome survives here, save the memory of
her naval power; scarcely anything of mediaeval Christianity,
save the presence of the great poet, whose Divine Comedy
marked the end of the Middle Ages.   More Byzantine than
Constantinople herself, Ravenna is not only the Portsmouth
of Augustus, the Italian Ravenglass ; not only the residence
and burial-place of Theodoric ; she is the city of Justinian
and the Exarchs, the richest treasure-house of early Christian
art and ritual.

A dozen miles from the most southern of the seven
mouths of the Po, the Thessalians founded the ancient
colony of Ravenna.   They were succeeded by the natives
of Umbria, the Etruscans, and finally by the Romans.
Three miles from the old town Augustus decided to con-
struct a capacious harbour, as the station of the Roman
fleet which was to control the eastern half of the Mediterranean.   This naval base, with its arsenals, dockyards and
barracks, formed a small city, which borrowed its name from
the fleet, Classis.   The intermediate space was soon built
over.   Ravenna joined hands with Classis across the suburb
of Caesarea.   The capital of the Flaminian and Aemilian
provinces became one of the most important cities in Italy.

The principal canal, constructed by Augustus, carried the
waters of the Po through the centre of the city to the
harbour.   A network of subordinate canals permeated the

town and formed thoroughfares, crossed by bridges, navigated by boats, and lined by houses raised on piles. It was an earlier Venice. There still exist rings inserted in the walls of a house in the Corso, to which boats might be attached. The walls of the city were surrounded by water ; a deep and impassable morass stretched for miles, across which an artificial causeway, easy to guard or to destroy, connected Ravenna with the Continent. The morasses were interspersed with vineyards, and Martial declares that wine was cheaper than good water at Ravenna. The place itself was, like modern Venice, singularly salubrious, and for the same reason. The tides of the Adriatic daily swept and deodorised the canals and the lagoons that divided the islands of the marsh. The same waters floated every day the vessels of the neighbouring country into the heart of Ravenna.

The gradual retreat of the sea has left the modern town six miles from the coast. The waves pile up the sand, the streams bring down soil, so that the open shore yearly advances eight feet seaward, and at the mouths of the rivers much more than that. The process began long ago. As early as the sixth century A.D., the port of Augustus had been converted into pleasant orchards, and a lonely grove of pines covered the ground where the Roman fleet once rode at anchor. And meanwhile the soil of Ravenna has been gradually sinking, several inches a century, so that now the pavement of the Baptistery is below the average level of the sea, and the pavements of S. Vitale and S. Apollinare in Classe are awash with water.

The Piazza Maggiore, now encircled by palaces, is the ancient Roman Forum. The beautiful sculptured capitals

THE INTERIOR OF SAN VITALI, RAVENNA.

of the columns in the colonnade are probably relics of a temple of Hercules. The columns in this piazza recall the dominion of Venice. The Palazzo Communale is adorned with part of the Gates of Pavia, trophies of inter-communal warfare. Six sixteenth century gates alone remain of the fourteen, which were once in the circuit of walls, dating from Claudius Germanicus, Odoacer, and Valentinian III.

The great monuments of Ravenna cover an epoch of one hundred and fifty years. They illustrate three periods. The Churches and tombs of the family of Theodosius represent the Christian Western Empire ; the Churches and Mausoleum of Theodoric, the Gothic Kingdom ; S. Vitale and other Italo-Byzantine buildings represent the period after Justinian had recovered Italy.

(1) *Christian Western Empire.* The approach of Alaric so terrified Honorius, " distinguished above his subjects by the pre-eminence of fear as well as of rank," that he abandoned his palace at Milan for ever, and transferred the capital of the Western Empire to the safer retreat of the walls and morasses of Ravenna. Till the middle of the eighth century Ravenna remained the seat of Government. For the example of Honorius was followed by the Gothic Kings, and afterwards the Exarchs, who, representing the Imperial authority in Italy, occupied the throne and palace of the Emperors at Ravenna.

After the sudden death of Alaric (410) the Goths chose for his successor his brother-in-law, Ataulphus. Amongst the prisoners whom Alaric had carried off from Rome, was Galla Placidia, daughter of Galla and Theodosius I. Sister of the timid and vacillating Honorius, it is said that at the age of eighteen, so wonderful was the influence of her beauty

and the strength of her character, that, when Alaric was
before the walls of Rome and reducing the ancient capital
of Rome to the lowest depths of humiliation, she stirred
the people to a vile act of revenge, and put Serena, the
widow of Stilicho, the fallen General of Honorius, to death,
on the charge of friendship with Alaric. Moved by her
charms, Ataulphus now, in the hope of winning her for his
bride, placed his army at the service of the Empire, and
marching into Gaul, which was in a state of chaos, won it
back for the Emperor. Honorius detested the idea of
yielding to a barbarian the sister and daughter of Emperors,
whom he would have preferred to bestow upon Constantius,
his own General, who was desperately enamoured of her.
But Ataulphus made her his bride at Narbonne, and the
marriage thére, solemnised with Roman splendour, seemed
to symbolise that union between Goths and Romans, which
had long been the dream of many, and which was to be
realised in part by Theodoric. An assassin put an end to
Ataulphus' career, and Honorius gave Galla Placidia to her
faithful lover, the rough soldier Constantius, who was made
Honorius' partner in the Empire. Galla Placidia received
the title of Augusta, and a few years later this masterful
woman became Regent for her infant son, Valentinian II.
Her policy, which was the opposite to that of Honorius,
was to unite East and West, Constantinople and Ravenna,
against the threatened invasions of the vast barbarian hordes
which swarmed throughout Europe. The party at Ravenna,
which favoured the independence of the West, chose John
as the successor to the throne in opposition to Placidia's
regency. For Placidia the General Bonifacius declared ; the
General Aetius for John. John collected a fleet at Ravenna

and Aetius brought 60,000 Huns to his aid. The fleet, which was bringing an army from Constantinople to help Placidia, was scattered in a storm and their General, Ardaburius, was cast ashore at Ravenna. But, though a prisoner, he managed to hatch a plot within the city by which his son Aspar, advancing from the mainland, was enabled to enter Ravenna by surprise and seize John himself, who was put to death. For a quarter of a century Placidia governed, whilst the Arian Vandals began to dismember the Empire. Not a woman of great intellect, she was shrewd and very beautiful. The incapacity of her son, and the fact that she had on her side the Catholic clergy, have given her a greater reputation than perhaps she deserved. But at any rate she lives, lives here in Ravenna and keeps alive for us the century in which she lived and which has vanished elsewhere. The mausoleum which she built is the earliest monument of Byzantine art here. It is in the shape of a Latin Cross—the first in the West—with a domical vault. A low brick wall, a low, brick, tiled, octagon tower ;—so humble is the exterior that the beautiful mausoleum, in which Galla Placidia was entombed beside Honorius, her brother, her husband Constantius and her son Valentinian, it might easily be passed by. But within, the walls and arches are completely covered with mosaics of the rarest colour and design to within five feet of the pavement, and, below, up to the spring of the vaults, the walls are veneered in yellow marble. It is a casket of jewels rather than a mere mausoleum. At Ravenna, as at Constantinople, Palermo and in St. Mark's at Venice, mosaic work fills the place of the fresco-painting of Florence and the North, as the medium of artistic expression and decora-

tion.   In the North the architect strove to create vast spaces
to be illuminated by windows of immense breadth and
height, through painted glass of the richest, warmest hues,
in order that the interior of his church might glow with
light and colour, in contrast to the dull, grey skies without.
In the East, where sunshine is an enemy, where the shadow
of a great rock is an image of delight in a plain of torturing
glare and heat, the builder, by means of low domes and
narrow windows, aimed at the admission of only so much
light as should reveal the depth and coolness of the sombre
colours, deep blue and green and gold, of his bejewelled
walls.

The fifth century mosaics of the tomb of Galla Placidia
within, and the old brick walls without, have lost much of
their peculiar air and reality of antiquity in the last few
years.   The brick has been restored and repointed in
common with almost every national monument in North
Italy ; the hard lines and fresh monotonous colour of new
work have supplanted the irregularities and varied tones
of a building mellowed by the ages.   Mosaics, damaged
by damp and years, but hallowed by the atmosphere of an
immense antiquity and sanctified by the certainty of their
genuineness, have been patched up with modern *tesserae*,
utterly inferior in depth of colour and detracting by the
harshness of their lines from the mellowness and irregularity
of the originals.   The pattern has been preserved at the
expense of a great part of the spirit.   But even so the
chapel-tomb of Galla Placidia and the chapel of the Bishop's
Palace at Ravenna remain supreme triumphs of decorative
art.   The glow of colour is irresistible ; in architecture,
ornament and design the harmony of style, proportion

and period is perfect.   Through a blue sky, blue with
the depth of Eastern darkness, gold stars shine forth
upon Placidia's perpetual night.   And in this heaven of
stars, in the centre of the dome, a large Cross glitters,
watched by the symbols of the four Evangelists beneath.
Over the door, Christ, a youthful Shepherd, feeds one of
his sheep.   Over the altar He bears a Cross and burns
the writings of the heretics upon a brazier.[1]   On the
lunettes at the termination of the transepts, golden stags,
symbolising proselytes, advance through green-gold arabesques upon a blue ground to drink at the water-brooks,
the Fountain of Life.   Through the green grass the Apostles
walk, two and two, whilst pairs of doves sip from vases
around them.   The design, so simple and direct, is a marvel
of delicacy, richness and grace ; strongly reminiscent in
detail of classical work, the whole breathes the dignity of
the East.   The harmony of design and of colour—the deep
blue, dull red, the greens and gold and the pure shining
white, is marvellous.   And beneath these lowly domes,
decorated with the simple, beautiful symbols of the Christian
story, beneath this blue sky, aglow with the golden stars
and the sign of the Cross, lie the simple, mighty tombs of
the great Queen and of the two Caesars, Honorius II. and
Constantius II.

As late as 1577 Placidia herself was to be seen, like
Charlemagne in later times, wrapped in her Imperial robes,
seated on a throne of cypress.   But through the aperture
which revealed this marvellous sight, three children put in
a light ; the robes caught fire, and in a moment all that
remained of the daughter of Thedosius, the sister of

[1] Otherwise interpreted as S. Laurence and his gridiron.

Arcadius and Honorius, the wife of Ataulphus and Constantius, the Empress of Aetius and Bonifacius, the mother of Valentinian III., was reduced to ashes.[1] It matters little. Her presence fills the tiny tomb ; her memory survives in the splendour of these rare mosaics.

It was the intrigue of Placidia's daughter, Honoria, with Attila, which furnished the King of the Huns with his excuse for invading the Western Empire. Galla Placidia also built Santa Croce, of which the Campanile recalls the foundress, and, in fulfilment of a vow made during a stormy passage from Constantinople, the church of San Giovanni Evangelista (424). Reliefs in the tympanum of the fourteenth century doorway illustrate the occasion of that vow. The court in front represents the ancient atrium. The Church, but not the Campanile, was practically all rebuilt, 1747. Galla Placidia also built, for her Confessor, the Church of San Giovanni Battista, which was almost entirely rebuilt in the late seventeenth century. To the first half of the fifth century also belong the superb Baptistery of the Orthodox, founded by Archbishop Neon, 451, and the Chapel of the Archbishop, S. Pier Crisologo, adjoining the Cathedral. Like the tomb of Galla Placidia, the exterior of the low, octagonal Bapistery, with its red-tiled, flat-domed roof, is strangely insignificant, partly, perhaps, because the soil has sunk and reduced the elevation. It has the corbelled cornice and angle pilasters of later Lombard buildings. But, within, the glory of azure-blue mosaics gleam and glisten as brilliantly as they did nearly fifteen

[1] So writes Dean Stanley, but the mummy was very likely an imitation made at the end of the thirteenth century, the great era of fake and fabrication.

hundred years ago.   Here we have an early instance of the
adaptation of Pagan buildings and atmosphere to Christian
uses.   For in luxury, as in site, this Baptistery is the successor of a Roman Bath Chamber.   And the influence of
Roman art is as clear as the influence of Roman institutions.
For in the dome the Twelve Apostles on a blue ground,
holding crowns and divided by arabesques, encircle the
central figure, a bearded Christ on a gold ground, who is
being baptised in Jordan.   And the River Jordan is represented as a Pagan river-god.   Below the Apostles is another
circle of mosaic decoration, wherein, between light marble
columns, are represented the four books of the Gospel open
upon four altars, and, between them, four thrones of
dominion with crosses.   Figures of the prophets clad in
white on a gold background appear below.   All the mosaics
of the dome are entirely untouched by the restorer's hand.
The sinking of the building is indicated by the fact that the
bases of the column are now covered by the floor.

The mosaics in the ceiling of the Chapel of the Archbishop are also the original fifth century ones, almost
untouched.   Again a beardless Christ, a figure of solemn
dignity, is surrounded by his Apostles and Saints, and the
design, which includes crosses and birds, is wonderfully
beautiful.   The Madonna, and the two Saints, Vitalis and
Apollinaris, on either side, belong to the twelfth century.
The pavement is of marble and porphyry, " opus Alex-
andrinum."

The ivory chair, called the Throne of S. Maximian, with
its ivory reliefs, is a thing of surpassing loveliness, perhaps
the finest piece of ivory work existing.   The Cathedral
itself, but not the Campanile, was modernised beyond recall

in the eighteenth century. Little more than the beautiful marble columns remain of the original Church of S. Agata.

(2) *The Gothic Kingdom.* It was at Ravenna that Orestes, the last of the Generals who made and unmade Emperors at their will, overthrew Julius Nepos, and caused his own son to be elected Emperor—that Romulus Augustus who was destined to be the last Emperor of the West, and who, by the irony of fate, bore the name of the first King of Rome. At Ravenna, after Pavia had been sacked by the barbarians, and his father, escaping thence, had been slain at Piacenza, the boy Emperor was deposed by Odoacer, and the Empire of the West having fallen, the history of Italy began.

And at Ravenna, in his turn, Odoacer, after ruling Italy for a few years, fell at the hands of Theodoric the Goth, who came as the Representative of the Emperor, with the title of "Patrician," to reconquer Italy for the Empire. Odoacer had fought the invading nomad horde of Ostrogoths near Aquileia and had forced Theodoric to shut himself up in Pavia. But when the Visigoths, too, crossed the Alps and combined with the Ostrogoths, he was obliged to retreat upon Ravenna. There, for three years he withstood siege, for Theodoric could not blockade the port, till at last he captured Rimini and was able to collect a sufficient number of ships. Then famine began to press the beleaguered city. Many, says Agnello, the chronicler of Ravenna, spared by the sword perished of hunger. Odoacer surrendered on terms which were finally settled through the Archbishop of Ravenna. His own life was to be spared. On March 5, 493, Theodoric entered Ravenna in triumph. All the Clergy came forth to meet him, chanting Psalms ;

the Archbishop led the procession. A few days later the Conqueror gave a grand banquet to which he invited Odoacer. But the moment he appeared, soldiers rushed upon him, and Theodoric, drawing his sword, spitted his vanquished foe. " Where is God? " cried the murdered man. And Theodoric merely observed, seeing how easily his keen sword blade sank into his enemy's breast—" One would think he had no bones." He was proclaimed King by his Goths, and he ruled Italy as the subordinate of Constantinople. The whole civil administration remained in Roman hands : the army was composed of Goths. This dualism was maintained. There was no real fusion of the nations, but there was a long period of peace and prosperity, and during it a development of building in the municipal towns and a development of literature, as instanced by the presence of Boethius at Theodoric's Court.

After the fourth century Constantinople had become the artistic capital of the world. The Gothic wars must have almost wholly eradicated the traditions of Roman art. And now that Theodoric had set up a stable society once more, it was from the decorative art of the East that he borrowed ; the East, suitably enough, whence the rock of Christianity had been hewn. How that influence spread north and west is indicated by the fact that it was from Ravenna, from the palace of Theodoric, that Charlemagne obtained marbles and mosaics for his monumental church at Aix-la-Chapelle, and it was upon the plan of S. Vitale and the Eastern Churches that that church was built. For at Ravenna Theodoric preferred to reside, and here he would cultivate an orchard with his own hands, retiring to Verona on the Northern frontier, whenever danger threatened. And here he built himself a sumptuous Palace, of which only a later gateway or guard-house remains, ornamented with marbles taken perhaps from the original palace. The sea used to wash the gardens at the back, where the royal gardener loved to labour. The Palace itself was despoiled of its marbles and mosaics by Charlemagne, with the Pope's permission. A representation of Theodoric's palace in mosaic was put up in S. Apollinare Nuovo towards the end of the sixth century. It was in this Palace that he beheld the fatal vision of Symmachus' head. Legends have gathered thickly about the death-bed of Theodoric. The fact is that this astonishing barbarian was an enthusiastic Arian and had thrown Pope John I. into prison, to die there, because he favoured the Emperor's persecution of the Arian heresy. He secured the election of Pope Felix III. Then he died suddenly, whilst he was collecting men and ships to defend himself against the threatened combination of the Empire and the Vandals against him. Procopius relates that one day, when banqueting, Theodoric seemed to see a great fish, which had been set before him, glare at him and gnash its teeth, then turn into the likeness of Symmachus, head of the Senate, whom he had murdered, and father-in-law of Boethius, whom also he had murdered. The terror-stricken monarch took to his bed and died (526). And Gregory the Great records how a hermit on the island of Lipari announced Theodoric's death to a traveller who had left him alive and well. " I have just seen him pass with his hands fettered, dragged along by Pope John and Symmachus, to be thrown down Vulcan's crater at Lipari."

The bones of the mighty heretic were not allowed to rest in the wonderful Mausoleum, which his daughter Amalasuntha built for him. How the Catholics hated him may be gathered from the façade of San Zeno, at Verona. The bones of the Arian King were cast out, and the name of his mausoleum converted to S. Maria della Rotonda. His body is supposed to have been found by some labourers who were digging near the tomb in 1854. But they did away with the skeleton probably for the sake of the golden cuirass which they had also exhumed and of which a few fragments only were recovered.

This massive monument stands half a mile outside the city, in a garden of flowers where, in May, the nightingales sing all the day long amid the acacias. It is a circular building (520) of two stages, decagonal below, and with traces of a colonnade, which once ran round the upper story. It is roofed by an enormous flat dome, made of one block of Istrian stone, weighing some 470 tons. From this monolithic lid project enormous *handles*, so they appear, which may have been used for getting the stone in place, or perhaps they are imitations of small abutting arches, like those which surround the dome of Sta. Sophia at Constantinople. The names of the Apostles are engraved upon them.

Near the Palace of Theodoric stands the Cathedral which he built for his Arian Bishops, the Court Church, S. Martino in Cœlo aureo. It was catholicised in 560 by Archbishop Agnellus and re-named Sant' Apollinare Nuovo. The atrium and the apse have been removed and the exterior is plain, but, within, the walls of the nave present a spectacle of rare beauty and singular interest. The omission of the galleries, which were a feature of the Pagan basilicas, left in the Christian Churches a large bare wall-space above the arches and piers, which invited decorative treatment. This space—above the arcade supported on cipollino columns with Byzantine super-abaci and rough Corinthian caps—Agnellus filled with a blaze of mosaics, a silent procession of white robed Saints, a Christian version of the Panathenaic frieze. At the west end are views of the City and the Port. From Classis, on the left (it will be remembered that the women sat on the left side of the Church), issues forth a solemn and stately procession of Virgin Saints, bearing their crowns. They are divided into pairs by single palm-trees, and are led by the Three Kings, bearing gifts, to the feet of the Virgin, who sits, in the East, upon a star-embroidered throne, surrounded by four Archangels. From Ravenna, on the right, and the Palace of Theodoric, comes forth a line of Saints, who are led by St. Martin to Christ, who sits enthroned between four angels. Of even greater interest, and probably earlier, are the sixteen figures of teachers of the Church, between the windows, and above them the very early pictures in mosaic (unrestored) of the Christ-story. Here and elsewhere it will be noticed that the art of Byzantine mosaic is marked by its direct appeal, by the grave, yet sweet expression of the Saints portrayed, and by the Eastern dignity of the whole composition. The fact that the Crucifixion is not represented points to the early date of the design. In the Chapel of Relics there is a portrait of Justinian. It has been restored, like much of the other mosaic-work here. The Campanile—round as are the other Campaniles of Ravenna—perhaps dates from the ninth century.

Theodoric also founded the Church of S. Teodoro, afterwards dedicated to the Spirito Santo and rebuilt. The vestibule with eight columns of Greek marble, and the columns of coloured marble with Byzantine caps in the nave are remarkable. Theodoric, too, built an octagonal Baptistery for the Arians, afterwards dedicated to Sta. Maria in Cosmedin. The fine mosaic in the Dome is late sixth century.

(3) *The period of Justinian.* When Belisarius was winning back the Western Empire for Justinian, Ravenna was the last stronghold of the Gothic monarchy. The surrender of this impregnable city marked the triumph of the Emperor through his mighty general. The throne of the Gothic Kings was henceforth to be filled by the Exarchs of Ravenna, as representatives of the Emperor in Italy.

The period of Justinian's triumph is illustrated by two churches of supreme importance—S. Vitale and S. Apollinare in Classe, both begun a little earlier, under the Archbishop Ursicino, by Julianus Argentarius, " the Treasurer," both consecrated by S. Maximian, and both ablaze with the brilliant mosaics of the sixth century. Whilst S. Apollinare was built on the old plan of a Roman basilica, in S. Vitale we have the eastern and Byzantine type of building, now first introduced into Italy and destined to influence all the subsequent architecture of Europe.

S. Vitalis, the patron saint of Ravenna, was a soldier in Nero's army and a convert of S. Peter. He exhorted to constancy a Christian martyr whose endurance was failing and, when dead, gave him honourable burial. For this crime he was first tortured and then burnt alive. The Church of S. Vitale, largely built of material from the Amphitheatre, was completed, 547, through the generosity of the Emperor and Empress. It represents the triumph

of Byzantine art in the West.   In its construction the
tradition of Roman buildings is discarded.   It is neither a
basilica nor a cross in plan, but octagonal, with exhedras, a
choir to the East and a narthex.   Two stair-case towers
communicated with the women's gallery.   Within, a series
of round arches and domes, the favourite Byzantine domes,
wide rather than flat, are decorated by a continuous papering
of glittering mosaic carried over the vaults and arches.   All
angles are rounded off to take the tesserae.   Everywhere the
influence of Constantinople is evident.   Ravenna was now
crowded with Orientals, with Syrians, Armenians and Greek
soldiers.   Greek was the language of the Court ;   Greek
monks, seeking refuge from Arab invasions, filled the
monasteries ;   Greek and Oriental influences predominated
in the Church and were naturally reflected in ecclesiastical
construction and art.   Much of the carving was imported
and the patterns were Eastern.   Eight massive columns,
coated with marble, frame the central space.   They are
crowned by magnificent Byzantine-Corinthian capitals sculptured in rich bas-relief.   The beauty of these capitals of
Justinian's time has never been surpassed.   On the four
sides of them, in square panels, are carved tree-like forms
simplified almost to a fleur-de-lys.   Interlacing basket-work
fills the rest of the capital.   Similar examples are found in
Jerusalem, Constantinople and North Africa.   Impost-
blocks, interposed above these capitals, receive the springing
of the pier-arches.   This device became common in Byzantine structures, and seems to be a crude modification of the
fragmentary architraves or entablatures employed in classic
Roman building to receive the springing of vaults sustained
by columns.   But the chief glory of S. Vitale is the brilliant

mosaic work with which the walls are encrusted. This is, indeed, inferior to that of the Baptistery, the Galla Placidia tomb and Sant' Apollinare Nuovo ; the breadth of outline, the classic severity and strength is lacking in these designs. But, instead, a greater richness and fulness of detail, a more minute and elaborate splendour, a more careful and realistic portraiture characterise these brilliant pictures. They, too, have suffered from a restoration which is little short of disastrous to the colour effect and to the preservation of the spirit and actuality, which was the supreme quality of this wonderful monument. The mosaics illustrate (i.) the story of the founding and consecration of the Church, (ii.) the celebration of the Lord's Supper. The ground of the apse is gold ; in the centre of the dome, Christ, portrayed with all the dignity of noble youth, is seated upon the globe of the world. The four rivers of Paradise flow through green meadows, lily-dight, and purple clouds float over the golden ground. On one side a white archangel presents S. Vitale, to whom Christ extends a crown ; on the other, Ecclesius, the Bishop who began the building, offers a model of the Church (p. 25). The walls proclaim the union of Church and State in Imperial orthodoxy. Justinian and Theodora blaze in the purple and gold of their royal splendour. On one side Justinian, life-size, realistic, surrounded by his bodyguard of fair-haired Teutons, brings a donation to Archbishop Maximian and his clergy, who advance to meet him. On the other Theodora, her headdress glistening with real jewels, attended by the eunuchs and gorgeously attired ladies of an Eastern Court, stands on the threshold of the entrance-court of the Church. Mother-of-pearl is used in these mosaics. And the artist,

in his courtly flattery, has crowned with the halos of
Christian saints these life-like portraits of the coarse and
sensual features of the Emperor and of his vicious, cruel,
domineering wife.

Less good, but still of extraordinary beauty and interest,
are the mosaics which fill the quadrangular space. They
represent the Old Testament symbols of the sacrifice of the
Mass. On the vaulting, between green and gold tendrils
upon a blue ground, and green upon a gold ground, are four
flying angels upon globes, and below them four peacocks,
symbols of eternity. On the upper wall, above the apse, two
angels hold a shield with the sign of the Redeemer ; on
either side the cities of Jerusalem and Bethlehem, built of
jewels, shine forth beneath a cloud of buds and vine
tendrils on the blue ground above them. Then come the
Old Testament forerunners of Christ, Melchizedec, the High
Priest ; Abel, the Shepherd ; and Abraham, the Sacrificer ;
Moses, the shepherd and lawgiver ; Isaiah and Jeremiah,
the prophets ; the Four Evangelists ; and finally, Christ
Himself and His Apostles.

All the colour, symbolism and poetry of Christianity
triumphant, rejoicing in a new-found ritualism and splendour, are crystallised on these marvellous walls. If S.
Vitale were the only Church in Ravenna, Ravenna would
still be the most important town in all Europe for the study
of early Christian ritual and architecture. It is to be hoped
that the appalling frescoes which disfigure the Church may
be soon removed. The fifth century Tomb of the Exarch
Isaac, with its reliefs, should on no account be missed, but
it is sometimes not to be approached for the water that
floods the chapel in which it stands.

S. APOLLINARE IN CLASSE, RAVENNA.

Narses was the first and most powerful of the Exarchs, the viceroys of the Empire. Their power was soon limited, but the Exarchate, including Bologna and Ferrara, as well as Venetia and the Pentapolis, was never conquered by the Lombards. Not being a sea-faring people, they never reduced the cities on the coast of the Adriatic and Mediterranean. So for nearly two hundred years Italy was divided unequally between the kingdom of the Lombards and the Exarchate of Ravenna, and the seeds of political disunion were sown, which have borne fruit ever since. The Byzantine Emperors, afraid that the Exarchs might assert their independence, weakened rather than strengthened their hands, whilst the priesthood of Ravenna, encouraged by the Exarch, strove to maintain their independence of the Pope.

Ravenna was finally subdued by Ataulphus, the Lombard, and the long series of Exarchs was brought to a close when Pepin made it over as a temporal possession to the Pope. From 1295-1346 " Polenta's eagle " brooded over the city ; from 1346-1509 Ravenna was governed by Venice. Then Julius II. recovered it.

The Church of S. Apollinare in Classe was begun in 534, a few years after the death of Theodoric. It occupies the site of a temple of *Apollo*, and is said to have been built upon the spot where S. Apollinaris, who had been sent by S. Peter to preach the Gospel on the Eastern Coast, fleeing from prison at Ravenna, was overtaken and slain on his way to Rimini.

Of the old town of Classis, the Roman port, not a stone remains ; the suburb, Caesarea, is only indicated by the Church of Santa Maria in Porto Fuori, with its grotesque frescoes and a Campanile, part of which was once the light-

house of the Roman harbour. Here we have a pagan
Pharos converted into a Christian bell-tower. Conversely,
at Venice, and in our own fen country (*e.g.* S. Botolph's,
Boston), lofty Christian Church towers were used as light-
houses and sea-marks. Three miles of dykes and ditches
and malarial marsh-lands, whose spongy moss is lit by
marigolds and purple orchises, and whose stagnant pools
are decked by pink tamarisks and lilies, and long whispering
rushes, cover the site of the naval station of Imperial Rome.
Here and there the light green of springing rice in the
paddy-fields, or, as the result of recent drainage, crops of
grain and beet-root relieve the scene of desolation.   Then,
sheer out of the deserted, pestilential marsh rises a huge
round Campanile and a Church, encircled by the blue vault
of Heaven. The wide, marshy plain stretches away to the
horizon ; the scattered trees scarce break the monotony of
white, dusty roads, of yellow, muddy banks, of pools brown
and green with reeds and sedge.   But in the remote distance
the snowy Alps and Apennines glimmer through a purple
haze, and seaward the sky-line is broken at last by stone-
pines, through which glimpses of blue water shine, and
beyond the canal and moorland rises the dark green wall of
the Pineta, the tree-stems a shimmering blue or golden-red.
" Of all desolate buildings, S. Apollinare in Classe is the
most desolate.   Not even the deserted grandeur of S. Paolo
beyond the walls of Rome can equal it " (Symonds).   Shorn
of the broad, quadrilateral portico which once surrounded it,
stripped by Sigismondo Malatesta of the rich marbles that
once encased the walls, the façade disfigured by modern
workmanship and the whole buildings now by the necessary
repointing of the brickwork, the walls and columns green

with slime and damp, the bases of the columns sunk far below the level of the floor, and the pavement often flooded with brackish water, the plain, oblong building that survives, stands like a rock from which the sea that bore the Roman fleet has ebbed and left it, dreary, desolate, wonderful amid the ooze and wrack of time. It is a monument of melancholy isolation and romantic decay. But within, above a nave arcade of twenty-four antique Greek cippolino columns, run a series of (eighteenth century) portraits of the Archbishops of Ravenna, recalling the lost mosaics there, and in the apse the original sixth and seventh century mosaics give us the first picture of the Transfiguration. Amid light pink and light blue clouds a splendid cross with a half-length figure of Christ shines forth from a blue circle studded with gold stars and set with jewels. Below is represented the glorification of the Church of Ravenna, the rival of Rome, and the patron-saint, S. Apollinaris, in Bishop's robes preaching to his flock. Of the numerous early sarcophagi that of Archbishop Theodore is the most remarkable (sixth century). The baldachino erected by Petrus, a priest, in honour of Sant' Eleucadius (ninth century), now covers a fifteenth century altar.

The Pineta, or Bosco, as it is called, is gradually recovering from the disastrous fire and frost which nearly destroyed it last century. It was through the long alleys of those Imperial pines, whose innumerable tall columns, topped by evergreen caps, are laden with a valuable harvest of fir-cones, that Dante loved to wander—" Per la pineta in sul lito di Chiassi." Here, where the charm of solitude and silence was broken only by the whispering of winds and song of birds or the sudden rush of a storm through the tree-tops,

he would meditate his " poema sacro," buoyed by the hope
that, when completed, it could not fail " to melt the hard

DANTE'S TOMB.

heart of Florence." He would cross the marsh-meadows to
Santa Maria in Fuori (*Par.* xxi. 121), and be lost in reverie,
as he looked in S. Vitale upon the inscrutable, oriental gaze

of Justinian, whence he drew the inspiration for the sixth
canto of the Paradiso.   For to his " ultimo rifugio " at the
Court of Ravenna Dante had passed from Verona.   And
here, honoured and beloved by poets and disciples, soothed
alike by the courteous hospitality of Guido II. da Polenta,
and the gentle ministrations of his daughter, Beatrice, Dante
passed the evening of his days.

Ravenna, the cradle of Francesca, is the tomb of Dante.
He died in her service, from a fever caught in returning
across the swamps, after a fruitless embassy to Venice.   And
Ravenna rightly has the honour of being his last resting-
place.   The shrine to which the devotee turns his steps is
that restored by Bembo, 1483.   The ugly " little cupola,
more neat than solemn," was erected by Cardinal Gonzago in
1780.   The grim house of the Polenta, where Guido entertained him, stands at guard on the opposite angle of the
street.   The stately Campanile of S. Francesco, the modernised version of the Church which Neon built upon the site
of a temple of Neptune, and where Dante was originally
buried, vested in the blue habit of the Order he loved,
keeps watch over the spot where the exile found rest at
last.

> "Ungrateful Florence! Dante sleeps afar
> Like Scipio, buried by the upraiding shore!"

in spite of many subsequent attempts on the part of the
Florentines to obtain his bones.   But it is in the Pineta
that we feel his presence most.   And " Ravenna's immemorial wood," where

> "The shrill cicalas, people of the pine,
> *Make* their summer lives one ceaseless song,"

has memories, too, of other poets.   In the " haunted

grove of Chiassi " Boccaccio laid the scene of the loves
of Theodore and Honoria, and Dryden retold in verse
how the spectre huntsman, Guido Calvacanti, and his hell-
hounds pursued and tore in pieces the haughty maid who
had scorned his love, "renewed to life, that she might
daily die." [1] "Boccaccio's lore and Dryden's lay " drew
Byron to this forest solitude, through which he would often
ride during his two years' residence and work at Ravenna.
An inscription on the house he once occupied (Strada di
Porta Sisi No. 225) says that he was attracted to Ravenna
chiefly by desire to visit the ancient forest which inspired
Dante and Boccaccio.   But we know that there was another
attraction in the person of the Countess Guiccioli, which
kept him faithful to the charms of "that place of old
renown, once in the Adrian sea, Ravenna."

I like to remember that on the first occasion that I visited
Ravenna some fifteen years ago, returning from a long day
spent beneath the trees of the Pineta, I heard as I approached
the gates of Ravenna the Angelus begin to ring.   The
sound brought to my mind the lines from Don Juan, which
I quoted to my companion, not then at all remembering that
the succeeding stanzas show that they refer to Ravenna:

> "Ave Maria ! blessed be the hour,
>   The time, the clime, the spot where I so oft
> Have felt that moment in its fullest power
>   Sink o'er the earth so beautiful and soft,
> While swung the deep bell in the distant tower,
>   Or the faint dying day hymn stole aloft;
> And not a breath crept through the rosy air,
> And yet the forest leaves seem'd stirred with prayer.

[1] Watts' picture in the Tate Gallery, London, is an interesting
illustration of this poetic story.

Ave Maria ! 'tis the hour of prayer !
Ave Maria ! 'tis the hour of love !
Ave Maria ! may our spirit dare
    Look up to thine and to thy Son's above " ;

And then follows the *sauce piquante* of Byronism, the flippant, defiant *volte-face* contrasting with the intense emotional seriousness of the poet, the lover, the man.   It is interesting to recall that those haunting stanzas are written in a measure and a style which are a direct echo of Italian poetry, Italian cynicism and Italian wit.

Returning from the Pineta to Porta Sisi, we pass the *Colonna dei Francesi*, on the banks of the Ronco, the " broken pillar, not uncouthly hewn," which records the victory of Louis XII. over Julius II. (1512), and the death of Gaston de Foix, the hero-boy, whose tomb and monument we have seen at Milan, and whose memory is revived when, in the Museo, we gaze upon the recumbent statue of the Ravennese warrior (*Guidarello Guidarelli*).   He lies asleep in death, after the good fight fought, a very gentle and perfect knight, girt in exquisite armour.   This lovely work, which Dr. Ricci attributes to Tullio Lombardi, is one of the most perfect representations of the repose and peace in which a man should rest after his labours, as the Mausoleum of Galla Placidia and the Taj at Agra must rank as the most beautiful memorials of departed women.

CHAPTER XIV.

FERRARA.

THE main stream of the Po, which once brought her wealth and power, no longer flows by Ferrara. *La gran donna del Po*, as Tasso calls her, the rival of Venice, now lies surrounded by the many rivulets into which that mighty river breaks up " to rest in ocean with his sequent streams " (*Inferno*, v. 99). She has risen from what was once an immense stretch of marsh and fenland, much of which has been reclaimed, and she stands now like a jewel set in a green plain. Corn waves where once there was nought but sedge and reed, and nightingales sing among roses where once the wild swan circled overhead and mourned his friend Phaeton.

Ferrara first appears in the seventh century upon the right bank of the Po, just above its division into two main arms, the Primaro and Volano. This first settlement is represented by the suburb of S. Giorgio, where stood the first Cathedral. S. George was from the first the patron saint. In the sculptures of the portal of the Lombard Duomo he rides full tilt at the dragon ; and the warrior-saint in gleaming armour looks down on us from the fresco above the portcullis of the Castello. Ferrara gradually spread and developed on the left bank. The new city was surrounded by walls, but she was still vulnerable by water. The fleets of jealous Venice and jealous Ravenna combined to crush their prosperous maritime neighbour and to make good the claims of the Countess Matilda over a people whose self-government the Emperor recognised. The family of the Adelardi now appear as leaders of the Guelf faction, whilst the Torelli championed the Emperor. Under the Adelardi the city prospered. Begun by Guglielmo I. and continued by Guglielmo II., the new Duomo in the centre of the new city on the left bank of the Po is the splendid monument of their race.

Few towns have a greater individuality or a more striking charm than Ferrara. She has shrunk within her once impregnable walls like a kernel in a nut, although her

> "wide and grass-grown streets,
> Whose symmetry was not for solitude,"

are less deserted than they were a decade ago, for she shares in a revival of industrial prosperity with the rest of the North of Italy. Her girdle of incomparable gardens has vanished, the dreaming river, upon which the gilded bucentaurs bearing queens and duchesses used to glide, has been transformed into a dull canal. Avenues of chestnut trees and bare stretches of grass grow where once lay the marvellous pleasaunces of the Dukes, with their groves of myrtle and citron, their fish-ponds and summer houses and grottoes.[1] But the tradition of her splendid Court yet lives, and the fame of her poets is ever-green. The city is divided into two by the Via Giovecca ; one half is a winding labyrinth of closely-packed houses and narrow streets ; the

[1] Ferrara. By Ella Noyes. *Mediæval Towns Series.*

other the Renaissance city, with its broad, straight streets leading to the heart of it, which earned for the district which Duke Ercole laid out the title of the " first modern city of Europe." And in the centre, to which these streets lead, stand the two great buildings of Ferrara, the Castle of the Estensi and the Cathedral of the Adelardi and the people.

> " Il mile cento trempta cinque nato
> Fo qto templo a Zorzi csecrato
> Fo Nicolao scolptore
> E Glielmo fo lo auctore,"

So ran the old verses once inscribed in the mosaic decoration, and confirmed by the leonine Latin verses on the great central porch. They tell us that the Church, founded by Glielmo and " sculpted " by Nicolao, was consecrated in 1135 to S. George. Nicolao was probably the Nicolaus of S. Zeno at Verona, where the sculptures resemble those here in style and subject. The beauty of the west front and part of the south side, overshadowing the market, which survive from seventeenth century conversion, are the features which make this building memorable. The colour of the façade is of extraordinary richness and variety of tone. Opalescent pink and grey, cream and orange blend and change in the changing lights and leave an unforgettable impression on the mind, not to be expressed by the exact science of words. Of this façade the first storey, as far as the first arcade, belongs to the Adelardi era, and is in the Lombard style ; when the building of the Cathedral was continued, a storey in the new Gothic style was added. First an arcade with slightly pointed arches and simple moulding indicates the earliest introduction of Gothic, then yet another arcade with fully developed point, deeply recessed openings and rich clusters of columns indicate the maturity of that style towards the end of the thirteenth century. The façade was completed by the addition of three gables and a lovely open-arched gallery following the lines of the gables. To this period belong the inharmonious pointed arches and " *oculi* " above the round arches of the arcade on the first storey. This arcaded screen-front is perhaps the most Gothic in spirit of Italian façades ; it is at the same time highly instructive as an example of the use to which the Italian nature applied the Gothic curves and ornament to impart grace and lightness to the sterner forms of the Romanesque.

The same blending of styles is illustrated by the fine three-storied gabled porch which occupies the centre. Knotted shafts carry the front wall and rest on lions. The lower part, with the S. George and Dragon in the tympanum, and the quaint and typical Lombard carvings of monsters and animals, is the work of Nicolao. The upper stages, so graceful and rich in sculpture, with a Last Judgment filling the gable, which is remarkable for energy and grace and life, must be assigned to the beginning of the fourteenth century. The south side, which is partly disguised by the picturesque Loggia de' Mercanti, has an extraordinary upper gallery of Verona marble, in which almost every column is of different design.

The heavy Renaissance Campanile is faced with red and white marble, which harmonises well with the creamy-orange hues of the Duomo. The interior of the Cathedral has been ruined by frequent reconstructions in increasingly disastrous styles.

Guglielmo II. degli Adelardi was buried within the mighty

monument of the Cathedral he had built. The House of Este succeeded, through his niece, to his wealth and power. The Lords of Este sprang from the little town which nestles beneath the southernmost peak of the Euganean hills, and was once perhaps the capital of the Veneto, before the Roman era. They had established themselves in the marshy Polesine of Rovigo, " the land which Po and Adige lave," and extended their grasp southward in process of accumulating immense domains that reached from Genoa to the Adriatic. They represent the case of the feudal lords of the Trevisan Mark, who preserved their independence, and whose large estates tended to increase as the power of the Imperial government grew less, whilst their owners became lords of life and liberty as well as lands. From this time forward the story of Ferrara becomes the story of the splendour of the House of Este. Mainly Guelf in her sympathies, and weary of strife, Ferrara exchanged liberty for peace, and elected Azzolino, Marquis of Este, and his heirs, perpetual lords of the city. But through the dark, narrow streets and the frowning, vaulted lanes of old Ferrara for many years yet the battles of Guelf and Ghibelline, of Este, that is, and Salinguerra, were to be fought before the White Eagle of Este had made firm its grip, and the people hailed Azzo Novello perpetual Podestà. With feastings on the public piazza, with jousts and tourneys the investiture of the family granted by the Holy See was celebrated. If the choice had to be made between independence and anarchy, prosperity and freedom, it was perhaps wisely made. With courtly splendour, with joyous living, with material prosperity, which was, however, sapped at length by the demands of the Court, the Estensi rewarded the Ferrara merchants, engrossed in their maritime trade, for the surrender of their communal freedom.

Azzo Novello was a mighty man of war, and now that the Ghibellines had been crushed within her gates, he led forth the youth of Ferrara to fight the battles of the Guelfs at Parma and Fossalta.   The Torre de' Leoni, the rugged majestic tower which rises at the north-east angle of the Castello, commemorates in name and in the bas-relief on its north side the two lions, which the Marquis brought back from Frederick II.'s proud city of Vittoria (1248), after he had led forth the defenders of Parma to overthrow it (*see* Parma).

To the Marquis Azzo Novello, under whose beneficent rule Ferrara enjoyed a period of great prosperity, succeeded his bastard grandson, Obizzo, upon whom was conferred " full dominion to do all things according to his will, both just and unjust."   He appears to have used his powers to the full (*Inferno*, xviii. 55).   Relentless, bloodthirsty, determined, passionate, strong, he crushed his enemies and attained his ends.   Dante and the chroniclers affirm that he was slain at last by his own sons, but not before he had added Modena and Reggio to Rovigo, Adria and other smaller cities, which now formed the rich and powerful principality of the Estensi.   Under his strong hand trade developed, and Ferrara flourished as an oasis in the faction-torn desert of Italy.   The House thus established had many vicissitudes, but, in spite of all, maintained its power.   Usurping parties had their hour ; Venice and the Pope fought for so rich a prize ; the people were not always content ; over-taxation was never popular. There was one fierce rebellion when the people claimed a victim in Tommaso, the oppressive minister of Niccolo II. The Marquis sacrificed his minister, then haled the ring-leaders of the revolt to the scaffold, tied to asses' tails. And to prevent the repetition of so untoward an affair, he summoned Bartolino da Novara to build him a Castle which once for all should dominate the town.

Moated, portcullised, draw-bridged, machicolated, this grim Castello Rosso of the Estensi, with its massive square corner towers, is the most impressive mediaeval fortress in Italy, the very type and stronghold of feudal despotism. It casts a dense shadow over the still and gloomy waters that protect the dungeons, and frowns over the public square, a deadly menace once to the citizens who dwelt around it. The substitution of light Renaissance balconies for the great " Ghibelline " battlements and the addition of sixteenth century turrets to the towers, when the fortress was con-verted into a more peaceful Ducal Palace, has, in combination with modern municipal alterations, somewhat interfered with the military grandeur of the Castello Vecchio. But its air is still sufficiently over-awing. The dungeons still recall the tragedies born of family feud and jealousy and of ducal tyranny. But it has brighter memories to suggest.

About those frowning towers and dusky red-brick walls the song of Boiardo, of Ariosto still lingers in the air. The spacious courts and broad piazza recall the tournaments and pageants of the byegone dynasty. The magnificent marble halls, decorated by the brush of Dosso and of Titian, are redolent of the atmosphere of many a joyous wedding banquet, of many a dramatic performance, of many a contest of poetic skill and courtly chivalry, of philosophic discourse and the tales of love.

FERRARA CASTLE.

Hard by the Castello, and connected with it by a covered way, the ruling race lived in a stately Renaissance palace. Little of it now remains unspoiled. But from the Cortile, where once the famous ladies of the Ferrara Court passed with their attendant trains, where now the market women spread their wares, the lovely marble Scala Grande still forms the entrance stairway (1472).

It was in the dungeons of the Torre Marchesana, the Clock-tower of the Castello Vecchio, that Parisina and her lover were executed—Parisina, the fair and joyous daughter of Malatesta of Cesena, and Ugo d'Este, the handsome, knightly youth, one of her husband's innumerable bastards. Like that other pair of Parisina's House at Rimini, love led them to one death. Niccolo III.'s brutal revenge has obscured his reputation as a wise ruler, whose care for his people, skilful diplomacy and successful encouragement of industry prepared the way for the Golden Age of Ferrara.

Niccolo III. set the example to Northern Italy of sharing in the revival of Greek learning. He reopened the University, and invited the best scholars of the day to lecture at Ferrara. Students flocked from all the cities of Italy and from Europe to sit at the feet of those admirable Humanists and noble scholars, Guarino da Verona and Giovanni Aurispa. Guarino was the tutor of Niccolo's son, Leonello, the gentle prince whom he so wisely educated that he became the best ruler of his day. Leonello had been trained to war under Braccio da Montone, but under Guarino's direction, he preferred the bloodless battles of scholarship and the recreation of hunting—that was in the Este blood. He it was who established the habit of culture and the love of things beautiful, which passed into a tradition with the Estensi, so that Ferrara became the centre of art and learning and the embodiment of Italian Renaissance culture. This sensitive spirit, who excelled in the art of living beautifully, surrounded himself with everything that was beautiful and artistic. In his lordly pleasure-house, the Villa Belfiore, without the walls, which Roger van der Weyden and Angelo adorned with the works and ideas of their genius, and which was enriched with all the flowers of culture, products of goldsmith, craftsman, painter, sculptor, illuminator, the Prince would daily converse and theorise with the orators, poets and philosophers who attended his Court. No stone of that building, or of the other famous Este Villas, Belvedere, Belriguardo, and their exquisite country houses on the banks of the Po, remains. Under Leonello and his brother Borso, Ferrara was an island of peace and wealth amidst an ocean of bloodshed and exhaustion. Borso was as ambitious as his diplomacy was successful. He persuaded the Emperor to raise his states of Modena and Reggio into a dukedom, and Paul II. at length was induced to create him Duke of Ferrara. The golden age of this flourishing Court had begun. Without the artistic taste of his brother, Borso was a generous patron of art, a lover of pageantry and splendour, a magnanimous and kindly ruler, ready to do anything which might contribute to the reputation of the family which he represented. The building in which his memory is chiefly enshrined is the Palazzo Schifanoia, the Palace of Sans Souci (Shun care), which he completed and which stands now in a grass-grown street near the Court Church of Sta. Maria in Vado. Amidst the ruins of this beautiful villa, with its lovely Renaissance portal, whither the Este princes loved to retreat, we seem to listen again to the wonderful fairy tales which Matteo Boiardo would recite to those accomplished princesses, Isabella and Beatrice D'Este, beneath the acacias and lemon-trees, or to hear Duke Borso once more wind his horn in the chase he loved so dearly. For within, a series of frescoes, in part (E. wall) by Francesco Cossa, record, so far as they have survived seventeenth century whitewash, the daily round of Duke Borso's life and the personages of his Court, to the accompaniment of the symbols of astrology. It is a series of extraordinary interest, for in it the whole Court life of the fifteenth century, in all its picturesqueness and neo-paganism, still lives and moves and has its being. Borso, the central figure of the pageantry of old Ferrara, still rides forth a-hunting on his white horse, whilst his falconers and pages lead his favourite greyhounds in the leash ; he still looks on at the famous races for the *pallium* upon S. George's Day, when the Piazza was filled with crowds of spectators and scholars and courtiers, dwarfs and jesters, and fair ladies in rich brocades surrounded their Duke. In contrast to these scenes of feverish gaiety and revelling, in which the Ferrarese, spite of their taxes and poverty, were ever ready to indulge at the bidding of their pleasure-loving Dukes, it is interesting to remember that there was bred up here in Ferrara a thin, ascetic figure of a man, to whom the world, so full of misery and iniquity beneath a veneer of art and polish, seemed strangely upside-down (sotto-sopra). It is not strange that the sight of all " the wealth of the world and the woe " in this so joyous a city should have inspired Girolamo Savonarola with the text of his terrible denunciations. Ercole I., who married Leonora, daughter of the King of Naples, a most noble, pious, accomplished and courageous woman, succeeded Borso. He set himself to make the University the foremost, his Court the most brilliant, and his city the finest in Italy. He borrowed Alberti's Treatise on Architecture from Lorenzo de' Medici, and applied the principles of the great Renaissance architect to his improvements. New Churches were built ; a lofty Campanile was added to the ancient Duomo. Broad, regular streets and spacious squares were laid out, adorned with noble monuments and sumptuous palaces, set in lovely gardens. These streets, laid out upon a symmetrical plan, form the Addizione Erculea. It was an addition never destined to be justified by the development of Ferrara. The streets stand now grass-grown, silent, deserted, as the measure of the Duke's ambition and enthusiasm, and the secret of the shrunken beauty, the melancholy charm of the town. The genius of Biaggio Rossetti gave to Ferrara her triple zone of fortifications, besides the Church of S. Francesco and others. Ercole Grandi rebuilt Santa Maria in Vado. Outside the town the Duke laid out a wonderful park, which he stocked with stags and strange beasts, such as spotted giraffes, whilst every device to enhance the luxurious ease of a country villa, in which Renaissance princes, imitating Roman magnates, took so much delight, was applied to the villas of Belfiore and Belriguardo.

The Camerini of the Castello and the halls of the Schifanoia Palace were filled with precious works of art, the gems and cameos which Ercole loved, the tapestries and embroideries and metal-work made by craftsmen whom Leonora introduced to Ferrara, and with the luxurious carpets of the East. And under such princely patronage

there arose a little school of native artists, which later spread
to Modena and Bologna, training the hands of Lorenzo
Costa and Francia, and influencing the genius of Raphael
and Correggio. They were the scholars of Cosimo Tura,
who spent his life painting the portraits of the Este family,
creating altar-pieces for the Duchess Leonora's favourite
churches, and adorning with frescoes the villas and palaces
of the Dukes.

Side by side with painting, the sister arts of literature,
music and the drama were encouraged by the accomplished
Duke, who spent all his leisure in classical studies. Europe
was ransacked for tenors, lute-players and violinists: the
choir of S. Maria in Vado rivalled even that of Milan. A
stage was erected in the old Gothic Palazzo della Ragione on
the Cathedral Square, and here Latin comedies, translated
by the Duke himself, with interludes of music, morris
dances and masques, or plays written by Niccolo da Correggio, Matteo Boiardo or Ercole Strozzi, were acted on
every occasion of festivity. In the sunshine of ducal favour
a new school of Italian poets blossomed forth, who composed
songs and romances to be sung to Leonora and her gentle
daughters, Isabella and Beatrice. Thus Ferrara became a
centre of art and learning. Scholars flocked to the Court
where Matteo Boiardo shone, and where blind Francesco
Bello charmed all men by his improvisations.

For so splendid and luxurious a Court could not be content without the luxury of letters. Now and henceforward
the Este princes cultivated literature, therefore, as some rare
and beautiful plant with which they desired to adorn their
house. In response to their patronage, the art of Boiardo,
of Ariosto and of Tasso blossomed forth. And the scent of

those rare flowers of intellect sweetens forever the memory of the voluptuous tyrants who tended them for their pleasure.

Here in the intervals of his public duties,—he was governor of Modena and Reggio,—Boiardo composed, for the glorification of the house of Este, his epic, that graceful and ingenious blend of classic dignity and chivalric romance, the *Orlando Innamorato*. Here Ariosto, born, like Boiardo, at Reggio, catching the lyre as it fell from Matteo's dying hands, produced a sequel to that poem in the *Orlando Furioso*. Escaping from the profession of law, he had entered the service of the Duke's brother, the coarse, unscrupulous Cardinal Sigismondo, whose only comment on the poem was to enquire of Ariosto "where he had been for all that rot?" This was that Cardinal who built the Palazzo dei Diamanti, faced with some 12,000 facets of stone, an ugliness, a Renaissance millionaire vulgarism, which has however some meaning, since the Diamond was the emblem of Ercole, as the Unicorn of Borso. The charm of the building lies in the marble colonnade within, facing the delightful garden-court. This Palace is now a Museum of Ferrarese paintings.

This was the beautiful façade of Guarini's rhyme

"Bella porta, bell'entrata,
Bel canton, bella faciata."

The truly " beautiful portal " is that of the Prosperi palace, and the " beautiful entrance " that of the great Bevilacqua palace opposite, which belonged to the great family of that name, who possessed no less than five of the richest palaces in Ferrara. There is a great charm in these decayed, deserted palaces, with their blending colours of Verona

marble and terra-cotta mouldings, their double colonnades
and lovely cortiles ; but a charm greater and more simple
attaches to the little house in the Via Ariosto, which the poet
built for himself with the proceeds of his poem, where he
polished his verses and tended his garden with all the
enthusiasm of a James Thomson. Here he died. The
Duke had rewarded the poet, for his neatly turned comedies
of intrigue and for his superintendence of theatrical per-
formances and for his adulation of the House of Este, with
the governorship of Garfagnana, a wild district overrun with
banditti, who read and admired their governor's epic. The
amiable poet made no great fortune. But he was able to
build this house for himself—

> "Parva sed apta mihi, sed nulli obnoxia, sed non
> Sordida, parta meo sed tamen ære domus."

So, in the Latin distich, inscribed on the façade, the poet
described the history and the charm of this little house and
garden which he was content to call his own.[1] The verses
which he polished there are the ideal representation of the
Court life of old Ferrara, with its conventional chivalry and
self-conscious sentiment. The lovely pastoral scenes,
wherein errant knights and damsels so wisely wander, are
but reproductions of the pleasaunces and gardens of the
Dukes, of the superb summer palace Belvedere, which
Alfonso built upon an island in the Po, with its halls and
chapel decorated by Dossi, its stately terraces and stairs leading down to the river, its delicious gardens planted with
orange groves and box-hedges, adorned with marble loggias,

---

[1] This House is kept by the municipality. Ariosto's manuscripts, which
show his unceasing labour of revision, and other relics, are preserved in the
Public Library.

lakes and fountains. Ercole's sun was not unclouded. There was the conspiracy of his nephew, Niccolò. Coming unawares, in his absence, with five vessels from Mantua, Niccolò entered Ferrara by a breach in the walls, where they were being repaired. Leonora awoke to find the Palace surrounded. Springing out of bed, she fled with her infant son in her arms by the covered way to the Castello. The conspirators rushed into the palace, sacking and slaying. But the people rallied round their Duke. The cry of " Diamante! " triumphed. Ercole returning, appeared on the balcony of the Castello and publicly embraced his wife and children amid tumults of applause. Niccolò and several hundreds of his followers were beheaded. And now came the War of Ferrara, which gave employment to all the leading condottieri of Italy. The greed of Sixtus IV., who wished to acquire Ferrara for his nephew Girolamo Riario of Forlì, and the greed of Venice, who saw promise of extending her frontiers from Adige to the Po, and who was aggrieved because the Duke, in spite of the monopoly which the Republic claimed for her salt works at Cervia, persisted in making salt at Commacchio, led to a combined attack against Ferrara and her allies, Naples, Florence and Milan. The fevers bred of her marshes laid many of Ferrara's enemies low. But the Venetians, under the valiant Condottiere, Roberto di Sanseverino, supported by the Pope, utterly defeated the Ferrarese forces at Argenta, and Gaspare, son of Sanseverino, marching to the very gates of Ferrara, planted the lion of S. Mark in the ducal park. Plague scourged the city. Duke Ercole himself lay at the point of death in the Castello. But once more the high-born Duchess rose to the occasion. She sent her children out of danger to Modena, summoned the magistrates of the city, and harangued them from the garden loggia. Moved to tears at the womanly courage of her appeal, the citizens shouted the watchword of the House of Este, *Diamante!* and vowed to die for their Duke. They rushed in their enthusiasm to the chamber where Ercole lay, and covering his hands with kisses, assured themselves that their beloved Duke was still alive. Then they rallied bravely to the defence of the city. Every man who could bear arms in Ferrara helped to man the walls. Without, the peasants rose to harass the invaders. Help came, too, from Milan, for Lodovico Sforza checked the advance of the Venetians, whilst Ercole's brother-in-law, Alfonso, Duke of Calabria, himself rode at the head of fifty horsemen and a troop of infantry to the aid of the beleaguered city. To create a diversion Venice invited Charles VIII. of France to Italy. The Peace of Bagnolo was the reward of this bold stroke of diplomacy, whereby Venice acquired the Polesina and obtained the recognition of her rights with regard to Ferrara. The Pope died of rage, Lodovico received 60,000 ducats from Venice, and Ferrara retained her independence. Il Moro, who married Beatrice d'Este, has left his mark on Ferrara in the Palace, which he began to build for himself as a place of refuge in case of need, and of which the exquisite pilasters and capitals that he loved and the beautiful marble loggias give a hint of the imagined perfection.

Ercole's son and successor, Alfonso, had married one of the most famous and inexplicable of women, Lucrezia Borgia, who brought a splendid dowry of money and relief of tribute to Ferrara. The bride, whom Roman gossip termed daughter, wife, and daughter-in-law of the Pope, was hailed by Ferrarese Court poets as *pulcherrima virgo*, and was received with pageantry and splendour never surpassed at Ferrara. Very beautiful she certainly was. The mere sight of her completely subjugated her hitherto unwilling bridegroom. Her charm and accomplishments soon won golden opinions from every side. Young Pietro Bembo, the representative man of letters of his age, who had just joined his father Bernardo, to whom Ravenna owes the tomb of Dante, found her fascination irresistible. He praised in Latin epigrams her every word and act, her singing, dancing, playing, and when he left Ferrara, to succeed Poliziano at Urbino, Rome and Padua in the dictatorship of letters, the lovers kept alive and strengthened their friendship by a long correspondence. In the Ambrosian Library at Milan there is preserved a touching memento of this so famous liaison— Lucrezia's letters and a tress of her long, yellow hair. Lucrezia had been married to husbands of increasing importance as the power and ambition of the Borgias waxed. Nursed in that sink of all the vices, Papal Rome, daughter of such a father, sister of such brothers, not unnaturally, and probably not without some cause, the foul weeds of unutterable scandal have grown up and choked the fair fame of this beautiful, pleasure-loving woman. Her last husband had been stabbed to death on the steps of S. Peter's by the assassins of the Borgias. But this byword of infamy proved a model Princess, and won the golden praises of Ariosto as a second Lucrece, brighter for her virtues than the star of regal Rome. But the praise of the wits and poets by whom she was surrounded in her brilliant Court at Ferrara need not blind us to the fact that she brought with her to Ferrara something of the atmosphere of the Vatican. Jealousy, it was rumoured, was the cause of the death of Ercole Strozzi, the poet who had sung her praises, and who was found dead, wrapped in his mantle and pierced with many wounds.

"Two years earlier another dark crime brought the name of Borgia before the public. One of Lucrezia's ladies, Angela Borgia, was courted by both Giulio d'Este and Cardinal Ippolito. The girl praised the eyes of Giulio in the hearing of the Cardinal, who forthwith hired assassins to mutilate his brother's face. Giulio escaped from their hands with the loss of one of his eyes, and sought justice from the Duke against the Cardinal in vain. Thereupon he vowed to be revenged upon them both. His plot was to murder them and to place Ferdinand d'Este on the throne. The treason was discovered; the conspirators appeared before Alfonso. He rushed upon Alfonso and with his dagger stabbed him in the face. Both Giulio and Ferdinand were thrown into the dungeons of the palace, where they languished for years, while the Duke and Lucrezia enjoyed themselves in its spacious halls and sunny loggie among their courtiers." (Symonds.)

We cannot here trace the steps by which Lucrezia's husband, whose recreation was forging guns, and whose business in the world was to combat the cunning of the Medici and the power of the Papacy, succeeded in keeping the dominion of his House intact. The light of that House went out with the death of Alfonso II., when Ferrara lapsed to the Papacy as a vacant fief, and its individual history ceased. But that light had burned very brilliantly to the end. Under the last Duke the old glory of the Renaissance had been revived in a Court of regal grandeur. And amongst those who have rewarded the Duke's patronage of art, of music and of literature are Palestrina, Battista

Guarini, author of *Pastor Fido*, and Torquato Tasso. The latter rewarded his patron with the sonorous and magnificent Coronal of Sonnets, wherein, borne onwards by " the proud sail of his great verse," the poet celebrates the House of Este. And for the same brilliant Court the first great pastoral drama, *Aminta*, was written by Tasso, 1573.

A poet and the son of a poet, Tasso came to Ferrara in the service of Luigi, Cardinal d'Este, brother of the Duke. The service, which the Cardinal in admirable patronage exacted, was the completion of the great poem of which Tasso had already given promise. Encouraged by the sympathy of the two great ladies of the Court, the Duke's sisters, Tasso worked for several years, attracting universal admiration by his brilliant occasional verses, disputing successfully with the *élite* of Ferrara on the subject of love, and presently entering the Duke's service. And now began the romance of his life, the intense, Platonic devotion to Leonora, the Duke's sister, the hidden flame, whose light burns clearly in his poetry. There can be no truth in the story that he was thrown into prison as a punishment for his presumption. But his hopeless attachment may have helped to unhinge his mind, already vexed beyond endurance by the high tension of poetic work, by the intrigue and jealousy of a Court, and by religious melancholy.

The *Gerusalemme Liberata* is a fantastic romance of knight-errantry, a dream as ethereal as Correggio's angels, as unsubstantial as Correggio's clouds, chanted in lines that cannot die. But it is more than that. It is the national epic of the Roman Catholic Reaction.

The great outbreak of Protestantism had been countered by an equally violent outbreak of Catholic zeal. Ignatius Loyola passed from the convent of the Theatines at Venice to found the Order of Jesus at Rome. Popes, whose taste in art was exquisite, but whose lives were passed in sensual and intellectual voluptuousness, and who laughed at the sacraments they administered, had been succeeded by Pontiffs who rivalled the primitive anchorites in their austerity. The poetry of Tasso is the poetry of that age, and offers a similar contrast with that of Ariosto. Whilst treating of the heroic days of the Crusades, Tasso voices the spirit of an age when foreign tyrants had crushed both the early Renaissance spirit and Protestantism in Italy ; when Catholicism was putting forth its utmost strength to drive back the Ottoman and the Heretic. And now, when his great religious epic was finished, ecclesiastical Reaction demanded by the mouth of Silvio Antoniano that Tasso should adapt it to the reading of monks and nuns. These troubles, acting on a brain already warped by the unnatural discipline of the Jesuits, into whose hands he had fallen as a boy, led to violent outbursts of insanity. Frantic paroxysms of repentance for imaginary sins shook his reason. The mania of persecution seized him and filled him with morbid suspicion of those about him. He fled from his supposed persecutors, but returned again to Ferrara, and then a frenzied attack upon a retainer of the Court led to his being confined and chained as a dangerous madman (1579). The Prison of Tasso, that wretched cellar in the Hospital of S. Anna (Strada della Giovecca), has been visited by countless devotees, who, touched by the tragic story, have written their names upon the window and walls,

and vented their indignant verse upon the head of Alfonso.
Byron's outburst against the Dukes of Ferrara,

> " And Tasso is their glory and their shame.
>   Hark to his strain, and then survey his cell !
>   And see how dearly earned Torquato's fame,
>   And where Alfonso bade his poet dwell ;
>   The miserable despot could not quell
>   The insulted mind he sought to quench, and blend
>   With the surrounding maniacs, in the hell
>   Where he had plunged it," etc.

is magnificent but scarcely fair.   Tasso apparently received
all the kindness of a hospital in those days, and if the Duke
refused to release him, his reply to those who interceded
for him was that his only object was to cure him.   Tasso's
confinement was rendered doubly hard by the death of
Leonora : he wrote imploring a famous preacher to kiss her
hand in his name, and to tell her that he was praying for
her recovery.   The Duke's treatment was unquestionably
salutary ; the violence of Tasso's mania quickly subsided ;
the clear light of his high thought shone forth again
unobscured, save that he remained the victim of hallucina-
tions.   He still thought himself persecuted ; he held long
dialogues, as he supposed, with a familiar spirit.   But he
was given comfortable rooms, where he was able to carry on
an extensive correspondence and to compose.   At length he
had sufficiently recovered for the Duke to yield to the
frequent solicitation of the Duchess of Mantua, and to allow
him to retire to her Court.

POMPOSA.

Within the compass of a day's visit from Ferrara stand
the deserted buildings of the once great Benedictine monas-

tery of Pomposa. The superb eleventh century brick campanile, rising from the marshes, deserted by the river and man alike, and the Giottesque frescoes of the Church, make Pomposa very well worth a visit. There are problems too to be pondered in connection therewith. Grand and desolate as S. Apollinare in Classe, adorned with capitals rich and delicate as those of S. Vitale, this ancient Church that stands upon the Delta marked out by the sea and the streams of the Po, brings to the mind in many ways suggestions of Torcello and Ravenna.

CHAPTER XV.

PADUA.

Padua, the refuge, according to the fable, of Trojan Antenor, stands among the winding streams of the Brenta and Bacchiglione. Dante mentions the mound by which the Paduans restrained the Brenta, swollen by the melted snows of Chiarentana and the Alps (*Inf.*, xv. 7). To the south-west rise the "mountains Euganean"; the rich plain at the foot of those famous hills gave such wealth to the city as led to the proverb—*Bologna la grassa, ma Padova la passa.*

"Tyranny," says Lassels, "and too frequent murthers have much depopulated Padua." Within her walls

> "Those mute guests at festivals,
> Son and mother, Death and Sin,
> Played at dice for Ezzelin."

Ezzelino da Romano, sprung from the little rock fortress in the Veronese marches, the soldier to whom Frederick delegated the captaincy of the Imperial party, the supreme type and first example of the cruel monster into which, as we have seen (*Milan*) the tyrant was liable to degenerate, still lives as a kind of hero of horror in popular legend. Cruelty became his god, blood his only lust, power his unique desire.

Most terrible of all his successes, to which he marched by
every means of violence or treacherous craft, was when he
succeeded in entrapping 11,000 Paduan soldiers, only 200
of whom escaped the torments of his horrible prisons.   It
was not till he had fully established his power over Verona,
Vicenza and Padua that he began to give rein to his insane
lust for blood.   Then began a reign of terror at Padua,
such as, perhaps, the world has never seen.   All supporters
of the House of Este, especially, were marked down for
destruction, their palaces destroyed, their goods seized (1250).
New dungeons were constructed, specially designed to be
noisome, but still the prisons were filled to overflowing :
young and old, of either sex, noble and peasant, were seized,
starved, mutilated or destroyed.   Whole families, who had
incurred his displeasure or suspicion, were blotted out by
the infuriated ogre, after suffering the ingenious tortures
from which he derived sheer delight.

At length the Pope, aided by Venetians, who were jealous
of the tyrant's might, organised a crusade to rid the Mark
of this bloodthirsty maniac.   The Crusaders took Padua,
and, restoring her liberty, sacked the city with unbridled lust
and rapacity.   Then the miserable, mutilated thousands were
led forth from Ezzelino's horrible dungeons.   He meanwhile slaughtered all the Paduan burghers who were with
his forces at Verona, and made the most desperate and
brilliant efforts to recover Padua, and even to seize Milan.
He was crushed at last, wounded and taken prisoner, and
died like a boar at bay, rending from his wounds the dress-
ings which his foes had applied to keep him alive ; but this
"son of the Devil," as he was thought, left behind him a
progeny of monster despots, like Bernabò Visconti and

Galeazzo Maria Sforza, whose inhuman cruelties sprang also from unbridled lust and power.

Relieved from the tyranny of Ezzelino, " many-domèd Padua proud " enjoyed a period of democratic government and prosperity. She was free from internal faction—for Ezzelino's ferocity had almost extinguished the nobility— and at peace with her neighbours. Her wealth and spirit found expression in the four buildings which will engage our attention—the Salone, Il Santo, the Church of the Eremitani and the Cappella dell' Arena (1303). The first, the Palazzo della Ragione (1172), which rises between the Piazza dei Frutti and the Piazza dell' Erbe, and is approached by the tortuous streets with low and narrow *portici* characteristic of the town, derives its name from the vast Hall on the upper floor (1420). It much resembles that at Vicenza. The wonderful roof was copied, it is said, by an Augustine monk from a palace he had seen in India. Access to it is obtained from external arcades on the first floor, to which staircases lead from below. The second is the sepulchral Church of S. Anthony of Padua. Opinion concerning the exterior of San Antonio seems to be divided. I take it to be grossly ugly, save when a distant view lends some enchantment to the multitude of domes and octagonal brick minarets in this clumsy adaptation of Eastern effects to the pointed style. Tradition, surely in this case a lying jade, attributes these ugly proportions to Niccolò Pisano. The third is the shrine of Mantegna and other artists of the school of Squarcione ; the last the chapel of Giotto.

Padua was no stranger to inter-communal warfare. An incident in her history affords a good example of the trivial causes which gave occasion for strife. It happened that the

PADUA. A GLIMPSE OF THE PALAZZO DELLA RAGIONE.

people of Treviso gave a magnificent festival to the neighbouring towns, and provided for their amusement a mimic
Castle of wood, adorned with vair and ermine, purple and
scarlet, within which were entrenched the twelve most lovely
ladies of Padua.   The chosen youths of each city advanced
in bands to the attack, and the fair garrison made defence,
hurling in carnival spirit flowers and fruits and fragrant
perfumes at the besiegers.   At last some Venetians, fighting
prudently and delectably, as 'tis recorded, planted the banner
of S. Mark upon the wooden walls.   The blood of the
Paduan youth rose at the sight ; words led to blows ; the
banner of S. Mark was seized and torn.   The Trevisans
drove the combatants out of the town.   Insulted Venice
flew to arms and humbled proud Padua.   As a condition of
peace, the Paduans were compelled to send twenty-five of the
young men who had destroyed the banner to Venice.   There
they were treated courteously, and returned home with
honour.   But every year, down to the last days of the
Venetian Republic, Padua sent to Venice a tribute of
twenty-five hens.   These were set loose to be chased and
killed by the people, with whom the festa of the " Paduan
hens " was ever most popular.

Padua did not long retain her democratic independence.
War with Vicenza led to Can Grande becoming master of
Vicenza, and the Paduans elected Giacomo da Carrara as
Signore to defend them against Can Grande.   After long
conflicts with the Scaligers of Verona and the Republic of
Venice, Padua finally became a tributary of the latter power
(1405).   The city flourished under Venetian rule, and the
University developed in a remarkable fashion.

Just as the University of Oxford probably owes its existence to a migration of scholars from Paris, so the University of Padua (*Il Bò*) originated in the quarrels between the City and the University of Bologna. The students seceded for a while from that city (1222), and set up their schools under the protection of the Commune of Padua. Later secessions, the result of further troubles at Bologna, stimulated the vigour of Bologna's greatest rival. The first College, the Collegium Tornacense, was established in 1363, for six students of Laws. The Dukes of the Carrara family encouraged the University, Francesco Carrara (1399) giving the University the first building of its own, and under the patronage of the Venetian Republic, which forbade her subjects to study anywhere else, Padua became the veritable "quartier Latin" of Venice. The lamp of learning burnt in Padua's halls,

> " Once remotest nations came
> To adore that sacred flame,
> When it lit not many a hearth
> On this cold and gloomy earth."

The result was that Padua became a centre of humanistic learning, and, being so, attracted many young artists. Petrarch came to reside at Padua as a Canon of the Cathedral ; Squarcione, an amateur and travelled collector, trained a school of young artists to draw from his collected models (c. 1440). In his studio was trained Andrea Mantegna. Son of a small farmer, he was taught the science of painting and perspective by Squarcione, and in Donatello's bas-reliefs in S. Antonio he could find an example to hand of the great Florentine masterpieces.

Near to Giotto's Chapel of the Arena—for it is none but his—the vast and singular Church of the Eremitani, with

its immense, aisleless nave, contains some frescoes by
Mantegna, worthy of study perhaps beyond any other wall-
paintings in existence, as an example of the proper function
of the artist, which is to improve on nature, to decorate his
surroundings, to beautify his environment. These early
frescoes, though certainly cold and lifeless in form, reveal
the genius of the greatest of the Lombard masters, ere it
was freed from the cramping effect of a painstaking
apprenticeship. Mantegna left Padua to enter the service
of Lodovico Gonzaga at Mantua, and laboured under three
Marquises in the adornment of the Castello and the chapels
of the Gonzaghi with his masterpieces. The development
of the Paduan School may be followed in Il Santo and the
Pinacoteca.

In 1443 Donatello came from Florence to work for ten
years in the little house facing the Cathedral.[1] He produced for Padua two masterpieces. His first commission
was a High Altar in bronze and marble to the honour of the
popular Portuguese Paduan Saint, denouncer of the local
despot, who lies buried in the Church of S. Antonio. The
High Altar of Il Santo, with its marble setting and bronze
figures, is not Donatello's masterpiece as he left it. For it
was dismantled in the seventeenth century, and has only
recently been reconstructed, with much care and skill,
indeed, but without complete success in the placing of some
figures. Each of the figures and panels is worthy of the
closest study. The Madonna is supported by six Saints ;
S. Francis on her immediate right, S. Anthony, portrayed
as a homely friar, on her left. Nobody was more modern

[1] I am indebted to Lord Balcarres' scholarly monograph upon Donatello.

than Donatello, but this bronze Virgin, with the Child in her lap, gazing down the Church like some inscrutable, mysterious Queen of the East, is evidently modelled on Byzantine tradition, and seems at home in this Church with its Eastern domes and minarets. This bronze recalls to mind the sculpture of the western doors at Chartres. The arrangement of the hair, reminiscent of Greek sculpture, is as beautiful as the lustre and silken texture of it is lovely. The Crucifixion itself is a work of supreme excellence, a realistic yet imaginative and reverent portrayal of the grandeur of the living God, shining through the agony of the Man who died. Four panels record the miracles of S. Anthony ; the babe, who at his bidding proclaimed the chastity of its mother ; the absence of the miser's heart, to prove the Saint's text, " where thy treasure is, there shall thy heart be also " ; the healing of Leonardo, whose foot had been cut off in too literal obedience to the Saint's rebuke to a son who had tricked his mother ; and the refusal of a sceptic's mule to eat a sacred wafer. In all these bronze pictures the life-like disposition of the crowds, expressing by their attitudes the natural and various emotions of indifference and veneration, of excitement and awe experienced by the onlookers, is very remarkable. Four other bronze reliefs illustrating the symbols of the Evangelists, a tragic marble Entombment and a bronze Pietà complete the works of Donatello here, besides the choir of angels, plump choristers, of whom the worst are not possibly by Donatello, but the best are wholly pleasing in drapery, anatomy, expression and charm.

When Erasmo Narni, General Gattamelata, died in 1443, the Venetians granted the family of the great Condottiere, who had served them well, a site in tributary Padua on which to erect his monument. Donatello was commissioned in 1451 to cast the colossal equestrian statue, which was to prove so virile and animated a master-piece of bronze-portraiture.

In the course of travel sketched in this book, we are privileged to see the three finest equestrian statues in the world, that of Can Grande at Verona, of Colleone at Venice, and this, besides the memory of Leonardo's Francesco Sforza at Milan. And this, the first equestrian bronze statue of the Renaissance, was made by Donatello, with all the technical difficulties of casting on so large a scale to conquer, and with only the Horses at S. Mark's and the Statue of Marcus Aurelius at Rome to guide him in his art. The horse he made is a little too big for the rider, but it is full of life and spirit. Chafing and neighing as it is, the General sits easily in his saddle, unperturbed, strong but reticent, his hand outstretched in a superb gesture of command, the incarnation of control—over his soldiers, steed and self—a vivid contrast to the bravado of Colleone at Venice.

The tombs of this soldier-clan of Gattamelata in Il Santo, with the recumbent statues of mighty warriors resting in noble repose after the good fight fought, treated with great tenderness and remarkable grace, exhibit the influence of Donatello, whilst they suggest the later Warrior of Ravenna.

In an oval garden, which still preserves the outlines and site of an ancient Roman arena, stands a plain, undecorated chapel, with a simple oblong nave and apsidal chancel, built by Enrico Scrovegno, son of that Rinaldo whom Dante scourged ; built by him perhaps in atonement of his father's sins and for the use of the Order of the Cavaliers of Mary, which had been established for the vindication of the sanctity of the Virgin. It is one of the most famous buildings in the world. For Giotto came to decorate it in 1306.

It is characteristic of Italian Gothic that this alien ideal of architecture was always haunted by memories of the old basilica, covered with mosaics or paintings. And so, in Italy, the aim of Gothic structure is to provide broad, unbroken wall-spaces and a vast expanse of vaults over naves of extraordinary breadth, suitable for continuous stories in colour, without which the walls were not regarded as complete. Here in the Arena Chapel they are complete, and are painted by Giotto. Walls and roof are covered with frescoes by the master and his pupils illustrating the life of our Lord and of the Virgin, beneath which is a series of symbolical Vices and Virtues. At the west end is the Last Judgment ; on the eastern wall is a Christ in Glory. It is not necessary to analyse or catalogue these scenes. That has been done once for all by Ruskin (*Giotto and his work at Padua*). We may be content to observe that these pictures, often ludicrous for the weakness of their draughts-manship, if it were not that they convey the absolute sincerity and reverence of the artist, are famous in the world, not only as the work of him who was the forerunner and pioneer of modern painting, but also because of their truth, simplicity, directness and feeling. To depict in fresco-work the " gestures of living men, the incidents of everyday life and the portraits of living persons " was an innovation as important in the history of religion as of art. It meant the humanising of the Bible story, the bringing home of it as a story of human endeavour and destiny, without disguise or symbolism, to every worshipper, just as the translation of the Book revealed it to every cottage, without intermediary, in England or Germany. And these pictures, so simple and so direct, have all the pathos and tenderness of homely truth, as witness particularly the Appearance of the Angel to Anna, the meeting of Joachim and Anna at the Gate, the salutation of Mary and Elizabeth, the raising of Lazarus, and the exquisite Nativity and Deposition from the Cross. They are all the expression of a great genius, reverent and tender, who, brushing aside all that is false and superfluous, sought ever for the beauty of truth and life and love.

CHAPTER XVI.

VENICE.

WHEN Attila, King of the Huns, burst like a storm-cloud upon the Roman world, so terrible was the devastation which he dealt, that the grass, it was said, never grew on the spot whereon his horse had once trod. But this savage destroyer of men and cities undesignedly laid the foundations of one of the great maritime powers, of a Republic which was to revive the art and spirit of commerce and independence, and to live on through all decay and change, the supreme exemplar of the City Beautiful. Before the irruption of the Huns, the Veneti had established many flourishing towns in the district where the Po, the Brenta and the Adige flowed through innumerable channels into the Adriatic. But now from ruined Padua, from once wealthy Altinum, from rasèd Aquileia, the terrified citizens fled before the Scourge of God to the extremity of the Gulf, "where the Hadriatic feebly imitates the tides of Ocean."

Here they found, between the mainland and the open sea, a vast lagoon, whence some islands were emerging. Beyond lay low, narrow strips of land, which should serve both as a breakwater and a defence,—the first beginnings of the sandy Lido-shore, the popular bathing station of to-day.

The very foundations of Venice, like her people, were brought down by the rivers from the Alps. The Po and its great collateral rivers have for centuries, daily and hourly, been engaged upon the task of levelling the earth, bringing down with the Alpine snows vast masses of sediment and pebbles from the mountain tops, to form an ever-increasing belt of low land along the coast. We have seen this process at Ravenna. We find it again at Venice. For it was upon the patches of land so formed that the Venetian refugees, becoming the last of the European Lake-dwellers, drove the first piles of the city that was destined to become the bulwark of Europe against the Turks, and to " hold the gorgeous East in fee." Venice was originally only one of many settlements formed on the chain of marshy islands, which stretch from the mouths of the Isonzo to those of the Adige. These island-settlements were not at first intended to be permanent. But the systematic pressure of the Lombards followed upon the spasmodic invasion of the Huns.

It was decided to make the lagoons a permanent home. New cities were organised, churches were built, and, as the ancient Greek colonists carried fire from their mother city to light the altars in their new homes across the sea, so from the Roman settlements of Venetia the immigrants now brought their sacred vessels, their social organisations of class and guild, and even the very stones of their abandoned temples. Torcello and Burano succeeded to the inheritance of Altinum, Grado to that of Aquileia, Malamocco and Rivoalto to that of Padua. Heraclea and Chioggia rose to prominence. From Grado to Chioggia each island had its own Tribune, and was closely connected in a sort of confederacy with the others. In order to concentrate their powers of self-defence and obviate the disorders bred of faction and jealousy, the first Doge (Dux) or Chief Tribune, with sovereign powers, was elected at Heraclea in 679.

Unity and concord, however, were not obtained in a moment. There was a long struggle for pre-eminence between Heraclea and Malamocco (now beneath the waves), whither the seat of Government was transferred. But when Pepin began his attempt to reduce to obedience the lagoon-dwellers, who, thanks to their almost unassailable position, were already first in the race for emancipation from the Empire, it was found that the Lido-shore was no more secure than the mainland. Malamocco, like Heraclea, must be deserted, and safety found at last upon a little cluster of islands, in the very heart of the lagoons, safe from attack from the mainland, safe from attack by sea, yet lying not far from one of the openings in the sea-bank, the Port of Lido, approachable through the tortuous channels with knowledge, unapproachable without, washed twice daily by the tide, which rises and falls enough, but not too much, and fenced from the storms of the Adriatic by the guardian sands. Rialto was chosen as the new capital of the Venetian State. The element of rivalry and faction that arose from the discordant aims of Malamocco and Heraclea was removed, and Venice rose "throned on her hundred isles" (814). When we pass beneath the Rialto bridge, "that strange curve, so delicate, so adamantine, strong as a mountain cavern, graceful as a bow just bent," it assumes a new significance if we remember that here, rather than in the Piazza, was the original heart of Venice. Cassiodorus,[1]

---

[1] In a letter to the *Tribuni Maritimi*. The marble "Chair of Attila," as it is called, in the grass-grown piazza of Torcello, was probably the

BURANO. VENICE.

the Secretary of Theodoric, compared the early inhabitants
of the lagoons to water-fowl who had fixed their nests on
the bosom of the waves.   In this primitive document of
their existence, the islanders are described as earning their
livelihood by fishing and extracting salt from the sea.   You
gain an impression of these early settlements, and a memory
of unforgettable colour, from the streets and from the tiny
port of Chioggia, whence the fleet of painted fishing boats,
bragozzi, with their bold, subtly-curving bows, their dashing
figure-heads, and their deep red sails, streaked with orange
and painted in richest hues with brilliant devices,—a blazing
Sun, a Sword, an outstretched Hand, a Virgin or a Saint,—
issue forth at sunset and spread out over the Adriatic, like
butterflies, orange-red, hovering over the harvest of the sea.
They differ but little from the smacks of the days of Cassiodorus ; from the boats in which this adventurous, sea-faring
folk visited all the harbours of the gulf, and penetrated with
their wares into the heart of Italy by the secure navigation
of the rivers and canals.   The marriage, which Venice
annually celebrated with the Adriatic, was contracted in her
early infancy.

But most of all at Torcello can we trace and realise the
origin of Venice.   It is not necessary to know the history
of Venice in order to appreciate the beauty of her palaces ;
it is fortunately possible to admire the Adam and Eve on
the corners of the Doge's Palace without ever having read a
word of Ruskin ; and without the glamour of historical
association the waters of her wide lagoons show forth in the
ever-changing lights new beauties, and colours ever more

judgment seat of one of these local island tribunes, ere Venice had risen,
like Aphrodite, from the sea.

refulgent, to those who have eyes to see. But just as the rays of the setting sun, falling on the façade of some admired, familiar Palace, reveal new glories of tone and colour in the water-stained marbles, so in the mellowing light of history, a city beautiful, a city of the soul, such as Venice, shines forth more beautiful. Not long ago the traveller came to Venice imbued with the sweet melancholy of Childe Harolde's passionate lament. He saw in her palaces only the monuments of a vanished greatness, and in her beauty only the symptoms of decay.

Then " the Austrian reigned and an Emperor trampled where an Emperor knelt." Then, as in the Venice which Ruskin described, " her thirteen hundred years of freedom done," " empty halls, thin streets and foreign aspects " flung " a desolate cloud over her lovely walls " (*Childe Harold*). Men looked back with regret and indignation to the glory of her youth, to the great days of Candia and Lepanto, and compared with the Piazza, deserted save by Austrian soldiery, the pageantry and splendour of the Republic, when Venice was " the revel of the earth, the masque of Italy." That is not altogether the atmosphere of modern Venice. The blood of national life pulses once more through her veins. The bustle of the modern revival of industrial activity, born of the Risorgimento, is not indeed here so evident as in Milan, but it has stirred something of her former vigour to life again in the lovely form of the past Mistress of the Sea. This has resulted in uglifications, necessary and unnecessary. The smoke of factories on S. Elena, Murano, in the Giudecca, and of steamers is the price we pay for modern prosperity and modern conveniences,— this and the whistling and disastrous wash caused by the hurrying penny steamboats.   But in the matter of destruction, of building and of re-building, the Venetians seem possessed by an utter recklessness and disregard for loveliness which is hardly credible.

However short one's time in Venice, it is wise to spend one day in a voyage to Torcello, a voyage not in a steamer, but in a gondola.   The life and charm and beauty of Venice are to be found and felt in ever-increasing force upon the broad, bright expanses of water, over which she hovers, poised in the tremulous air, it seems, like some giant white sea-bird, and upon the sea, which pulses through her dark canals as blood flows in a man's veins.   Pictures and churches and palaces—there are enough of these to fill a life-time with study and delight, but learn Venice first, to the sound of the rhythmic cadence of the dipping oar, to the lapping of the water against her walls, and to the music of the gondolier's cry ; learn Venice first in the peaceful, desert-like silence of the lagoon, shimmering through lights of silver and pearl, or in the green paths and purple byeways of her narrow, sun-streaked, shadow-laden *calli*.

The gondola is not only the most beautiful and luxurious of carriages, beautiful in poise and curve, luxurious in the whispered poetry of its gliding motion, but it is also the best conceivable adaptation of a rowing-boat to the environment of narrow canals.   The gondola glides more easily because it does not rest upon an even keel, and for the same reason it offers a securer foothold to the oarsman, steersman and look-out in one, who stands upon the *poppe*.   He, so standing, balanced by its subtle curves, can ply a *single* oar, propelling and steering in the same stroke, as with a canoe-paddle, bringing the whole strength and weight of legs and back and body to bear, and at the same time able to see ahead, and to exchange signals with the approaching, unseen gondolier. *Premi-é, Ah premi!* (press on your oar and omit the backward stroke = turn to the left), or *Stali-é, Ah stali!* (hold the water with your oar on the upward stroke = turn to the right). Rowing a gondola is a fine art, and a most fascinating but arduous exercise. Merely to retain your balance and, by constant pressure of the body through the arms, to keep the oar in the *forcola* is not so easy as it looks ; to take the sharp corners of the narrow canals, especially in a cross wind, without accident to the much-valued *ferri* and important paint, to learn the tides and the pathways of the waters, takes years of practice. A row of gondolas is drawn up ready for hire or for ferry-work at each *traghetto* or ferry station. They are bright with brass and polished iron, but their trappings and *felzi* (cabs) are jet black, in accordance with the sumptuary laws of the seventeenth century, which were rendered necessary by the mania for extravagant display. We start, perhaps, from the Piazzetta, and enter upon that breadth of silver sea, across which the front of the Ducal Palace, flushed with its sanguine veins, looks to the pearl-white dome of S. Maria della Salute, Longhena's masterpiece (1631), reared on a noble flight of steps. Opposite the Ducal Palace the Campanile of San Giorgio Maggiore on its island is reflected in the glittering water, which stretches away, past the Arsenal [1] and the Gardens, to the Lido and the open sea. On the angle, below the *Salute*, the low Dogana, full of character

---

[1] Described by Dante, *Inferno XXI.*, in famous lines that apply entirely to-day to the *squeri*, or dockyards where the gondolas are built and repaired.

and original charm, juts out upon an angle, dividing Venice
from the islands of the Giudecca, where stands Palladio's
Church of the *Redentore*.

This is the gateway to the Grand Canal, the "finest street
in the world," the veritable Golden Book on whose monumental façade the entire Venetian nobility has signed its
name. Every house is a palace, every palace a masterpiece
of colour and design, eloquent, too, of the romances of
family history.

The earliest houses of Venice were built of wood, but
when the treasures of the exhaustless East were poured
into her lap, and she could boast barges and vessels enough
to bring building materials, these were soon exchanged for
walls of brick. It was impossible to bring sufficient solid
stone to use constructionally as at Bergamo or Verona, but
the brick was veneered with Istrian marble and alabaster,
with discs of porphyry and glowing mosaics, or covered from
top to bottom, like the Fondaco dei Tedeschi, with frescoes
by Titian and Giorgione. Few gardens remain of those
that once surrounded the houses of the Venetians, and it is
strange to remember that there was once an orchard in front
of S. Mark's. But the Venetians love flowers ; and they
coax vines to grow over tiny pergolas, just as Londoners
grow flowers in their window-boxes and back-yards. For
as Venice grew, every inch of pile-driven foundation became
valuable. The result is reflected in her architecture. There
was here no room for the shady arcades of Bologna. But
instead, in order to the enjoyment of the evening air and
shade, the beautiful Venetian balconies were added. Lack
of space caused an absence of recesses and a general flatness
in the façades, which was, however, relieved by arcading,

by the steps and doors and halls open to the canal, and by the posts in front of them, of varied colours, to which the Venetians, even in Cassiodorus' day, tied their boats like horses.

" Is it true, Signorino," my gondolier asks, " that in London the horses run in the very street? "

The exigencies of the scarce foundations probably account for the absence of orientation in the Churches of Venice. For the same reason, when, after passing beneath the Rialto bridge (c. 1590), we leave the serpentine Canal and turn into the narrow *calli*, making eastward for the open Lagoon, we find that the houses have sought the sky, forced up like crowded trees, to seek in height the space which was denied to them in breadth. Niggards of every inch of land, the Venetians made their streets only just broad enough to allow passage for a citizen, whilst for traffic and for promenade, in barge or gondola, the water of the canals was and is the highway.

And now we are making our way over the desert of silent water. Across the grey-green or opalescent shallows our tortuous track is marked by huge white stakes, *briccoli*, through fields of black sea-weed, and brown and yellow sand-banks fringed, perhaps, with white by the rushing tide. Here and there, clad in a scanty shirt, fishermen knee-deep in mud search for sand-crabs. It was from flesh so tanned and aglow with sun and sea as theirs, from figures made beautiful by the superb exercise of the oar, as your gondolier's yonder, from the familiar sight of men wading through the lagoon, and the play of water-lights on limbs, that Tintoretto caught his inspiration for that rare treasure of the Ducal Palace, his Bacchus and Ariadne.

Before us rises a succession of low-lying islands, stepping stones, as it were, to the mainland. Often, as we approach them, so soft and luminous is the harmony of water and light, of broad lagoon and distant mountain, these islands seem like dream-lands suspended in the pearly, vaporous air. In the distance is the purple outline of the far, fair Euganean Hills, where Petrarch spent his declining years ; to the north the blue wall and snowy peaks of the Alpine chain girds the whole horizon. We pass first the Campo Santo, San Michele, where in graves beneath the cypresses, brushed by the wing of the sea-gull, washed by the waters of the lagoon, the " poor dead " of this sailor-folk find their good repose.[1] A cloud of smoke from the glass-factory streaks the sky above Murano, Murano whose ancient basilica (tenth and twelfth century) earned Ruskin's eloquent love. Next, on the right, dark green cypresses shade a brown-roofed monastery, upon a tiny island, where, if any-where, the peace and penitence of the " blessed solitude " which an inscription on the cloister invokes, should be found. One solitary stone pine, the most artistically effec-tive tree in the world, save perhaps one in Borrowdale, leans out from the corner of the wall over the waste lagoon. This is the Island of S. Francesco del deserto—the island where S. Francis, returning from the East, stopped by chance, and, when he chanted matins, the little birds sang the responses for him. Francis, rejoicing, stuck his staff into the ground ; it became a tree for their shelter. Part of that tree is enshrined in the cloister garden.

[1] " Buon riposo ai poveri morti." Modern Venetians are a sailor-folk only in a limited sense, however. I remember once when I took my gondolier for a sail upon the Adriatic, his cries of delight at being *for the first time* " sul proprio mare " soon turned to groans.

We glide on past the lessening line of *pali*, disturbed only by the wash of a steamer, which we consign to its proper place,—but that, I am told, would not be navigable,—*troppo secco*. We watch all Nature's doings reflected in the ever-changing mirror of the lagoon, blue haze and purple cloud or silver noon-light, as later, to sound of guitars and Venetian song, we shall watch the stars come out and the moon, and see the deep, infinite blue of the sky repeated in the soft bosom of the water by San Giorgio. A few fishing boats or sandolos with sails drift slowly past us, steered by an oar astern. Or a barge upon which a huge haystack is afloat, carrying a sail painted with some bold and flaming device, approaches.

It is curious how much of local colour there is in the every-day details of life and architecture. A haystack on a barge at Venice is an unforgettable, individual thing, communicating the spirit of the place with as eloquent a charm as an English bee-hive stack on a Surrey farmstead. Not long ago, in the parts about Rimini, you may have noticed the declension of a haystack, built round a central pole, as Mr. Home has drawn it. There is a local note about the little charcoal pots, which were all the means of warmth available on the snow-bound heights of San Marino. North and south and east and west there is a peculiarity in the smell of very town and land ; in almost every detail of architecture there is an individuality of period and place. See, we are passing through Burano, past a low grass stretch and ruined walls on either side of us. A Campanile a-tilt and a lonely cypress end the long low line of white and brown houses. It is an island of fisher-folk and lace-makers. And the local note here is the chimneys, the quaint, bell-

THE DETRITION OF AN ITALIAN HAYSTACK.

mouthed chimneys, as typical of the old Venice we shall learn
to know from the canvasses of Gentile Bellini and Carpaccio,
as are the round chimneys of our Lakeland cottages or the
red-brick stacks of our Tudor houses.

Across a waste of brown sedge and brushwood, amid
sodden fields and dreary flats broken by lifeless inlets, in
solitude and poverty rises the mighty Campanile[1] of
Torcello. Its shadow falls on grass meadows and sea-
marsh ; upon a deserted piazza, a ruined bridge, a Church
(Sta. Fosca), and a Cathedral. It stands, not to awaken
regret, but pointing to the sky in pride and hope. For
Torcello was one of the first stepping stones to Venice,
scene of the first launching of the Imperial province of
Venetia when she put out to sea. Lost among little villages,
that stand out white in the distant shadow of the misty
plain, lie the sites of Heraclea and Altinum.[2] Across the
grey shallows, cut by the blue serpentine channels which
divide us from the mainland, the Roman patricians fled with
their dependants before Attila, Theodoric and Alboin, to the
sand-banks which had long served them as watering-places
and merchant ports ; fled to found this *New Altinum*, and
to cover these grassy meadows with their palaces, their
gardens and churches. They fled, but their flight was
orderly and reasoned. They brought with them the very
stones of their ruined home to build the new. The marbles
of their churches were brought across the lagoon to adorn

[1] Both tower and church have been horribly restored within the last
ten years.

[2] The abandonment of Altinum was not final or complete. Some of the
refugees would return after each invasion. Altinum retained a certain
importance down to the ninth century. (*Molmenti.*)

TORCELLO.

their new Cathedral ; pillars, capitals, pulpits, the Bishop's throne, the marble screen of the choir, the pavement and the font of this island Church followed in the track of the exiles from their mainland temples.

Capitals therefore the most perfect, and mosaics the most striking distinguish this noble Church, which was rebuilt in 1008, and stands forth as witness to the new school of architecture, the result of native national Venetian life impressed upon the Byzantine type and tradition. The Virgin in the apse, in blue mosaic on a gold ground, gazes in stately calm towards the turmoil and terror of the Last Judgment at the east. And this apse, with its ambo and episcopal throne, dates from the seventh century,[1] Sta. Fosca, adjoining, from the ninth. Here, then, on these desolate sands, in a silence broken only by the bells that boom and tinkle from the distant towers of the neighbouring islands, or by the wash of the waves and swishing of the rushes in the winds, survive the tower and churches of the mother of Venice.

The Roman merchant-princes, who fled thus to Torcello and finally concentrated their power, as we have seen, at Venice, brought not only the stones of their deserted cities, but also their social organisation and their trade with them. Untainted by Goth or Lombard, unpolluted by feudal or Teutonic influences, undisturbed by struggles between conquerors and conquered, between Lombard noble and Italian serf, Venice lived on, as her chroniclers boast, the legitimate daughter of Rome, long after Rome had ceased to be pure Roman. The tradition of a great commercial state, ruled,

[1] The Arian persecution had produced a further migration from Altinum and the Bishops then (seventh century) removed their see to Torcello.

in utter contrast to the feudal ideal, by "royal merchants, whose argosies o'ertop the petty traffickers" (the genius of Shakespere seized as ever the salient characteristic), was a direct inheritance from the Roman province whence they came.   These noble merchants of Venice governed her as their patrician forefathers, the Curials of Padua and Aquileia, had governed ten centuries before.   Manin, the last of the Doges (1797), was truly called the last of the Romans.[1] It is this unity of Venetian society, fisherman, salt-maker, vine-grower, gondolier, clinging as clients to the great patrician traders of a Roman province, which makes the history of Venice so different from that of other Italian towns.   It is reflected in her architecture.   There was here no ceaseless struggle between baronage and people, no communal revolt, no rising of race against race to throw off a foreign yoke.   No huge, embattled palaces therefore line her canals, houses of war such as fling their dark shadows over the streets of Florence ; no towers that speak of family feud and almost daily revolution, as at Bologna.   Of all the towers which rose like a branchless forest from her islands, there is none whose office was other than that of guiding her merchantmen, or watching against her foes, or summoning to prayer.   Her palaces are open to the water, houses of united citizens unperturbed by faction, bright with marbles and frescoes, broken with arcades of fretted masonry, and, in place of machicoulis and forked battlements, their

[1] The old Roman life, which became strange even to the Capitol, lingered unaltered, unimpaired, beside the palace of the Duke. The strange ducal cap, the red ducal slippers, the fan of bright feathers borne before the ducal chair, all came unchanged from the ages when they were the distinctions of every great officer of the Imperial State. (Green, *Stray Studies*.)

roof-terraces are wreathed with Arabian imagery of golden globes suspended on the leaves of lilies. And since there was no " popolo," there arose no democratic Broletto ; only Halls [1] of the merchant-guilds decorated with all the wealth of commerce and resources of art, only a Ducal Palace, where the old senatorial houses of the fifth century lived on, ruling and administering the State, only the Cathedral of S. Mark, the treasure-house of the trophies brought home by the city's merchant-fleet.

The immigrants brought with them, then, the embryo of the Venetian patriciate. They brought also the inheritance of Roman trade. The port of Aquileia had long been the emporium of a trade which reached northwards to the Danube and eastwards to Byzantium. The Roman merchants of Venetia simply transferred this trade and the commerce of Padua, Altinum or Concordia, to Grado, Torcello, Rialto.

It was natural that, with this tradition of trade and with her geographical position, the new Republic should at first turn her back on Italy and her face to the East. Byzantium was her nursing mother, and poured into her the milk of her art, her commerce and her customs. That fact also is reflected in the stones of Venice.

When the first business of uniting the islands on which she stood, of draining the marshes and guiding the streams into canal-streets and bridging them with wooden bridges was completed, Venice faced the task of consolidating her power. Under her great Doge, Pietro Orseolo II., she laid

[1] The Scuola di San Marco and the Scuola di San Rocco, "one of the three most precious buildings in the world," which Tintoret decorated with the labours of 18 years, and which Ruskin has described.

the foundation of her supremacy in the Adriatic. The attacks of the Saracens and Normans in Sicily, the raids of Sclav pirates, who swooped down upon their merchantmen from the creeks and bays of the Dalmatian coast, compelled her to form a navy. She crushed the pirates ; the Doge of Venice assumed the title of Duke of Dalmatia (1000), and a ceremony was instituted which was afterwards developed into the famous function of the *Sposalizio del Mar*. Henceforward in every sense Venice is always a city " just putting out to sea " for trade and conquest. She developed her glass factories and metal foundries, her fisheries and salt-pans, and became the emporium of the trade of East and West. Whilst her profitable enterprise in the Holy Wars, and the choice of her as the starting point for the Crusades, were developing her wealth, prestige and her commerce in the Levant, Venice could not hold altogether aloof from the politics of the mainland. She joined the Lombard League, but since a disastrous war with the Emperor of the East had prevented her from taking any share in the battle of Legnano, the capital of the lagoons was chosen as the meeting-place where Frederick Barbarossa and Pope Alexander III. might come to terms (1177). The Emperor crossed the lagoons from Chioggia, and advanced to the front of the Basilica, where, upon a lofty throne, the Pope received him.

" I will tread upon the aspic and the basilisk," said the pontiff, as he placed his foot upon the Emperor's neck, " the lion and the dragon will I trample beneath my feet." " Not to thee but to Peter," protested the Emperor. " Both to me and to Peter," haughtily returned the Pope, while his foot pressed more firmly upon the humbled monarch. So the apocryphal story runs, but it represents at least the fact that Frederick's concessions were humbling the imperial authority beneath the spiritual heel of Alexander. The successful accomplishment of the truce there struck added glory to the State. During the Pope's stay she celebrated the festival of La Sensa, and the pontiff handed to the Doge a consecrated ring, with which to wed the sea. Henceforth this famous ceremony was performed with immense pomp and magnificence ;

"The Doge in his robes of state, together with the Senat in their gounes, embarked in their gloriously painted, carved and gilded Bucentors, inviron'd and follow'd by innumerable gallys, gondolas and boates, filled with spectators, some dressed in masquerade, trumpets, musiq and canons, having rowed a league into the gulph, the Duke at the prow casts a gold ring and cup into the sea (*Evelyn*),

declaring in the words "Desponsamus te, Mare," that Venice and the Sea were forever one, and the Sea held in subjection by her lord. This famous scene may be easily conjured up after a glance at the historical pictures in the Ducal Palace and Accademia, or by the sight of the loyal reception of an honoured visitor to modern Venice, when all the canal is hung with carpets and bunting, and State gondolas, fantastic and gorgeous, are escorted at utmost speed by crowds of laughing and excited spectators.

Under the Dogeship of Enrico Dandolo in the fourth Crusade, Venice became the most important State in Europe. Coldly calculating, she stood Sphinx-like amid the nations, unstirred by any motive of enthusiasm or chivalry, and, guided by her commercial interest alone, she used the fervour of the faithful for the extension of her trade and dominion in the East.

The Lion of S. Mark was planted upon the Imperial towers of Constantinople (1204). It was even debated whether the Venetians should not remove to the capital of the East as a seat more worthy of their achieved and promised greatness. They decided to remain, and set themselves to invest the Republic with her due majesty of splendour, and to transform their thatched, wooden huts into marble palaces, fit to house the wealthiest merchants in Europe, citizens of the commercial capital of the Mediterranean.

Abroad, they devoted themselves at first to the expansion of their maritime empire. This policy involved prolonged and bloody warfare with Genoa in the Levant, which was brought to a close, after many vicissitudes, by the splendid victory of Chioggia (1380). The whole Genoese fleet surrendered, and Venice was left in undisputed maritime supremacy of the Mediterranean. She had obtained the carrying-trade of the world. Already by the beginning of the fourteenth century she could boast of over 3000 ships scattered upon the world's waterways. The spirit of commercial adventure had been stimulated by such explorers as Marco Polo, who, returning from China, Tartary, Japan, the Indies or Labrador, to his old home near the Church of S. Giovanni Crisostomo, laden with precious stones and clad in old Tartar clothes, fired the imagination of the people with tales of the wonderful cities and the millions of treasure he had seen—Messer Marco *Milione*, they called him. So, by 1363, Petrarch could write,

"They carry our wines to England, our honey to the Scythians, our saffron, our oils and our linen to the Syrians, Armenians, Persians, and Arabians; and wonderful to relate, they convey our wood to the

Greeks and Egyptians. From all these countries they bring back
in return articles of merchandize, which they distribute all over
Europe. They go even as far as the Don. They quit their vessels
and travel to trade with India and China, and after passing the
Caucasus and the Ganges, they voyage as far as the Eastern Ocean."

So far Venice has been facing Eastwards, and the influence
of the East is reflected, clear as noonday, in the colour and
style of her architecture, based upon Byzantine models and
wrought by Byzantine workmen ;—in the arcading of the
Byzantine palaces that line the Grand Canal, in the shape
and decoration of the shrine, which was at once the treasure-
house and temple of her commercial glory. S. Mark had
been adopted as the Patron of the Republic early in the
ninth century, when three traders stole the Evangelist's body
and smuggled it to those Rialtine islands, where, 'twas said,
he had once been driven to land. The foundations of a
resting-place fit for so great a Saint were laid, in 829, upon
the site of a basilica founded, according to reliable authority,
by the Eunuch Narses, and dedicated to the ousted patron,
San Teodoro. That is why, erect upon the two huge familiar
granite columns of the Piazzetta, red and grey, spoil of
Syria, the statue of Theodore stands side by side with the
Lion of Mark (1178), to watch over and ward the sea-going
ships.[1] The basilica of 829 was destroyed by a fire during
a revolt of the people against the Doge in 976. The present
building was begun, 1063, by the Doge Domenico Con-
tarini. His successor, Domenico Selvo, began to overlay
the bare brick walls with mosaic and the decoration which it
took two centuries to complete.

[1] Cf. the well-known legend of the ring presented by S. Mark to the
fisherman in a terrible storm which seemed to threaten the very existence
of the city.

The design of the new Church was modelled on the
Church of the Holy Apostles at Constantinople ; the old
basilica type was discarded ; the eastern type of a cruciform
Church, with the later addition of a western narthex and
high leaded cupolas rising above the dome, was adopted.
To this temple of their patron-Saint the merchants of
Venice brought trophies of victory and spoils of war and
commerce from every quarter. Pillars of porphyry and
groups of statuary,[1] Byzantine bas-reliefs, tablets, inscriptions were added to the basilica, already adorned with
Christian and Pagan relics from Aquileia and Altinum,
columns from Rome, friezes from Byzantium.

In sharp contrast with the narrow, irregular alleys and the
network of bridged canals behind it, the Piazza di S. Marco
opens out into a blaze of light and life and colour. What
once it was may be gathered from Gentile Bellini's picture in
the Accademia ; what it can be now may be realised on S.
Mark's day, when, a marvel of gorgeous vestments and
colouring, the procession, issuing from the Duomo, wends
its way round the square. The countless ordered arches of
the Old and New Procuratie (designed sixteenth century by
Buono and Scamozzi) line the sides of the great square, like
soldiers at attention, who guard the approach to the gorgeous
fane of the Queen of the Sea.

The Piazza is trapeze-shaped, but once a glorious Campanile rose to contract it into a harmonious parallelogram
and to bring into proper relation that wonderful group—the
Ducal Palace, the Church, and the blue-dialled, fifteenth
century Clock-Tower. Once, for the mighty watch-tower,

---

[1] Cf. the group near the Porta della Carta in the Ducal Palace, brought
from Acre.

ST MARK'S, VENICE.

which had seen the French Crusaders follow Dandolo when he put to sea, which beheld the bands of Tiepolo routed by Gradenigo, and the Doge, Marino Faliero, beheaded on the Palace stairs by the vigilant, triumphant Ten, fell on July 14, 1902, collapsing on its base in a dense, grey cloud of dust, and destroying Sansovino's lovely Loggietta at its base.[1]

The Church of S. Mark, thus framed and guarded, flashes in the distance across the chequered pavement, " a multitude of pillars and white domes, clustered into a long, low pyramid of coloured light ; a treasure-heap, it seems, partly of gold and partly of opal and mother-of-pearl, hollowed beneath into five great vaulted porches, ceiled with fair mosaic, and beset with sculpture of alabaster " (Ruskin). The façade has three openings on either side of the central porch, which is marked by groups of columns of porphyry and verde antique on both stages. The porches themselves are enriched by cipoline, jasper and pentelic marbles. The grandeur of the central door is increased by three flanges of sculptured ornament " carved and undercut with marvellous patience, composed of a bushy spiral of leaves, foliage, flowers, fruit, buds, angels, saints and monsters." Fantastic animals adorn the bronze panels of the door. A Last Judgment in feeble seventeenth century mosaic crowns the arcade. The story of the discovery and translation of the body of S. Mark from Alexandria is told in seventeenth and (fifth Porch) thirteenth century mosaics in the lunettes of the other four doorways.

Above the central porch, upon the gallery which runs round the Church, are the famous horses of Corinthian brass, green and gilt in the sunshine, reared back on their haunches,

[1] The Campanile is now (1908), after many delays, well-nigh half re-built.

their manes straight and cut like those of the frieze of the
Parthenon, full of life and vigour and action. We look
involuntarily for the vanished triumphal car to which they
must once have been harnessed. They have travelled far.
They are supposed to have adorned in succession the Arch
of Nero and the arch of Trajan, and to have been trans-
ported by Constantine to Constantinople. They were taken
by Napoleon to adorn his triumphal arch in the Place du
Carrousel, and were restored by the Austrians (1815).
Whatever their birthplace, their pedigree is Greek. And
they are part of the spoil brought by Enrico Dandolo from
the hippodrome at Constantinople to the proud Republic
who had harnessed the horses of the sea.

The row of porches form the first storey of the façade.
It is bordered by a balustrade of white marble. The second
storey contains five arches, of which the central, largest one,
is adorned not by mosaic, but by four antique pillars and
glass. The ribs of these arches diminish into the ogival
point, enclosing a semicircular tympanum. They are
separated by late fifteenth century Gothic pinnacles and
turrets. Superb, nude, life-size figures of slaves are placed
in the curve of the arcades. On their shoulders they bear
amphoras, depressed for emptying. These amphoras are
hollowed so as to serve as rain-spouts, and the slaves themselves are gargoyles. From the ogival point of the big
central window, on a dark-blue background gemmed with
stars, a gilded lion of S. Mark, with a halo and outstretched
wing, and a claw upon the opened Gospel, looks out over
the sea, watchful and terrible. And above, a statue of the
Evangelist, erect on the gable-end, receives the homage of
the neighbouring Saints.

THE PIAZZETTA, VENICE.

The lateral façade, facing the Piazzetta, is covered with
bas-reliefs. Here, as in the main portal, occur those
symbolical subjects with which we grow familiar—birds,
griffins, animals in pursuit of their prey, children half-
devoured by dragons, men hunting, boys fighting. Notable
are two pairs of armed figures clasping each other ; Greek
Emperors, or Crusaders in porphyry, or Harmodius and
Aristogeiton,. as the varying explanations have it. The
short column of porphyry with a white marble capital is the
old edict stone, where the laws and notices of the Republic
were proclaimed to the people. Here, as on the western
façade, are medallions, marbles of every hue, monsters,
saints, malachite, enamel, mosaic, bas-reliefs of peacocks
spreading their tails, brought perhaps from some temple of
Juno, rich foliage cut acanthus-wise, capitals of richest
design, all the wealth of the world in material, colour and
fancy brought together to adorn this temple of the Venetian
Saint. And on the north side, guarded by crouching lions of
red marble, the same mixture of designs, of rich materials,
of Christianity and of Pagan myths is repeated.

Ceres, a lighted pine-torch in each hand, in a chariot
drawn by dragons, searches for her lost child, side by side
with an early bas-relief of Abraham's sacrifice, Pagan and
Christian art and myth intermixing in a manner characteristic
of the Venetian spirit even of to-day, which confuses the
old lore and the names of the old gods with the simple,
priest-led piety of fisher folk.

There was not, as there is not, anything austere in the
Venetian temperament. Architecture, to satisfy this people
living under new conditions, must have something more
than the perfect proportions of old types. It must express

the joy and fulness, the wealth and wonder and colour of
their new life, and contain within itself features drawn from
all quarters of the earth, the harvest of the east and north
and south which their argosies gathered. Heirs of all the
ages, Pagan colossi of Mars and Neptune find a place in
their temple among the Saints or Adam and Eve ; Ceres,
Abraham and Bacchus are equally admitted to the sacred
throng ; the Virgin heeds not the neighbourhood of the
Venus she has supplanted. Gothic mingles with Byzantine,
and is transformed into the new Venetian type.

From the glare and heat and brilliancy of the Piazza, we
pass through the narthex into the dim, cool depths of a
golden sea. The domes, the walls, even to the angles of
the arches, are covered with gold and richly-tinted mosaic.
It is a sea of colour, sea-green, sea-blue and gold, obliterating
with its soft-swelling waves all the lines of moulding, as it
does all care for the details of the structure. There is
nothing tawdry or garish here, nought but a soft harmony
of colour and curve. Fane of the Queen of the Adriatic,
the very pavement of this typical example of an eastern
Church borne over the seas, symbolises, in its wave-like
undulations, like that of Sta. Sophia, the stormy waters of
life and the familiar, harvested sea, which washes the very
walls of the houses of the Venetians.

The interior of S. Mark's is the second volume of a vast
illuminated Bible. Exquisite thirteenth century mosaics in
the atrium without have prepared the catechumen by their
simple story of the Old Testament ; now, within the mystic
building, the story of the birth and passion and glory of
Christ is told. The sombre domes, encrusted with those
brilliant cubes of gilded crystal made at Murano, form a

background for this story, for black-winged angels, for trees
that typify the Garden of Olives or the genealogy of the
Virgin, whose fruits are Kings and Saints, for Paradise with
the legions of the Blessed, for all those who by prophecy,
preaching or martyrdom have borne witness to Jesus.
" Everywhere near the picture is the text ; the inscriptions
rise and fall or run about in the form of legends in Greek,
Latin, Leonine verses, versicles, sentences, names, mono-
grams, specimens of the calligraphy of all countries and all
times ; everywhere the old black letter traces its script on
the page of gold in between the jambs of the mosaic "
(Gautier). And in the central Dome Christ appears in
Glory, surrounded by a vast circle of heads and wings
disposed in circles, glittering, palpitating, quivering, alive
with flame and colour, and the exaltation of worship and
delight.

S. Mark's is an epitome of Venetian art. Just as in the
mosaics, the stiff Byzantine forms pass to the Giottesque
spirit of the Baptistery figures and thence to the designs of
Titian, Pordenone and Tintoretto, so, on the façade, the
Gothic arch with its wealth of ornament rises above the
Byzantine narthex, and the bold fourteenth century sculpture
of the Dalle Mansegne rises beside the Renaissance altars
of the Lombardi and the bronze work of Sansovino.

And now Venice turned her face towards Italy, and, under
the stimulating guidance of Francesco Foscari, thanks to the
military genius of great mercenary generals like Colleoni [1]
and Gattamelata, established a mainland empire. Her

[1] The great Condottiere (*see* Bergamo) bequeathed (1475) a large
portion of his wealth to Venice on condition that his statue should be
erected on horseback in the Piazza di S. Marco. The law forbade the

dominion included Bergamo and Brescia, and, at its greatest, was bounded by the Alps, the Adda, the Po and the sea. That her rule as a mainland power was mild and beneficent is shown by the fact that the towns to which, during the war of the League of Cambrai, she had rendered their liberty, voluntarily returned to her allegiance. Expansion on the mainland was a political necessity ; hers was not merely a campaign of greed. Venice, afloat on the lagoons, could not afford to have her ports and supplies controlled by a hostile power. But expansion and aggression are like the reverse sides of a hollow cone. Venice had long been the envy, she now became the common dread of the Italian powers. Her aggressive policy towards Milan and Ferrara seemed to indicate that she aimed at the subjugation of all Italy north of the Apennines. The League of Cambrai was formed (1508).

Pope and Emperor, France and Spain, Ferrara and Mantua joined hands in an attempt to reduce the Venetians to the position of " humble fishermen," and to divide her territories among themselves. Julius II. declared that he meant to cut the claws of the Lion of S. Mark. A French

placing of a monument upon the square of S. Mark. By an ingenious quibble the Piazza in front of the Scuola di S. Marco (Campo di S. Zanipolo) was allotted by the Senate for the statue which Andrea Verrocchio, pupil of Donatello, and tutor of Leonardo da Vinci, was commissioned to execute. The example of the Gattamelata statue at Padua (q.v.) inspired the conception of Andrea's model : he died before it was completed ; then the vigorous genius of Alessandro Leopardi breathed into the monument all the life and strength and energy, all the grandeur and all the fire, which had marked the mighty General it commemorates. It was he who designed and executed also the beautiful pedestal of this triumph of Renaissance sculpture, and who cast the bronze bases for the red standards of S. Mark in the Piazza.

army crossed the frontier, and Papal troops invaded Romagna. The Venetians were completely defeated on the plains of Ghiar' Adda. " In one day," says Macchiavelli, " the Venetians lost all they had acquired with so much labour in 800 years." This was true, for though she made a heroic, and, for a while, successful effort to hide her exhaustion, her vital energy was sapped by that struggle, and by her prolonged wars in the Levant, where she was, throughout the fifteenth and sixteenth centuries, compelled to fight for her life with the new, aggressive power of the Turks. But more disastrous to her prosperity, perhaps, was a victory of peace. " This is the worst piece of news that we could ever have had," a Venetian merchant noted in his diary, when he heard of Vasco da Gama's voyage in 1497. The discovery of a new sea route between the Indies and the north struck an overwhelming blow to the Venetian carrying trade and to Venice as an emporium betwixt East and West.

For two whole years, along with the other industries of Venice, the Press of Aldus was paralysed by the forces of the League of Cambrai. In 1462 Adolph of Nassau had pillaged Maintz and dispersed its printers over Europe. In 1466 John of Spires established himself at Venice, and before the close of the century nearly 3000 books had been issued by the Venetian presses. Among them were the first editions of the great Greek authors, for Aldo Pio Mannucci, " Roman and Philhellene," had chosen Venice as most conveniently placed for obtaining Greek compositors and for distributing his completed works, and there in a house near S. Agostino had cast his Greek type and set up his press. Strikes and war and the insecurity of copyright, difficulties of obtaining authentic editions, these and a thousand other obstacles were met and overcome. With incredible enthusiasm and by unremitting toil, this noble artist accomplished his design. In beautiful type, adapted from the handwriting of Petrarch and cut by Francesco— perhaps Francia—of Bologna, the Aldine Library of Greek, Latin and Italian Literature was printed and published to the world at prices astonishingly moderate.

Nor did Aldo neglect the moderns. He published Erasmus. The establishment of his press at Venice marks, then, not only an epoch in the history of learning but in the history of the world.

Throughout all this period there was, at Venice, a unity of purpose and a uniformity of development wholly unlike that of the faction-riven Lombard cities. The years from 697 to 1229 witnessed the slow, orderly progression from a Republic, dominated by a Doge, the Judge and General, who ruled in concert with a representative Council, to a close Aristocracy. This was partly the result of the traditional organisation I have sketched, partly the outcome of a wise dread lest the dogeship should become a hereditary despotism. First the election of the Doge was transferred from the people to the Grand Council, then his judicial powers were put into commission in the form of a Senate, the Quarantia. Next all questions of peace and war and supplies were assigned to the Senate of the Pregadi, interposed between the Doge and the Grand Council. Both these Senates were elected by the latter, in which the practical sovereignty was thus centred. So, according to the old, happy simile, the constitution of Venice was a pyramid resting upon the basis of the Consiglio Grande, and rising through the Senate and the College to the ornamental apex of a Doge.

By the crisis of 1297-1319 the Grand Council was restricted to a few noble families. A close hereditary oligarchy was established. The finishing touch was given to this development when the famous Council of Ten was instituted (1311), whose supervision of all magistracies soon enabled them to control all the foreign and domestic affairs of Venice. The object for which this arbitrary and terrible authority was created was the suppression of such conspirators as Tiepolo, and the institution of a permanent, centralised body to direct the policy of Venice. That it was successful is proved by the acquiescence in its rule. " The Venetian bowed in silence and obeyed, knowing that all his actions were watched, that his government had long arms in foreign lands, and that to arouse revolt in a body of burghers so thoroughly controlled by common interests would be impossible " (Symonds). For among the inhabitants of the lagoons, from the lowest fisherman, who earned then as now a scrannel existence by catching crabs in the mud-banks at low tide, to the most powerful noble, whose rich argosies were abroad on every sea, there was a unity of purpose and interest. All alike were merchants of Venice. There were no idle nobles, and to the labours of the great this free and prosperous people felt that they owed their prosperity and freedom. They were ready therefore to fight under them the naval battles of the Republic and to obey the decrees of the tyrannous Council of Ten, as the engine of an oligarchy which did after all derive its sanction from the people.

The Doge's Palace, that wonderful sea-borne palace of the ancient mistress of the sea, enshrines the very spirit of the Venetian Republic, proud and orderly and free, developed through ages almost undisturbed by interference of the Church and intrigues of despots, the mausoleum of her historic memories, the temple of her noblest art. For when the fear of faction and of foreign invasion was over-past, a building with loggias and porticoes, undefended, open to the land and sea, arose upon the site of the old feudal palace (811-1172), with its flanking towers and crenulated walls. The building is of three stories, which rise in bold geometrical progression, the upper being nearly equal to the two lower in height. It is to be remembered that the gradual raising of the pavement, now many inches above the old base of the columns, has altered the proportions and adds to the top-heavy effect.

In vivid contrast to the richness of the lower stages is the plain unbroken wall above ; but whereas the sculpture and mouldings below are of purest white, the wall-surface of this upper portion, added later for the sake of the Great Council Hall, is chequered with a delicate diaper of marble, a coating of pale rose, which affords the supreme example of the application of colour to a public building. A large window and balcony in the centre take the place of the windows of the original design. The massive colonnades and loggias of the lower half date from the fourteenth and fifteenth century and are pure Venetian Gothic. The exquisite tracery of the magnificent upper arcade, *La Loggia*, the simple, pointed arches, the superbly carved (and wonder-fully restored) capitals of foliage, and the figures of the open, lower arcade have been elaborately analysed and rendered famous by Ruskin. Plain moral lessons, the stories of Noah and Tobit, of the Fall, of the Judgment of Solomon, are

S. MARIA DELLA SALUTE, VENICE.

inculcated by the groups at the exposed angles, and in the lower range of capitals the Virtues and Vices, fruits and animals, the Labours of the Months, trades, sciences, arts— *quicquid agunt homines,* all the medley of human life, are represented with a richness of invention and a skilfulness of craftsmanship unsurpassed in Europe.

The Doge's Palace represents the orderly development of the Republic. Out of the dark recesses of the Rio del Palazzo, spanned by the Bridge of Sighs (c. 1600), rises the third side of the building, an ornate Renaissance façade by Antonio Riccio (late fifteenth century). Riccio's Adam and Eve face Sansovino's colossal Mars and Neptune at the top of the Scala dei Giganti within the splendid inner Court (1464-1554).

The pride, the luxury, the mundane splendour of Venice in the sixteenth century are reflected in the mirror of the art of Jacopo Sansovino, who was summoned by the Doge, Andrea Gritti, to adorn the proud Republic with products of his skill in architecture and in sculpture. He built the Zecca, the Library, the Scala d'Oro of the Ducal Palace. With the receptivity of genius he absorbed the atmosphere of voluptuous pomp and conscious pride which were the keynotes of the Corinth of that age, and with a superb, full-blooded rhetoric he eloquently expounded in marble and in bronze the neo-pagan sensuality of the time.[1]

At the top of Sansovino's stair Tintoretto's S. Mark greets us, " hurtling through the air like ancient Saturn, with two superb women, Force and Justice, and a Doge who receives from them the sword of leadership and war-

---

[1] In the bronze door of the sacristy of S. Mark he introduced life-like portraits of himself, of Titian, and of Pietro Aretino.

fare." Within, all the walls and ceilings of the offices of State,—the spacious chambers where the Senate assembled, where Ambassadors approached the Doge, where the Savi deliberated, where the Council of Ten conducted their inquisition,—designed by Palladio, Aspetti, Scamozzi, Sansovino, are hung with the pictures of Tintoretto and Veronese, of Titian and Pordenone, of Palma the younger and Bonifacio, encased in framework of carved oak and overlaid with burnished gold. All the genius of the city laboured to perpetuate in this Valhalla the heroes of the Venetian State, Doge and Generals, sailors and merchants, who won the victories, here recorded, and accumulated the treasure and splendour of the city, of which this is the apotheosis.

That is the meaning of these endless sea-fights, these ships with curved prows like swans' necks, locked in the death-grip, galleys with banks of oars, broken and confused in deadly turmoil, battlements hurling forth showers of arrows ; this tumultuous strife of combatants, wrestling in wild fury of battle, crushing an assailant or remorselessly flung into the raging sea ; these crowds of Illyrians, Saracens and Greeks, their bodies bronzed by exposure and lacerated by the conflict.   It is the painted story of Venetian greatness.

That one idea is the keynote of all this treasury of art ;— the apotheosis of the splendour and the might of Venice, of the vigour and patriotism of her sons, over which Venezia herself, the type of Venetian beauty and Venetian glory, presides, the Renaissance goddess, the Venetian Pallas of the painters.   For the Triumph of Venice by Veronese is the epitome of it all.

I have scarcely told one half of the story of Venice, nor, in this case, is the half greater than the whole. The details of the palaces and churches, the analysis of such treasure-houses as S. Trovaso, of S. Giovanni e Paolo, and the Frari, the Mausoleums of the Republic, where in the Doges' tombs the pure Gothic form flowers in all its loveliness ; of S. Giorgio degli Schiavoni, the little shrine of the Slavonian sailors, which Carpaccio made perfect ; of S. Sebastiano, which Veronese made glorious with his immense and daring canvasses ; of Palladio's buildings, S. Giorgio Maggiore, the plague-church Il Redentore ; and S. Francesco della Vigna ; of Sanmicheli's masterpieces in the classical style ; of the Arsenal and that gem of Venetian Renaissance, the Church of the Miracoli ; of Santa Maria Formosa, with its memory of the Brides of Venice, ravished by the Pirates; of the decadent buildings of the baroque age, whereof Alessandro Vittoria was the genius ; the Scuola di San Rocco, the Scuola di San Marco ; of the charm and the fables of the islands, such as S. Nicolo and S. George of the Seaweed ; of San Erasmo, of Fusina, I must leave untold. These the traveller will visit at leisure and in turn with Ruskin's eloquent "Venetian Index" or Mr. Okey's reliable guide in his hand.

He will visit, too, an he be wise, the Accademia, and, his imagination fired by the pictures there, will recreate for himself the vision of the Venetian war-galleys beating out to sea, and of argosies unlading at the quays the treasures of the East ; of the splendour and the joyousness and the simple faith of the people of the canals ; of the proud and stately merchant-nobles and the gay, laughter-loving Bassanos, gaily clad, who paced the piazza or made merry at marvellous banquets ; of the music, and the blond hair of the Venetian Courtesans,[1] which the painters loved; of the many-hued and stately processions from the sea to the Palace of the Duke, from San Marco to the sea. He will trace here and in the Churches the development of the Venetian School of painting from the time when the Umbrian masters, Gentile da Fabriano and Pisanello, were employed to decorate the Ducal Palace (1419), and, influenced by them, Antonio Vivarini arose, founder of the school of Murano, and master of Jacopo Bellini, who studied also at Padua. Jacopo called the elder of his two great sons Gentile after his beloved master. Under the influence of Gentile and Giovanni Bellini, tenderest of Venetian painters, Vittore Carpaccio was trained. Cima da Conegliano, with his backgrounds of blue mountains and romantic architecture, brings to Venetian colouring a breath from the mainland, whither the Republic was now turning her eyes. With the advent of Giorgione (Gipsy and Soldier, Giovanelli Palace ; Miracle of S. Mark (?), *Accademia*) a new epoch opens, which culminated in the work of Titian, Palma Vecchio, Tintoret and Paolo Veronese. Tintoret's Miracle of S. Mark sets the seal on the beauty of Venetian painting. He and his younger contemporary, Veronese, are the lyrical poets of neo-paganism, giving expression with superb triumphant mastery of

[1] The repetition of this type in Venetian art was the result of the Oriental semi-seclusion in which women were kept. Those who were seen in public were of the class whose existence depended chiefly upon the cultivated loveliness of their physical charms. And, since this tint of hair was so highly prized, every device known to modern hairdressers was used to bleach, dye, "sophisticate," tint, treat, and curl it with tongs.

THE ISLAND OF SAN GIORGIO, VENICE.

technique to the neo-pagan delight in sensuous joys, in voluptuous women and mighty men, in the physical delights of light and shade and colour, singing like skylarks of the gladness of sea and air and the pomp and beauty of this Venice that hovers over the waters, trembling with life and movement, and sparkling in the brilliancy of change and light and colour. Carpaccio, Titian, Tintoretto, Veronese express the material magnificence, the colour, the splendour, the full, free, sensuous, gorgeous life of the proud and prosperous Republic. It is, indeed, characteristic of all Venetian painters that they are wholly concerned with the objective world as a thing of beauty, simple and real, to be repeated and represented, selected from and improved, but not moralised over or commented upon. Living in the heart of a city whose life-blood throbbed so steadily and fully through song-laden, palace-lined canals, to piazzas bright with the most gorgeous and varied costumes of East and West, in the midst of lagoons which entranced the eye each hour with a new vision of changing delight, existence passed before them like the scenes of a pageant, and all their concern was to arrest and reproduce their so vivid impression of these kaleidoscopic, sensuous joys.

They have their devotion, but it is simple and joyous, without a trace of mysticism or gloom. The new spirit of the Renaissance inspired them, too, to humanize the altar-pieces and cloister-frescoes upon which they toiled. Titian's Madonna Assunta is not so much the Mother of God as the radiant type of motherhood. Tintoret's Apostles are Venetian peasants. But the chief motive of the Venetian painters is light in the wonderful Venetian life around them—the architecture of their lovely home, the bright costumes, and beautiful people—the strong men, graceful, musical children, and fair-haired women, the glory of the lagoons.

Carpaccio and Gentile Bellini, when called upon to decorate the Halls of the merchant companies, could think of nothing more exquisite than the representation of the daily life of the great Republic that was visible without.

The whole spirit and all the physical charm of bygone Venice is embalmed in the canvasses of these painters. But it is not till we have learnt Venice on the lagoons, and seen, across the opalescent waters, the snowy Alps, tinged to amethyst by the setting sun, not till we have seen the sky "roofed with clouds of rich emblazonry," and earth and sky "dissolve into one lake of liquid fire," as Shelley saw it when he rode with Byron on the Lido, that we can fully understand how Titian was inspired to paint the rich masses of red and blue and the faces flushed with sunlight, which arrest us in his *Assumption*, or how the quays of Venice, ablaze with the naval pomp of the world, how her palaces of porphyry and frescoed walls reflected in the moving waters, and how the flesh of her people, ruddy and glowing and russet-brown with the soft sea-wind and the sun, stirred her colourists to their splendid raptures in paint. The greatest of colourists sprang from a city of colour, and from the soft tones and diffused lights, born of the mingling of sky and water, they learned that art of rendering an atmosphere luminous and suffused with colour, which distinguishes them from the painters of the mainland.

CHAPTER XVII.

VICENZA.

I KNOW no pleasure in life like that of returning to Venice, and no pain of its kind like to that of leaving it. But at least on this voyage we leave it for Verona. And on our way Vicenza lies at the northern base of the Monti Berici, astride the Bacchiglione. It is crowned by a coronet of low wooded hills ; masses of dark foliaged trees show against white palaces and red-roofed villas. Beyond a brown distance of plains rise the Alps, tumbled like lumps of sugar in a basin. We enter the city by the Porta del Castello, the old tower with its bold, brick machicoulis, covered by a square battlement under a flat roof.

This is the city of Palladio, and in the palaces of this, his native town, more even than at Venice, the greatness of the Renaissance architect is revealed (1518-80). I confess that it was not till I had seen the Palazzo Giulio Porto ; the Basilica Palladiana, with its two stories of colonnades surrounding the Gothic Palazzo della Ragione ; the Museo Civico, and the Teatro Olimpico at Vicenza that I realised at all fully how great an artist was this architect, and how sadly his reputation has suffered through imitations of the Palladian style.

Leo Battista Alberti once complained that a slight alteration of the curves in his design for S. Francesco at Rimini would make a discord in his music. The perfect balance and proportion of the parts, attained by geometrical accuracy and expressed with simple lucidity, was the ideal, the pattern laid up in Heaven, after which the architects of the best Renaissance period strove. The melody of lines and the harmony of parts was the music of their marble symphonies. This ideal, the poetry of proportion, the organic connection of the members and the chaste simplicity of the whole, was here achieved by Palladio. His imitators have reproduced again and again the features of a classical building, according to the precepts of Vitruvius, but have lacked the artist's sense of beauty and style. They have overcrowded their Doric and Ionic columns, overlaid their pediments and façades with ornamentation, and yet dubbed their buildings Palladian. The curse of the imitator, in literature as in art, is that he reproduces a detail or a trick of style and mistakes it for the essential. The imitators of S. Mark's at Padua produced S. Antonio, just as our modern London builders with their mania for cupolas, minarets and domes—forms totally unsuitable to our climate—have crowded Whitehall with a number of feeble, ineffective curves of domes, through lack of the imagination needed to perceive what would be the appearance of these curves when erected and viewed from below.

Returning for a moment to the Palazzo della Ragione, with its enormous hall arched by a huge timber roof, and its Gothic front cased by Palladio with open arcades, it is worth observing that the Hall was burnt in 1389, and the walls of the upper portion, with marble in diaper, recall the Ducal Palace at Venice. The slender brick campanile and

BASILICA PALLADIANA FROM PONTE LUCIA, VICENZA.

the two Venetian columns—emblems of the town's subjection to Venice, 1404—group with the Palazzo into a charming picture.

From Vicenza to Verona the train runs at the foot of the mountains, through a fertile plain, dotted with hills, clad with luxurious vegetation and crowned with mediaeval fortresses. Here Bacchus rides triumphant on the vineladen trees, and the white wine of Soave vies with the red vintage of Val Policella. We pass the ruined castles of Montecchio, of Bonifacio and of Soave, the magnificent feudal stronghold of the Scaligers, on the banks of the Adige, before we come to the chief scene and monument of their greatness.

CHAPTER XVIII.

VERONA.

VERONA is and always has been a place of the utmost strategic importance. It commands the outlet of the narrow defile, the *Chiuse*, which is the key of the Brenner pass. That pass is the lowest and easiest of all the Alpine roads, and affords easy communication with the valley of the Inn and the upper waters of the Danube. And, to the east, the pass of the Pear Tree leads to the lower valley of that mighty river, where the barbarian hosts were ever gathering. Standing at the meeting-place of great highways, the Via Gallica, the Via Postumia, and other roads running north and south and east and west, Verona is the gate through which the Goths always entered Italy, and through which " the current of northern life enters still into its heart through the mountain artery, as constantly and strongly as the cold waves of the Adige itself." This Roman Colony became the natural halting-place of the Teutonic immigrant tribes, who abandoned the cold, dark forests of their German bogs to bask in the golden sunshine of Italy. It was afterwards made by the German sovereigns the capital of the Mark of Verona, for the defence of the frontier.

There are some *Roman* columns in the Baptistery, San Giovanni in Fonte, and the remains of a Roman Theatre, recently uncovered, are interesting enough. The huge walls built by Theodoric, in triple courses of brick and stone, crowned now by the walls and forked battlements of San-micheli, have eclipsed the fortifications of the Emperor Gallienus. But there are at Verona two Roman monuments of great interest. The vast amphitheatre, which was included within Gallienus' walls, is a building of the familiar oblong shape, so vast that over 20,000 people could easily be seated in it, so skilfully arranged that it could be emptied in a few minutes, built of great blocks of stone and Roman mortar, on such a Titanic scale that it stands, terrible in its vastness and desolation, ready at a moment's notice for a display as of yore, whether the gladiatorial fights and water-shows under Trajan, the burning of Christians under Diocletian, the jousts and tournaments under the Scaligers, or the bull-fights under Napoleon. It was here that SS. Fermo and Rustico were placed upon a pyre to be burnt alive—*taeda lucebis in illa*—but were saved by rain, which extinguished the flames. They had little reason, however, to be grateful for this miraculous respite. Their escape was held to prove that they were magicians, and they were immediately dragged away to the banks of the Adige and beheaded. The Church of S. Fermo contains their relics.

There is a bridge outside Bologna which when first I saw there came into my mind the first line of that rollicking poem of Catullus, in which, good Veronese, he pleasantly satirises the municipal pride of a rival town ;—

"O Colonia quæ cupis ponte ludere longo,"—

and refers to the games upon the town-bridge which long formed a part of municipal delights (*see* Pavia). Com-mentators do not seem to be certain whether Bologna was the Colony referred to. Perhaps it was Verona itself. In the Ponte della Pietra there survives a noble example of the Roman Bridge. It spans the " yellow waves of the rushing Adige," which almost encircles the city, which has brought inundation and disaster countless times upon her, and, as the commercial highway from the north for goods and timber, has brought prosperity also to Verona, *la degna* (the worthy). Since the last terrible flood of 1882 a vast and expensive embankment has been built to curb the unruly river, which has had the inevitable effect of spoiling for the artist the once picturesque banks, and has made Verona look like Paris. But the old Roman bridge has withstood the floods, and still recalls the sound of Catullus' verse. The main part of the city lies upon the right bank. Upon the left bank the ground rises rapidly ; the city walls and towers and serrated battlements boldly climb the irregular outline of the hills, and upon the ruins of the Palace of Theodoric (*see* Ravenna) rises a modern barrack.

At Verona died Alboin, King of the Longobards, whilst still in the first flush of his victories (572). In a drunken orgie he seized a bowl made of the skull of Cunimund, King of the Gepidae, whom he had slain with his own hand, and whose daughter, Rosamund, he had married, and invited his Queen to " take a draught in her father's company." In revenge she invited Peredeus, a man of great strength and daring, to murder him. Peredeus shrank from the task, till Rosamund approached him in the guise of a waiting maid with whom he had an intrigue, then, revealing herself, threatened to inform the King of their meeting unless he accomplished the murder. One afternoon, when the drunken monarch was sleeping off the effects of his mid-day potations, Rosamund tied up the sword that hung at the head of his couch. She then admitted Peredeus, who with difficulty slew the defenceless monarch.

In the days of Communal freedom Verona did her utmost for the Lombard League and to check the ambition of Frederick Barbarossa. When the Emperor was returning from Rome (1154), the Veronese would not admit the Imperial forces within their walls. They constructed a bridge of boats, by which the army crossed the Adige. But scarcely had the soldiers gained the opposite bank, when enormous pieces of timber, swept down by the current, destroyed the bridge. Frederick never doubted that this was a snare laid for him by the Lombards, and marched home ravaging and spoiling through the Milanese territory. Several buildings date from the years that immediately followed the peace of Legnano ; the Palazzo della Ragione (1185), the Casa dei Mercanti and that glorious tower, the Torre Civica, which records that it was the work of the Commune " free, prosperous and victorious," rise from the Piazza dell' Erbe, the ancient forum, one of the most picturesque market squares in Italy, in the centre of which stands the ancient Seat of Judgment.[1] And the basilica of S. Zeno was finished in 1178.

The magnificent brick Ponte di Castel-Vecchio, with its characteristic parapet and forked battlements, spans the broad and rushing Adige on the western verge of the city. The vast main arch is not in the centre ; the remaining two, descending rapidly to the north bank, give a strange, down-hill appearance to the bridge. The main arch is connected

[1] A marble column marks the satisfaction of the people with the rule of Venice.

PONTE CASTEL VECCHIO OR DEGLI SCALIGERI, VERONA.

with that grand yet simple pile, the Castello Vecchio, with its towers and lofty walls and forked battlements, which Can Grande II. built in the fourteenth century.

Beyond it, far from the bustle of the town, stands San Zenone Maggiore, the noble church which, in its splendid proportions and perfect detail, represents the highest achievement of Lombard twelfth century work.

"There is a breadth and simplicity about it," says Street, "and an expression of such deep thought in the arrangement of materials and in the delicate sculpture, which with a sparing hand is introduced, that one cannot sufficiently admire the men who planned and executed it."

The pious and learned S. Zeno, eighth Bishop of Verona, died in the year 380. The Church which does him honour is one of the finest and most characteristic of Lombard Churches. The building is of red brick, broken by courses of rich-coloured stone, but the façade is a glorious composition of red and white marble and stone of the warmest yellow. Verona marble is no new thing to those who have made the pilgrimage of this book, but there is ever something marvellous and strange in its many-coloured depth. For the *mandorlato* of Verona, besides the almond-blossom tints from which it takes its name, boasts many another tone and modulation of colour, passing from pink and creamy yellow to orange red. And this marble, which harmonises so happily with the rose-tints of terra-cotta, which the Lombard builders elsewhere used sparingly as a jewel, reserving it for slender shafts and noble sarcophagi and the couchant lions of their porches, is at Verona used as freely as brick or stone, for her balconies and doorway arches, her

writhed pillars and the façades of her churches, and for her
" sombre, old, colonnaded aisles."

In front of the doorway detached shafts, resting on
monsters, support a low canopy. The sculpture on the
façade, " the expression of the introduction of Christianity
into barbaric " minds, is by Nicolaus and Guglielmus, whose
work we have seen at Modena and Ferrara. Here, in rude,
sincere fashion, on the lintel and upon the very early bronze
plates of the door, the labours of the months and the story
of the Old and New Testament are illustrated.

" Everywhere we detect the undecided spirit of the
twelfth century, the relics of Roman tradition and the
blossoming of fresh discoveries ; the grace of an architecture
preserved and the gropings of sculpture in its beginning."

In the right hand corner occurs the legend of Theodoric
as the wild huntsman riding headlong in chase of the stag,
which leads him to the gates of hell (see Ravenna). From
this western entrance a flight of steps leads down to the floor
of the nave. From the top of them, the vision of timber-
roofing and the lofty, simple walls of the nave, and of the
mysterious crypt, which appears through three open arches,
supported beneath the raised choir by delicate red marble
columns with characteristic capitals, tender and grotesque,
is one of singular and impressive charm, which dwells in the
memory forever. The sculptures are chiefly in Lombard
jesting mood, tame compared with those of S. Michele, yet
full of riotous imagination and the joy of good hunting.
Outside, the cloister, with its small brick arches and coupled
shafts of red marble, is lovely, and the stately Campanile is
magnificent. Near S. Zeno is the monastery Church of San
Bernardino, with the exquisite Renaissance *Cappella Pelle-*

grini, an almost perfect example of pure classical work by the great Veronese architect, Sanmicheli. It is not far from the Porta Palio, one of the most noble gateways built by that mighty genius. The shell of the Duomo, its beautiful, canopied porch, and the cloisters are very similar to those of San Zeno. Among the reliefs behind the columns and griffins of the portal are statues of Roland and Oliver, the paladins of Charlemagne, executed also, according to the inscription, by Nicolaus (1135). The Assumption of Titian, bronze crucifix by Gian Battista da Verona, and the superb Renaissance marble screen by Sanmicheli are the chief treasures within.

The Cathedral occupies the site of a Roman temple [of Minerva?], traces of which, especially a mosaic pavement, are to be seen. The Baptistery—probably on the site of a Roman Bath—contains a delightful twelfth century Lombard font.

"A plague on both your houses!" Shakespere, choosing an episode in the feuds of Montecchi and Cappalletti (Montague and Capulet), has made the family factions of Verona and the other Communes part of the common knowledge of mankind.[1] The Montecchi were Ghibellines, the Cappalletti supporters of the Guelf Counts of San Bonifazio. The former, driven out, appealed for aid to the man whose name lives as the typical monster of despotic cruelty, "the cruellest and most redoubtable tyrant that ever existed among Christians" (*Villani*). We cannot here trace the steps by which Ezzelino da Romano (*see* Padua), starting as a feudal lord of the Mark, with his stronghold at Bassano, by

[1] The tombs shewn as those of Romeo and Juliet are good examples of the economic law of tourist demand and local supply.

treachery and cunning, by perseverance and force, warring with the Counts of San Bonifazio, whose stronghold was at Soave, warring with this town and that, warring for Frederick with the Lombard League, made his hold upon Verona at last secure. In the midst of the bloodshed and strife through which he was endeavouring to make good his position as arbiter of the Mark and Lord of Verona and Vicenza, an extraordinary incident occurred. Fra Giovanni of Vicenza, a Dominican monk, like Peter Martyr, that prophet of persecution under whose direction the stakes were lit in Milan, began to preach, in Italy feud and faction-torn, a gospel of union and reconciliation. From Bologna, where his eloquence had moved not only multitudes, but even hereditary noble rivals to abandon their enmities, where he had been chosen as a law-giver to revise the statutes of the city, he passed in triumphal procession to Padua. The Carroccio of the city went forth to meet him, and the standard which had led the burghers to many a bloody battle, floating upon it, heralded the arrival of the prophet of peace. Thus he passed from city to city, everywhere, even at Romano, the nest of the savage Ezzelino, joining in good-will hands that had been stained in fierce fraternal conflict. The towns clamoured for his help in revising their constitutions. At length he felt the moment had come when he might extend to the relations of the cities the healing balm which he had poured upon their internal feuds.

On the plain of Paquara near Verona he summoned the burghers of the towns to meet him. Over a quarter of a million people, representatives of the leading cities of Lombardy, attended this national assembly on the banks of the

Adige, and listened to the eloquent sermon of the inspired monk whilst he exhorted them to enter into a solemn covenant of Lombard union. " My peace I give unto you." His success was little short of miraculous. Unfortunately, it unbalanced him. He demanded titles for himself, the lordship of Vicenza, the supreme authority in Verona. Every demand was readily granted to the new-found Saviour of Society, who after altering the statutes of the towns, himself condemned sixty Veronese citizens to the stake as heretics. The Paduans revolted against his tyranny, and an appeal to arms put an end to his prestige for ever. The peace produced by the emotion of this sermon lasted little more than a week. Finally, after incredible struggles and vicissitudes, Ezzelino made himself master of Verona.

After the death of that " Son of the Devil," Ezzelino, the Veronese, in order to protect themselves from the Counts of San Bonifazio, chose Mastino della Scala for Podestà. Under the rule of the Scaligers Verona entered upon the era of her greatest prosperity. Mastino was murdered in 1277. His brother Alberto was chosen Captain of the People to succeed him. Under his almost absolute, but wise and merciful rule, the town flourished and grew. His eldest son, Bartolommeo, welcomed Dante, the exiled Florentine, to the Court, and has his reward in the lines,

> " Lo primo tuo rifugio e il primo ostello
> Sarà la cortesia del gran Lombardo,
> Che in sulla scala porta il santo uccello." [1]

> —*Par.* xvii. 76 ff.

[1] Thine earliest refuge and inn shall be the courtesy of the great Lombard, who on the ladder bears the holy bird.

Bartolommeo was succeeded by his brother Alboino, who associated with him in the government his more famous brother, Francesco, that chivalrous and heroic knight, wise ruler, too, and skilled diplomatist, the noblest of Italian despots, Can Grande della Scala. In him were centred all the hopes of those who wished to see the Imperial cause triumphant in a united Italy. The "Dog of Verona," Dante prophesied (*Inf.*, i. 85 ff.), should be lord of all "the land 'twixt either Feltro," and his rule bring widespread good to Italy.

With astonishing vigour and success, Cane, born under the influence of Mars, began to fulfil the prophecy of Dante's vision. One after the other the towns of Alta Italia fell before his conquering sword. Brescia, Vicenza, Padua, Cremona, Parma, Reggio, Mantua and Treviso owned his might. "He fortified Verona against the Germans ; dug the great moat out of its rocks, and built its walls and towers" (Ruskin). Rich and powerful, tall and graceful, gifted with the art of fair speech and a noble courtesy, the young warrior was hailed by his contemporaries as the ideal Prince. He died before he could fulfil the hopes which had been placed in him. Can Grande was the first of the Italian despots to patronise art and letters. The splendour of his Court equalled the splendour of his achievements in the field. All eminent men of the day found a welcome here ; deposed despots and exiled Ghibellines rubbed elbows with banished poets and wandering artists. "Each guest had his separate apartment separately served, and decorated in harmony with his fortune, with symbols of Triumph for a warrior, of Hope for an exile, of the Muses for a poet, of Mercury for an artist, of Paradise for a preacher." And, to cheer them, the walls of the Scaliger Palace rang with the song and laughter of jesters, jugglers, fools and musicians. Hither came Giotto to do "some pictures for Messer Cane" (*Vasari*), and the school of Veronese painting sprang up under the influence of that Master and in the sunshine of such royal patronage. This School by a regular succession of painters passes from Altichiero, Jacopo d'Avanzi, and Pisanello, leading to Francesco Morone and Liberale da Verona and his pupils. Hither, too, came Dante to pass some of the few years that remained to him ere he won his way to his last home at Ravenna. Here, like the Aeneas of his "master and guide," he felt the bitterness of exile, "how hard it is to climb another's stair, how bitter to eat another's bread." Here, as he wandered among the ruins of the vast Arena, the structure of his *Inferno* was suggested to him, so Benvenuto says, though perhaps the grand circle of the mountains, with their giant towers and titanic walls of rock, the range of the Trentino and the Primiero Dolomites that bound the northern horizon of Verona, might rather be the source of the imagery of the poet's dream. Here gossips would point to his grave face and firm-set lips and solemn gait, and would whisper that his "beard was crisped and his hair darkened by the heat and smoke of the Hell which he had visited." And, in more holiday mood, he looked upon those

> "Who o'er Verona's champain try their speed
> For the green mantle."—*Inf.* xv. 124.

in the famous annual race for the *pallium*,[1] run on the first Sunday in Lent, in which the competitors were stark naked,

[1] Cf. the Palio at Siena, the Pallone of Bologna, the Regatta at Venice.

and therefore "for reasons of modesty a high standard of speed was demanded by all who should take part therein." The foot-race and the chariot-race are no longer, but *sunt quos curriculo*,—the dust of the motor-car and the motor-bicycle clouds the race-course now.

The Piazza dei Signori teems with memories and buildings of the Scaligers—the Palazzo della Ragione with its lovely external staircase, the old Palace built by Mastino I., the beautiful Renaissance "Loggia di Fra Giocondo," erected by the Venetian Government in 1497, and, behind it all, that lofty, simple, almost unbroken piece of brickwork, culminating in the light, strong shafts and heavy balconies of the belfry-windows, the unforgettable campanile of the Palazzo dei Signori.

But the supreme monument of the Scaligers exists in the wonderful series of Tombs in the tiny burial ground of Sta. Maria Antica adjoining this Piazza, which was the centre of their life. Within a beautiful and intricate iron grille, which shows the *ladder*, the badge of the Scala family, beneath a confused mass of pinnacle and shaft, a crowd of saintly and warlike figures watch and wait. Tyrants and warriors, murderers and exiles, heroes, fratricides, they all sleep here at length the last long sleep.

The monument of the greatest of them, Can Grande I. (1335), "the consummate form of the Gothic tomb," forms the portal of the Church. Upon a simple sarcophagus, sculptured with shallow bas-reliefs, showing the chief incidents of the hero's life, and forming a groundwork for fully relieved statues representing the Annunciation, the Lord of Verona lies in civic robes. But above, upon the lofty canopy supported by four pillars, the mail-clad warrior is seated upon a noble war-horse, made, it must be remembered, before Verrochio and Donatello had formed the model of equestrian statues.

The knight's helmet, dragon-winged and crested with the dog's head, is "tossed back behind his shoulders, and the broad and blazoned drapery floating back from his horse's breast,—so truly drawn by the old workman from the life, that it seems to wave in the wind, and the knight's spear to shake, and his marble horse to be evermore quickening its pace, and starting into heavier and hastier charge, as the silver clouds float past behind it in the sky" (*Ruskin*).

Next in date, as perhaps in merit, stands, at the corner of the cemetery, the striking tomb of Mastino II. Here, too, on a sarcophagus, beneath the outspread wings of guardian angels, is a recumbent figure ; and above, the Captain of the People, sword in hand, rides on his war-horse. The sculpture of the figures, as of the delicate, decorative foliage, is very fine.

"Horse and horseman ride with their faces towards the setting sun, as all in life must ever ride ; the effigy below lying so that, at the last day, the beams of the daystar in the East may first meet its view and awaken him that sleepeth here in peace" (*Street*).

The tomb of Can Signorio (d. 1375), executed during his life-time by Bonino da Campione, is more sumptuous and more florid, but very beautiful. It betrays the more elaborate method of the Renaissance, and less directness of design. Here again the device of a recumbent and an equestrian statue is repeated. A crowd of figures, warrior Saints and Virtues, rise amid flowering marble into a pyramid like a bouquet in a vase ; while the sky shines through the infinite interstices of the scaffolding.

It is natural, and wise, to pass from the Tombs of the Scaligers to the Church of Sta. Anastasia, outside which, upon a red marble sarcophagus beneath a canopy formed by a simple Gothic arch, richly-cusped, lies the recumbent effigy of Can Grande's friend and councillor, Guglielmo da Castelbarco. It is the most perfect monument of a city which boasts the most perfect monuments in Italy, a thing so convincingly beautiful in its simplicity and purity of style and tenderness of feeling, that it is only necessary to repeat Ruskin's words concerning it, " pure and lovely, my most beloved through all the length and breadth of Italy—chief, as I think, among all the sepulchral monuments of a land of mourning."

Nor is this perfect tomb the only beautiful thing here. The Dominican Church itself (1260-90), which owed much to the generosity of Guglielmo da Castelbarco, is, albeit unfinished, a most perfect specimen of the red-brick pointed style in Verona. With its rich brick cornices and heavy, pinnacled buttresses and portal of marble, red and white and grey, it forms an exquisite harmony of delicately-tinted stone and of terra-cotta ornament and moulding. From porch to pavement, from fresco to columned aisle it presents a rich and delicate scheme of colour, in which mason, painter and pavement-worker have subordinated and combined their arts to the production of a perfect whole. And this effect is heightened by the simplicity and space procured by the short-ness of the Choir, the open bays and general ground-plan of an Italian Gothic Church.

I have to leave unmentioned many of the treasures of art and architecture, including the works of Sanmicheli, which may be seen in almost every street by those " who trudge about through fair Verona." How to bid farewell to this city of marble and stately campanili, this home of rich palaces and lovely balconies, through whose pierced traceries many a fair Juliet has whispered to her Romeo? There is a garden, the garden of the Palazzo Giusti, on the hill-side across the river, the higher level of which is reached by an avenue of ancient cypresses bordered by fair flowers. Hence, through the city, out of which the towers and churches rise up into the serene sky, far above the turmoil of the crowd below, the eye follows the winding Adige past the Palace of Theodoric, under the battlements of the Scaligers' mighty bridge, till it straightens out into a silver arrow and points through the green vineyards to the hills of red marble above the waters of Garda. Southwards, in the very heart of the blue Lombardic plain, bounded by the distant Apennines, gleam the domes and the white lakes of Mantua ; eastwards lies Padua, beneath the " many-folded " Euganean hills ; and beyond, Venice rests upon the bosom of the sea. To the north-east, " touched into a crown of strange rubies as the sun descends, there is the snowy cluster of the Alps of Friuli."

" You have thus beneath you at once, the birthplaces of Virgil and of Livy : the homes of Dante and Petrarch ;[1] and the source of the most sweet and pathetic inspiration of your own Shakespeare; the spot where the civilization of the Gothic kingdoms was founded on the throne of Theodoric, and where whatever was strongest in the Italian race redeemed itself into life by its league against Barbarossa. You have the cradle of natural science and medicine in the schools of Padua ; the central light of Italian chivalry in the power of the Scaligers; the chief stain of Italian cruelty in that of Ezzelin ; and, lastly, the birthplace of the highest art ; for among these hills, or by this very Adige bank, were born Mantegna, Titian, Correggio, and Veronese." (*Ruskin*).

[1] " They keep his dust in Arqua, where he died."—*Byron*.

VERONA FROM THE GIARDINI GIUSTI.

LAGO DI GARDA.

But there is yet another Veronese, " Mantua Vergilio gaudet, Verona Catullo." Catullus, " tenderest of the Roman poets, nineteen hundred years ago," lives here, but most of all his passionate presence is felt upon the waters of the Lake he loved and upon his " almost-island, olive-silvery Sirmio."

The extraordinary charm of the pure Italian scenery of the Lago di Garda is not to be discovered in one summer's day ; it must be learnt, as Catullus learned it, by weeks of peaceful yachting, watching the deep blue of its waters and their ever-changing hues of silver, green and azure, fishing in its clear blue depths, and passing from the broad, low basin of the southern extremity at Peschiera into the narrowing strip banked by the majestic cliffs and screens at the northern head. Lacus Benacus, the Romans called it, and, like Como, it is quickly stirred from smiling peace and azure haze into the white-foamed waves of a dangerous sea beneath the lash of sudden squalls that rush down from the gullies in the mountains on the north-eastern and north-western shores. - " Fluctibus et fremitu assurgens, Benace, marino," as Vergil says. Take a boat from Peschiera,

> " Phaselus ille, quem videtis, hospites,
> Ait fuisse navium celerrimus."

It is just such a skiff as Catullus describes. When you ask the boatman where the timber for his boat and oars comes from, you know the answer beforehand. He points to the pine-woods yonder, beyond Riva, in the Austrian Tyrol. . . .

> " Ubi iste antea fuit Comata silva."

As the clouds pass over the Lake and the water deepens from a foot to a thousand feet, the colour changes from green to grey, from ultramarine to azure-blue. At length, after ten kilometres made with sail and oar, we reach the little promontory of Sirmione. A fringe of golden rushes leads the eye up to a mass of olive-trees and bays. Our skiff runs under the drawbridge and portcullis of the mighty

SIRMIONE, CASTLE OF THE SCALIGERS.

Castle which the Scaligers built upon the point, with its heavy machicolation and swallow-tail battlements. The discovery of sulphur-springs upon this sweet and haunted spot has led to an outbreak of hotels, which somewhat mar the atmosphere of it. But in these days, in order to enjoy anything, it is necessary to shut our eyes to the ugly and keep them open to the beautiful. Regrets are vain, save where we can use our influence to prevent or undo uglification. It is better to imagine and appreciate than to yield

ourselves to mad Ruskinian rage.   Otherwise we could not
see Venice for the Germans or England for motor-dust.
After all, it is on the lake rather than at Sirmione, or amid
the ruins of Catullus' villa there, that we are most aware of
the love and hatred of Catullus.   The little volume of
his immortal verse, so simple, vehement and polished, the
direct utterance of the personal passion he felt so intensely
and expressed with all the vigour and scholarship of a Swin-
burne, scholarship not impeding the lyrical stream, passion
finding vent in verse illuminated by scholarship, sounds upon
these azure waters with a ring as true, with a music as
lovely, as when first he praised his yacht, or buried his
mistress' sparrow, thanked Cicero for a speech, lampooned
Caesar and his friends, or said *Ave atque vale* to his lost
brother.

CHAPTER XIX.

MANTUA.

From the lakeland villa and the birthplace of Catullus one passes naturally to the home of Vergil. *Mantua me genuit*—the remembered phrase drew me to the town, as to the birthplace of the "landscape-lover, lord of language," the supreme artist and colourman in words. It was not a false instinct. From the moment the train began to descend the slopes of the Italian Alps, lines and phrases, read in the *Georgics* many a time, and hitherto perhaps but half-realised, descriptions of vineyards and agricultural implements, of times and seasons, of crops and stock, of the works and days of the Roman farmer, have haunted my memory. I have recognised with delight the plough which the poet described, and seen through many a mile the vine wedded to the elm as he directed. And now we are in the fields "whence Vergil drew his immortal honey." True, the old Etruscan town, the city of the Gonzaghi and of Giulio Romano, has no more of Vergil than of Etruscan to offer us. It is, indeed, as fascinating as it is unhealthy.[1]

The waters of the Mincio, spread out into three shallow lakes, lie about the city, and make a malarial marsh of the

[1] Or was. The recent draining of the lakes and marshes will prove an enormous boon, except to the artist.

surrounding land. Mantua is a city with a moat of lakes ;
the battlements and towers of her walls and Castello are
reflected in still, miasmic waters. But it is not in the *Piazza
Virgiliana*, buzzing with merry-go-rounds, nor in memorial
statues that we find ourselves in contact with the poet's
mind.

A CAPITAL OF THE ARCADING OF A STREET IN MANTUA.

Mantua me genuit—Mantua was my birthplace—so runs
the famous epitaph ; but it was about the poet's tomb at
Naples that legend busied itself. Vergil seems never to
have made any long stay at Mantua, and the place is barren
of tradition concerning him, though in the Middle Ages
several places in the neighbourhood bore the poet's name,
and were pointed to as having been frequented by him, his
villa on the Mincio, the wood, and the cave two miles from
Mantua, where he would retire to meditate. And it is

amongst these woods and water-meadows that we may best commune with the poet's soul. For the charm of a local note always sounds through Vergil's most exotic cadences; with him, the poet and the observer always illuminate the scholar. Mantuan scenery colours even his Sicilian eclogues. Here, the "wielder of the mightiest measure ever moulded by the lips of man" would sometimes coin his golden phrases, licking his verses into shape, so he said, as a she-bear licks her cubs, till "all the charm of all the Muses flowered in a lonely word."

Here, in part, we may fancy, the artistic perfection of the *Georgics* was achieved, born of study and experience acquired from Mantuan agriculture, and directed to the glorification of labour, the virtue of the Roman race, which his patron had desired him to preach, since Augustus, with the piercing gaze of his profound statesmanship, had perceived that virtue to be necessary for the maintenance of the Empire. It is here, we may fancy, that, escaping from the applause of the Emperor and his admiring Court, the poet composed and polished part of that great national epic, which is both the introduction to and the noblest criticism of the history of Imperial Rome. The *Aeneid* is the mirror of the ideals of the Augustan age, as *Paradise Lost* reflects Puritan England, and the *Divine Comedy* mediaeval Catholicism. Vergil is the Tennyson of ancient Rome, as Aeneas was its Arthur. But Aeneas is ever "the master of his fate, the captain of his soul." He is the personification of the grandeur of Rome's destinies. Patriotism was the religion of ancient Rome, as, apart from personal passion, it was the only motive of Roman poetry. And Vergil, born in these Mantuan fields, far from Courts and Kings, to be the prophet of Roman duty and the poet of Roman Imperialism, glows with this intense religious flame of patriotism.

Foreseeing clearly, as Augustus foresaw, that the decline and fall of the Empire would proceed from greed, passion, and self-indulgence, he embodied in his hero the national ideal of the manhood of duty, of self-sacrifice and of self-control. More than this. He perceived that a new era had dawned ; that the establishment of the Empire was a step which might lead to the regeneration of which the world stood in need. And, writing in Messianic language, he hymned the birth of an expected child, hailing in him, the boy Scribonia never bore, the coming of a national hero and ruler, divinely inspired, who should deliver and redeem not only Italy, but the whole world, from the darkness and wickedness which characterised the age. *Tu Marcellus eris.* Such was the spirit of the Mantuan poet, whom Dante chose, " My master thou and guide," to lead him through the regions of Hell and Purgatory to the gates of Paradise.

It is recorded that Carlo Malatesta, Regent in the fifteenth century, flung into the Mincio with iconoclastic zeal a statue of Vergil, which once adorned the Piazza di S. Pietro, because the people paid him the homage due only to a Saint.

The Christians, indeed, had long regarded this pure and lofty spirit with compassion, as worthy to have been a Christian, as one whose only fault was his pagan spirit. The same motive which led the monks to adapt the shrines of pagan deities to the fanes of Christian Saints, prompted them, when the study of the great Latin authors could no longer be burked, to enlist in the battle against barbarism

the pagan poets whom they had hitherto regarded as deadly
foes. Ovid was bowdlerised, and sugared with unexpected
morality ; Vergil was credited with allegorical significance.
The beauty of his style, it was insinuated, almost entitled
him to be regarded as a Christian. Pity for so pious a soul,
who had just missed the salvation offered by Christ, was
inculcated. The tradition that S. Paul visited his tomb at
Naples was invented. The verses of the Mass of S. Paul
which used to be sung at Mantua, and the *Image du Monde*
describe S. Paul's grief when he found that Vergil, who
had so clearly foretold the birth of Christ, was dead, and
that he was too late to convert him, " *Ah! si ge t'éusse
trouvé, Que ge t'éusse à Dieu donné!* "

The expectation of an immediate regeneration of the
world in an era of happiness, justice, love and peace, which
inspires the poem we have referred to, the connection of this
expectation with the birth of a child, and the ancient
authority of the Sibyl on which the whole prophecy is based,
were declared to constitute unmistakeably a Messianic prophecy. Vergil, with the Sibyl, was hailed as a prophet of
Christ. They were admitted, in sacred art and mysteries,
into the company of David and Isaiah. And in the pictures
of Vasari at Rimini, of Raphael at Rome, the student will
find the Roman poet transfigured into a Christian prophet.

Thus, when the pall of the Dark Ages had settled down,
and the light of all the stars of Literature had gone out,
the dim, borrowed glory of Vergil as a semi-Christian
personality had survived, and diffused a strange, mystic
light. He passed, in popular imagination, from poet to
philosopher, from philosopher to prophet, from prophet to
magician. For he had been almost deified by the Romans ;

his tomb at Naples had come to be regarded as a Temple. His poetry formed the staple of education in the schools of the grammarians. Then, in an age when miracles and marvels formed the basis of nearly all literature and thought, legends began to gather round his name. He grew into a wonder-worker in popular tradition : the old tales of other wizards were re-made and fathered upon him, till Vergil, the Augustan poet, stood forth, reincarnated as the benevolent magician and sorcerer, and, wrapped in the mysterious mantle of a wizard, waited on the extreme verge of the Dark Ages to lead Dante, as the type of human reason, through the realms of Hell and Purgatory. " Pretty, i' the Mantuan ! "

The Via Sagliari leads to the heart of Mantua, the Piazza dell' Erbe. Arcades with a wonderful variety of capitals culminate in a corner house of very rich terra-cotta work and pillars. From this point the busy scene of the fruit-market reveals itself beneath the Clock Tower and the, much altered, thirteenth century Palazzo della Ragione. The communal existence of Mantua, of which this is a monument, has no remarkable features. That it was sufficiently occupied with fighting its neighbours is indicated by the chroniclers, who enumerate five wars with Verona within a very short space of time. One of these wars is memorable for the recorded snipping off of 3000 noses from captured combatants by the victorious Mantuans. The development of the city awaited the ascendency of the Gon-zaga dynasty. First the rising democracy committed political suicide by deputing the Buonacolsi to govern them (1270), after the Guelf aristocracy had been destroyed in a period of the most violent faction fights. Then, in 1308,

Lodovico Gonzaga defeated the clever and unscrupulous Buonacolsi, and ruled as Imperial Vicar. Under this dynasty of wise and beneficial rulers, who, besides keeping the love of their subjects, maintained, by their hereditary valour and skilful diplomacy, the liberty of the city against the encroaching power of Milan and Venice, serving first one, then the other of the rival States, Mantua increased rapidly in prosperity. The Gonzaghi were genuine lovers of art and literature, though they had fewer pennies to spend upon the patronage of artists than many other despots. Gian Francesco I., the fourth Gonzaga, employed Bartolino da Novara, architect of the Castello Rosso at Ferrara, to build the strong Castello di Corte, with four massive machicolated flanking towers, commanding the Ponte di San Giorgio, the entrance to the city across the lakes formed by the waters of the Mincio. This bridge he rebuilt, and the Lombard-Gothic Duomo, which in after years Giulio Romano transformed into a late Renaissance building, also owed much to his patronage.

Gian Francesco Gonzaga II. (1407-44) brought the Humanist, Vittorino da Feltre, one of the most wise and admirable of schoolmasters, to educate his sons, Lodovico and Carlo. And here in a house, so wisely ordered that it was held to be a " sanctuary of manners, deeds, and words," Vittorino trained in body, mind and morals many of the noblest and most honourable of the Italian youths of his day. This Gonzaga did much to encourage agriculture, by draining the marshes—an end towards which so much has been done of late years—and by establishing the manufacture of cloth, the staple industry of Mantua till the sack of 1630. Lodovico was responsible for the great era of art in Mantua,

Torre dell' Orologio in the Piazza dell' Erbe at Mantua.

for he invited Andrea Mantegna to his Court (1459), and the great painter, who was treated with the utmost kindness and generosity, worked here for fifty years in the service of the Gonzaga family. He commemorated the entry of Lodovico's son into Mantua as Cardinal-Legate, illustrating that splendid spectacle and portraying all the members of the House in noble frescoes—now sadly ruined—in the Camera degli Sposi, the Marquis' nuptial chamber in the Castello. It was on this occasion that Poliziano composed in three days his famous drama, *Orfeo*.

It was to the Castello di Corte that, with pageantry and music, with song and feasting, with tournament and carnival, Francesco Gonzaga welcomed the wedding party who, in a richly-carved Bucentaur, had escorted up the Po from Ferrara his bride, Isabella d'Este, so beautiful with her rippling golden hair, " *una donna piu bella assai che 'l sole*," so wise and accomplished that her kinsman, Niccolo da Correggio, the valiant knight, the polished courtier, the gifted poet of the Court of Ferrara, dubbed her " *la prima donna del mondo*."

Francesco Gonzaga, by his restless activity, his military ardour and clever diplomacy, raised Mantua to the front rank of the smaller Italian States. He was appointed Captain General of the League, which was to have cut off the French King's retreat. After the wretched victory of Fornovo, he was hailed as a second Scipio. Of his own valour there was no question, nor of his disappointment— " If others had fought as we did," he wrote to his wife, " not a single Frenchman would have escaped." In a deserted byeway at Milan, the Via San Simone, stands the little shrine of Our Lady of Victory, to commemorate this

" famous victory," and here the altarpiece painted for the occasion by Mantegna, now in the *Louvre*, was hung. The site of the shrine and the cost of the altarpiece were the penalty exacted from a Jew, who had removed a statue of Our Lady from the wall in this street. Later, when the Venetians, after their defeat by the League of Cambrai, surprised and made prisoner the Marquis of Mantua,—a feat which caused the choleric Pope, when he heard of it, to fling his cap upon the ground and curse S. Peter—Isabella took up the reins of government at Mantua. And she it was who, by her diplomacy, saved the city from the clutches of Cesare Borgia, of Louis XII. and of Francis I.

The delicate perfume of the presence of that most gentle and accomplished Lady still hangs about the beautiful suites of rooms in the Castello and in the vast Ducal Palace, begun by the Buonacolsi and completed by the Gonzaghi, which all her life long she was busy adorning with consummate works of art.

She filled her apartments with editions of the classics from Aldo's press, with gems and rare brocades, with viols and lutes of exquisite workmanship, and commissioned Bellini, Perugino, Mantegna, Francia to paint for her pictures of allegorical subjects, sketched out by her own poetic invention. Here, in her famous studio of the Grotta, here, in the suite known as Il Paradiso, looking across the flashing waters of the lake to Vergil's birthplace and the green meadows through which the Mincio flows to join the Po, here, whilst Columbus was discovering the New World, the Gonzaga princesses sang Petrarch and Vergil to the lute. To the classical beauty of Mantegna's allegorical " Triumphs," this admirable patroness added the softly-rounded forms of Correggio's treatment of similar themes, the brilliant colours of Lorenzo Costa's palette, and the quaint forms of Dosso Dossi's echo of the old Romance, contrasting with the grand manner of Titian's gloomy portraits and brilliant Saints, with the same exquisite landscapes bounded by the far blue peaks of Cadore.

Isabella, after the fashion of the times, amused herself with the jests and tricks of Court dwarfs and clowns ; the suite of low rooms and passages which she built in the Castello for these pigmies can still be seen. The fortune of war and the barbarity of soldiers have dealt hardly with the collections of this perfect flower of Italian womanhood in the time of the Renaissance. Her treasures were dispersed when the German soldiers sacked Mantua for three whole days in 1630. They were bought partly by King Charles I. and partly by Richelieu, and are now scattered through the Museums of Europe. The tombs and monuments of the Gonzaghi in S. Francesco were rifled by the French after the siege in 1797. But amongst ruined frescoes and damaged decorations there survives the lovely marble doorway and medallions which Cristoforo Romano carved for Isabella's studio.[1]

Mantegna, the much-prized painter of the Mantuan Court, was buried in S. Andrea, in a chapel decorated at his own expense. Over the grave was placed a bronze bust, which is a masterpiece of nervous character drawing. It was under the patronage of Lodovico Francesco that Leo Battista Alberti came to Mantua and designed the chapel of the Incoronata in the Duomo, and the Churches of S.

[1] I cannot too strongly recommend to the reader Mrs. Henry Ady's two delightful studies of the Renaissance—Isabella and Beatrice d'Este.

Sebastian and S. Andrea (1472). The latter church, aisleless and barrel-vaulted, one of the earliest and best examples
of the style of the classical revival, was founded to receive
the Sacred Blood, said to have been brought to Mantua by
the Centurion Longinus. The building is the masterpiece

ηΑΝ ΒΟΝΙΗΟRΗΤ ΌΑ·ΔΟΗΔΗΟRΒ3Ο · ΒRΑΜ·ΚΑR·QVΑSΤΑ·
ΟΡΑ · δΒV·ΑΗΟ 1444

A CAPITAL OF A HOUSE IN MANTUA.
The inscription is carved on one of the beams supported by the pillars.

of him who remodelled S. Francesco at Rimini. It is in the
form of a Latin Cross, with a dome at the intersection.
(The present dome is eighteenth century.) The façade is
a skilful adaptation of the idea of a Roman triumphal arch.
But even more than Alberti, Giulio Romano has made
Mantua his own. It was at the request of the Marquis

Federico Gonzaga that Castiglione brought this pupil of Raphael to this city, and for the Marquis Giulio designed (1525) the Palazzo del Té (so-called apparently from the T shape of the building) on the marshy ground outside the Porta Pusterla.

"This most noble of Italian pleasure-houses remains to show what the imagination of a poet-artist could recover from the splendour of old Rome and adapt to the use of his own age. The vaults of the Thermæ of Titus, with their cameos of stucco and frescoed arabesques, are here repeated on a scale and with an exuberance of invention that surpass the model. Open loggie yield fair prospect over what were once trim gardens; spacious halls adorned with frescoes in the vehement and gorgeous style of the Roman school form a fit theatre for the grand parade-life of an Italian prince. The whole is Pagan in its pride and sensuality, its prodigality of strength and insolence of freedom. Having seen this palace, we do not wonder that the fame of Giulio flew across the Alps and lived upon the lips of Shakespeare; for in his master-work at Mantua he collected, as it were, and epitomised in one building all that enthralled the fancy of the Northern nations when they thought of Italy."[1]

Isabella Boschetti, the beloved mistress of Federico, reigns as Psyche supreme among the goddesses on the ceiling painted by Messer Giulio within the sumptuous walls of the Palazzo. It was for her that Federico built the noble palace della Giustizia, also decorated by Giulio, whose own house confronts it.

[1] J. A. Symonds, *Renaissance in Italy*.

CHAPTER XX.

CREMONA.

As Vergil to Mantua, so violins entice one to Cremona. The site of Stradivari's house in the Piazza Roma alone rewards a wasted pilgrimage. The Cathedral, almost entirely built in by adjoining houses, is, as a whole, strangely ugly. Two immense transepts, added later, dwarf and hide the original nave, aisles and semi-circular apses. But the Torrazzo, the red-brick Campanile, which rises in a simple, unbroken succession of stages all but 400 feet into the blue sky, is magnificent. It is of this tower that the Cremonese, justly proud, boast

> " Unus Petrus est in Roma,
> Una Turris in Cremona."

It is connected with the Duomo by a series of loggie. The west end of the Cathedral, which has the usual porch resting on lions, is screened by an open arcading. The interior, which suffers from recent crude restoration and gilding, rejoices in a pulpit decorated with bas-reliefs by Amadeo (1482), which he designed for a tomb of the martyrs S. Mario and S. Marta, as well as the frescoes by Bellinesque Boccacino, chief of the Cremona school of painting. I shall always remember it chiefly as the first Church in Italy where I saw this welcome notice conspicuously hung :—*Per rispetto alla casa di Dio, e per l'igiene, si prega di non sputare sul pavimento.*

Cremona, like Piacenza, was a fortress founded by the Romans to check the raids of the Gauls. It was destroyed and restored by Vespasian, and, after suffering much at the hands of Goths and Lombards, reappears in the twelfth century, extraordinarily bellicose even for a Lombard Commune, and gradually supplanting Pavia as the second city of Lombardy, second only to Milan in power and pugnacity. As the chief supporter of Frederick, 1213, Milan, Piacenza and other communes invaded her territory and at Castel Leone surrounded her forces. But, fighting with the courage of despair, the Cremonese won a complete victory, and captured the Carroccio of Milan and 4000 prisoners.

With other Guelf Communes Cremona revolted from Henry of Luxemburg. He wreaked a prompt and terrible vengeance. Three hundred nobles and chief citizens, who had been sent, barefooted and with ropes round their necks to implore pardon for their indiscretion, were thrown into prison to die. The city was fined and sacked; the walls and towers were destroyed and the moat filled up. From this time Cremona sinks into insignificance, passing eventually into the possession of the Visconti and Sforza.

Opposite the Torrazzo is the thirteenth century Palazzo Publico, with its fine Renaissance portal. Here, as in the cloisters of the Certosa, the courts of the Ospedale Maggiore at Milan, and on the façade of the Duomo at Crema, is revealed in its most lavish splendour the Lombard treatment of moulded clay as ornament. Here again we find the richest fancy in device, acanthus leaf and tendril of the vine framing and veiling laughing Cupids and gladsome, dancing angels, whose hair streams in the wind and whose mouths are filled with song.

Cremona was the scene of the meeting of Dominic and Francis, when some Franciscans brought muddy water from their new well, and besought the two patriarchs to make it clear. There, so the story runs, Dominic said to S. Francis " Father, bless this water in the name of the Lord." But Francis replied, " Nay, father, for thou art greater than I." Then Dominic made the sign of the cross over the water, and lo! the waters of the well were purified.

CHAPTER XXI.

BRESCIA.

BRIXIA, "the beloved mother of my Verona," *Veronae mater amata meae*, as Catullus calls the gallant little town, lies at the foot of loftier Alps, between Lago di Garda and Lago d'Iseo, amongst smooth, rounded, turf-clad slopes that remind one, in their texture and anatomy, of the sheep-cropped rolling Border fells. The city nestles in a hollow between two main eminences, on one of which is the Castello. It is a town of curving streets and unexpected arches, with peeps of the fells opening up beyond. Brixia and Verona were the chief towns of the canton of the Cenomani, whence the streams of Celtic invaders washed away the Etruscan settlers in Northern Italy (c. 400 B.C.). Thanks to its manufactory of iron ware and weapons, to which it owed its prosperity in the Middle Ages and owes its prosperity now, it became a flourishing Roman Colony. An interesting relic of the days of Vespasian (52 A.D.) is preserved in the site of the *Museo Civico*. Passing through a plain and most unpromising exterior, we find ourselves in the very presence of the Roman gods. The fragments of an ancient Corinthian Temple of Hercules are strewn about the entrance, and broken columns that rest upon a massive substructure. Within are several altars, whereat mankind used to worship.

Here are many Roman " remains," stored and catalogued, but chief among them is the bronze, over-life-size figure of the Victory who used to grace the Roman arms. It is a very precious antique ; but from it we learn how poor, life-less, and imitative a thing was Roman plastic art. For it is false and imitative from head to toe ; the pose is false and stupid ; the fall of the drapery false, impossible, unob-served ; the movement stiff and false. It is second-hand and second-rate. It carries the mind back to the Louvre at Paris, to the Venus of Milo, to the Victory of Samo-thrace. It suggests both. For being dead, it yet desperately recalls the things that live.

Brescia has had to bear the brunt of the first onslaughts of innumerable invaders. Inured to conflict, hardened by the bracing mountain air, the inhabitants, by their fortitude in many a siege and death-struggle, earned for their city the proud title of L'Armata.

Sacked by Goths and Huns and Lombards, Brescia after-wards passed from a leading position in the Lombard League into the clutches of successive tyrants, who overwhelmed her with the might of Milan, Padua or Verona. Then at the beginning of the fifteenth century she submitted to the more beneficent sway of Venice.

Several heroic feats of arms brighten the pages of her war-like annals. Her repulse of the Visconti, in spite of famine, plague and every horror of a ruthless siege, was the reward of heroism and determination unsurpassed in history, when even the women and children fought by the side of the citizens on the ramparts. Her valiant resistance to Frederick II., after his victory at Cortenuova, turned the tide against his victorious arms.

Exasperated, it is said, by the long siege, the Emperor bound the Brescian captives to the front of the towers which were moved up against the walls. But the prisoners exhorted their fellow-citizens to let them die for their country. The Burghers revenged themselves by hanging their German captives by the arms over their walls. At length a brilliant sortie inflicted such loss that the Emperor broke up his camp and, having made a truce with Brescia, withdrew to Cremona, where his army disbanded.

Yet a second time Brescia broke the Imperial hopes of establishing organised government in the Lombard towns, when the Guelf party, having expelled the Ghibellines under Matteo Maggi, were besieged by Henry of Luxemburg (1311). They made a desperate resistance. Tebaldo Brusati, their leader, was captured, but refused to invite the citizens to surrender as the price of his own life. He was dragged to death at a horse's tail. When at length the day of capitulation came, and the walls of Brescia, strong in men and strong in arms, were broken and the gates sent to Rome, Henry's army had dwindled away and his resources were well nigh exhausted.

The treaty of Cambrai (1512) gave Brescia to France for a while. Then a force of Venetians surprised the city, cut to pieces every Frenchman they found and drove the garrison into the Castle which still dominates the town. Gaston de Foix, Duc de Nemours, hurried from Bologna to their relief, caring nought for the snow and morasses that would have arrested the march of any other general of that time. He defeated the Venetian army under the walls and took the town by storm. The spirit of this brilliant and determined soldier, who set the example to his men of descending the ice-clad slopes from the castle to the town in his socks, was echoed by the famous knight, *sans peur et sans reproche,* the Chevalier de Bayard, who led the forlorn hope and whose name, echoed as a battle cry, led the Venetian Commander to exclaim, "These Bayards grow in France like mushrooms ; the cry in every fight is Bayard." A terrible massacre of the Venetian troops followed. Bayard had been wounded and was carried to the house of a woman who was in an agony of terror for the honour of her two fair daughters. But Bayard, with a chivalry strange to the times, claimed not the conqueror's right. He treated the girls with courtesy, and dowered them with the ducats which their mother proffered as their ransom. On his departure the grateful maidens presented this " incomparable flower of chivalry " with a pair of bracelets woven with the gold of their own fair tresses.

The stubborn courage characteristic of Brescia is exemplified in the career of her most famous son, Arnold of Brescia, a pupil of Abelard, who was burnt alive at last in Rome for the daring persistency with which, in an age of luxurious and profligate ecclesiasticism, he preached the doctrine of a pure priesthood devoted to poverty and religion.

Alessandro Buonvicino, *Il Moretto,* a devout, ascetic painter of genius, so much praised, and, as it seems to me, overpraised, by Pater, and the vigorous Romanino, are the two native artists for whose sake, and for its bracing air, Brescia is now chiefly visited.

The centre of the town forms a very picturesque group of buildings. True, the white pinnacles which have been added to the Torre del Popolo are very distressing, but still the Piazza Vecchia, with its Venetian Clock-Tower, Torre, charming portici, and the ancient Cathedral Dome beyond, forms a delightful picture. The Loggia itself (the Municipio), a building of magnificent proportions, dates from the Renaissance period. The deep, simple colonnade in front and the chaste window-mouldings by Palladio relieve the excessive ornamentation by Tamagnino and others. It is crowned by a very rich and charming frieze of *putti* by Sansovino.

From walks beneath the ruined Castello there are magnificent views, across the huddled mass of houses, of the plain and the hills. Away to the West, beyond the empurpled rocks, rise the snow-clad heights of Monte Rosa.

CHAPTER XXII.

BERGAMO.

FROM Brescia the train skirts the foot of the Bergamasque Alps, passing, half way, the Lago d'Iseo.

A funicular railway leads up from the commonplace, modern town to the ancient city of Bergamo. The Città Alta hangs poised on the summit of one of these mountain promontories which run out into the sea of the Lombard plain. So to pass within the gates of this old-world Bergamo, to surmount its ramparts and to climb the narrow, steep and winding streets which lead up, past the piazza with its stately Broletto, to the Cathedral, is to transplant oneself to mediaeval Italy, to the age of the Condottieri. This spot, so grim and so commanding, is fit breeding-ground for some fierce warlike spirit or some great marauding brigand of romance. And indeed, close by the Cathedral, in what was once the Sacristy of Santa Maria Maggiore, in that tiny gem of decorative art, the Cappella Colleoni, lies the mighty soldier of fortune, Captain General of the Venetian army, Bartolommeo Colleoni, who first saw light in Bergamo (1400). The ruins of the massive castle-home of the Colleoni,—forked battlements and machicolated towers, within a curtain-wall and drawbridge, lie at Malpaga, some ten miles away. The Great Condottiere prepared his

The Piazza Garibaldi at Bergamo. The Palazzo Vecchio on the left.

immortality upon earth with all the care of a Renaissance Bishop.   More successful than many, he secured two post-humous masterpieces to keep his memory green.   At Venice he lives in Verrocchio's magnificent equestrian statue ; but for his last resting-place and that of his daughter, he chose the rich tombs within the chapel designed by Amadeo in the city of his birth, and worthy to be compared with the Cappella Portinari at Milan.

One end of the picturesque Piazza Vecchia is enclosed by the Broletto, rude, almost, in its simplicity, with its charming open stairway, its three windows and remains of the old Ringhiera (balcony).   Through the plain open arches we catch a glimpse of the apses and of the elaborate colour-scheme of the North Porch of Sta. Maria Maggiore.   It is approached by seven steps of alternate black and white marble, and is supported by columns of warm red Verona marble, the last of those " porch-pillars on a lion resting," that we shall record.   Above, in marble of red and grey, rides S. Alessandro and his attendant Saints ; it is topped by a canopied Madonna.   Tinted marbles, red, yellow, black, white, grey ; shafts twisted, moulded, carved ; rich traceries and rare imaginations perpetuated in the mellow stone, as in the marvellous Chase which circles round the arch, Saint and beast, bird and hunter, shepherd and soldier, are all mingled in this wonderful Porch in a most harmonious variety of colour and fancy by the rare technique and spirit of the sculptor.   And, by the side of it, is the façade of a small chapel, which makes even this revel of the Lombard mind in art seem tame and plain.

We have seen that Giovanni Amadeo, who came hither from the Certosa, and returned hence to work at Milan and

Pavia, though he certainly lacked the sense of form and the purity of style of the great Tuscan sculptors, is distinguished by his prolific fancy and his genius for rich decoration. And here the exuberance of his imagination has found full play. Varied marbles, jet black and white, flushed a roseate hue or tinted creamy yellow, are employed in every shape and design of sculpture and architecture and encrusted on the shrine. Statuettes and pilasters, medallions, busts and bas-reliefs ; Patriarchs and Roman Emperors, Saints and Pagan gods, virtues, cupids, graces, angels, caught in a net of loveliest arabesque, are mingled in the true Renaissance spirit of indifference to meaning or belief, in glad acceptance of all that is beautiful and joyous in art or story. And, as upon the walls of S. Mark's at Venice, the story of Hercules and his labours is balanced by the story of Adam and his Fall told in marble at the base, to the accompaniment of sweet music made above by the most charming of children untouched by toil or time, unstained by the sins and sorrows of the world. The tomb of the great Condottiere within, consisting of two sarcophagi, is also a highly elaborate work by Amadeo.

There is something very appropriate in the contrast between this ornate memorial of the soldier's triumphant, virile career, and the chaste tomb of his daughter Medea. For in the recumbent statue in which Amadeo has immortalised her incomplete existence, he has embalmed all the charm and all the pathos of her virginity, all the innocent expectancy and yearning of a pure young maid in its first outlook upon life, together with something of the anguish of the parent, who has seen his hopes of a perpetual progeny so cruelly frustrated. In the presence of the delicate loveliness of this portrait of Medea, sleeping in marble so tenderly wrought, we are hushed to silence ; admiration is speechless—speech might rouse the gentle girl from her long, sweet slumber.

It is said that when this tomb was moved from the monastery, which Colleoni built in memory of his dear dead daughter, the skeleton of a small bird was found among the remains of the youthful girl. Her father had placed the bird alive there—*passer deliciae meae puellae*—because she had loved it.

Huddled close to S. Maria Maggiore and the Broletto, is the Cathedral. It is a building of little interest, dedicated to the martyr S. Alessandro, standard-bearer of that Roman Legion of Christians, who mutinied when Maximian summoned them to persecute their fellow-Christians in Gaul and were all put to the sword (286).

We pass on and upwards. Half a mile beyond the Porta S. Alessandro and the limits of the Città Alta is the Castello. The view from this point is wonderful. Minute, abrupt hills rise out of the many-coloured plain, blue and brown and green. Behind, the mightier mountains are veiled in amethyst haze. It is the background of an early Italian picture. The monotonous level is broken only by lines of poplars and mulberry trees, the tall, white campanili of tiny villages, the tower of distant Cremona, and silver threads of streams. Bergamo lies at the junction of two fertile valleys, named from the Brembo and the Serio, tributaries of the Adda. And beyond the Adda, stretching to the Lambro in the West to Lecco on the North and southwards to Milan, lies the Brianza. This is the richest part of the garden of Italy, and upon the miles of fair vineyards, carefully tended orchards and mulberry plantations the eye lingers lovingly, proud of the strenuous labour of men and women, grateful to Nature who here, at least, has chosen to reward that labour bountifully.   And again one realises with what wonder and what desire the starving hordes of barbarians, and the plundering brigades of regular armies must have gazed, when from the barren, freezing hilltops they first beheld the fair, fat, sunny plain of Lombardy lying at their feet.   With these or other thoughts returning, we find our way at eventide to the steep ramparts with which the Venetians fortified Bergamo.   The shadows are deepening in the ancient, narrow streets: at every angle lofty houses, white-faced, brown-roofed, glower grimly upon us.   One of these was the dwelling place of Bartolommeo Colleoni himself, who bequeathed it for an orphanage to the city.   The shadows in the picturesque old Piazza are purple; tower, loggia and staircase of the Palazzo Vecchio and the striped pavement of the square blend into a perfect picture.   From the busy modern town that lies far below, the twinkling white lights of the lamps come out, like stars, one by one, shining through the deepening blue haze beneath.   And suddenly a bell rings out, then another, then a peal, then a chorus.   The Church bells are calling the Angelus.   Backwards and forwards, above, below, from old town to new, from new to old, they answer and echo and re-echo, clanging, crashing, tinkling, booming, harmonising now, now joining in so strident a discord, as might make Donizetto, the Bergamasque composer, turn in his grave.   They die away at last, in a gradual succession of diminuendo, over the distant, disappearing plain.

From Bergamo one passes naturally—and very wisely— to one of the most lovely, and to the Englishman or Scot, one of the most homelike of Italian Lakes, the Lago d'Iseo. Lacus Sebinus, the Romans called it, after the town of Sebum, now Iseo. The cult of the Egyptian Isis led, it is said, to the change of name. But thought and history, memory and architecture, art and learning, I put them all from me as I wander up the rich and verdant Val Camonica, by the clear waters of the Oglio, enclosed by mountains wooded to their crests, or, lazily drifting beneath the clear blue of an Italian sky, between shores clad with Italian vegetation, gaze up at the precipitous peaks of Monte Adamello, that towers above sweet Lovere. I put them all from me, for the grateful sense of peace, which the serene, woodland scenery and the amethyst rocks of the Sabine Lake impart, for the sake of the dear association it brings to me of an English Lakeland home.

INDEX

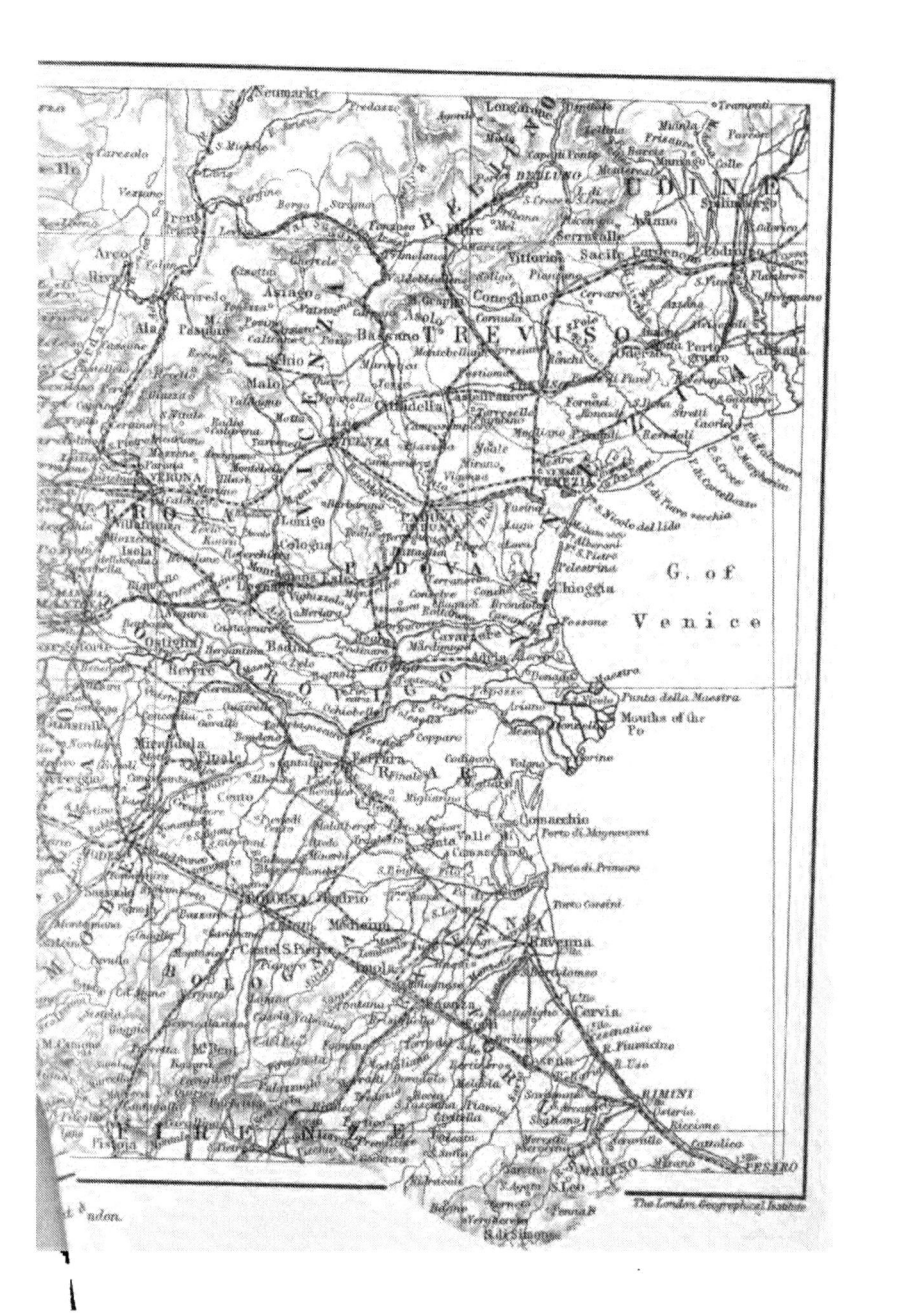

CPSIA information can be obtained
at www.ICGtesting.com
Printed in the USA
BVHW040556050719
552677BV00007B/106/P

9 780343 869519